Making Feminist Politics

Making Feminist Politics

Transnational Alliances between Women and Labor

SUZANNE FRANZWAY and
MARY MARGARET FONOW

UNIVERSITY OF ILLINOIS PRESS
Urbana, Chicago, and Springfield

© 2011 by the Board of Trustees
of the University of Illinois
All rights reserved
Manufactured in the United States of America
1 2 3 4 5 C P 5 4 3 2 1
∞ This book is printed on acid-free paper.

Library of Congress Cataloging-in-Publication Data
Franzway, Suzanne.
Making feminist politics: transnational alliances between women
and labor / Suzanne Franzway and Mary Margaret Fonow.
  p. cm.
Includes bibliographical references and index.
ISBN-13: 978-0-252-03596-8 (hardcover: alk. paper)
ISBN-10: 0-252-03596-8 (hardcover: alk. paper)
ISBN-13: 978-0-252-07792-0 (pbk.: alk. paper)
ISBN-10: 0-252-07792-X (pbk.: alk. paper)
1. Women in the labor movement.
2. Feminism—International cooperation.
I. Fonow, Mary Margaret, 1949– II. Title.
HD6079.F73   2011
331.88082—dc22   2010042433

Contents

Acknowledgments vii

Abbreviations ix

1. Feminist Politics and Transnational Labor Movements 1
2. Sexual Politics, Activism, and Everyday Life 24
3. Sexual Politics, Labor, and the Family 47
4. Political Spaces: Centers, Conferences, and Campaigns 67
5. Feminist Politics in International Labor 87
6. Women's Activism in the International Metalworkers' Federation 108
7. Another World Is Possible for Women, If . . . 125
8. Conclusion: The Future of Feminist Politics in Global Union Movements 139

Notes 147

References 153

Index 177

Acknowledgments

Duets are not uncommon in publishing, but they are perhaps rarely as beneficial as they have been to both of us during the process of writing this book. With one of us in the United States (Fonow) and one in Australia (Franzway), we have found that the need to interpret our different perspectives (sometimes even language) and geographical standpoints has often led us to new questions and, we hope, useful insights. This would have been much less possible if we had not been able to communicate regularly both physically and virtually. Our universities, Arizona State University and University of South Australia, have contributed to this through grants for travel, sabbaticals, and Internet technology.

We have been inspired and informed by networks of activists and scholars; formal groups include UNESCO Women's and Gender Studies Research Network, Working Women's Centre (South Australia), SAUnions Women's Standing Committee, Women in Male Dominated Occupations and Industries (WIMDOI), Research Centre for Gender Studies at University of South Australia, International Metalworkers' Federation, International Labour Organization, Global Union Research Network (GURN), Institute for Policy Studies, International Institute of Social History, World Social Forum/s, International Sociological Association's Research Committee 44 (Labor Movements), American Sociological Association (Labor and Labor Movements, and Sex and Gender Sections); informal groups include union feminists in Australia, Canada, New Zealand, the United States, and the United Kingdom.

We would also like to thank individuals who have contributed to our work in numerous ways: Max Adlum, Eileen Boris, Linda Briskin, Chilla Bulbeck,

Dorothy Sue Cobble, Raewyn Connell, Sandra Dann, Michelle Hogan, Jenny Holdcroft, Stanlie James, Sally Kitch, Sue Ledwith, Valentine Moghadam, Kathie Muir, Barbara Pocock, Elisabeth Porter, Louise Portway, Leila Rupp, Rhonda Sharp, Verta Taylor, Claire Williams, and Ara Wilson. We have been supported by the great skills of research assistants and copyeditors: Valerie Adams, Debjani Chakravarty, Eva Lester, Rosalee Gonzalez, Yue Ma, Virginia Mapedzhama, Kate Leeson, and Sue Breckenridge. In particular, we wish to thank our editor at the University of Illinois Press, Laure Matheson, for her generosity and persistence is bringing this book into being. We have also received expert help from Jane Little, senior coordinator in the School of Social Transformation at Arizona State University.

We thank our dear ones for their encouragement, their good humor especially over our absences in the name of the book, and their care. Suzanne wants to thank especially Neil, Sam, and Mele, as well as Charlie, who appeared during the project. Mary Margaret thanks her dear partner, Corinne Dillon.

Finally and importantly, our thanks go to those women who agreed to be interviewed and whom we cannot thank directly, as well as to the many union feminists who are working to make feminist politics every day. We are not the only people who owe them an enormous debt.

Any errors or flaws are our responsibility.

Abbreviations

ACTU: Australian Council of Trade Unions
AFL-CIO: American Federation of Labor and Congress of Industrial Organizations
AFM: Articulación Feminista Marcosur
AMWU: Australian Manufacturers Workers Union
CEDAW: The Convention on the Elimination of All Forms of Discrimination against Women
CLC: Canadian Labour Congress
COSATU: Congress of South African Trade Unions
DAWN: Development Alternatives with Women for a New Era
FIOM-CGI: Federazione Impiegati Operai Metallurgici
GUF: Global Union Federation
ICFTU: The International Confederation of Free Trade Unions
ILO: International Labor Organization
IMF: International Monetary Fund
ITUC: International Trade Union Confederation
JTUC: Japanese Trade Union Confederation.
LGBT: Lesbian, Gay, Bisexual, and Transgender
OECD: Organization for Economic Co-operation and Development
UN: United Nations
UNESCO: United Nations Educational, Scientific, and Cultural Organization
WICEJ: Women's International Coalition for Economic Justice
WMW: World March of Women
WSF: World Social Forum

1
Feminist Politics and Transnational Labor Movements

In 2000 the World March for Women gathered in Ottawa, Canada, to demonstrate the broad and growing support across the globe for equality and justice for women. Walking among the posters, union banners, and flags proclaiming each group's identity and concerns was one young woman holding a single rose. She was a nurse whose local union was on strike and who had traveled the long distance from Saskatchewan, because she felt she had to be there among other women, no matter how diverse their issues. In 2009 giant pregnant puppets sauntered through the opening ceremony of an arts festival in Adelaide, South Australia, part of a national campaign for paid maternity leave organized by women's organizations and trade unions. In 2005 in hot white tents in Porto Alegre, Brazil, women from a dozen different places, countries, organizations, movements, and NGOs, as well as individuals, worked to understand one another's experiences and concerns, and are both dismayed and hopeful to find how much they share.

Women's right to work and right to economic security are central to women's equality. Such rights are won through creative and persistent feminist politics. Little is gained unless women themselves can participate in the politics of economic and social justice. Without this capacity, the labor market, workplaces, and economic welfare become sites of discrimination and oppression of women. If women are not integrated into the organizations and associations of workers' rights, their needs and issues are ignored or excluded, resulting in skewed or discriminatory political and industrial agendas.

The powerful and unpredictable forces of globalization serve to heighten the need for feminist politics to mobilize around women's work and economic security rights. However, the magnitude of social and economic dislocations associated with globalization and global capital appear to limit progressive political activism.[1] The rapid spread of the so-called "credit crisis" across the globe is producing new threats to workers and new opportunities to undermine rights and conditions (Buvinic, Sabarwal, and Sinha 2009; World Bank 2009). Yet globalization has also provided opportunities for workers and their organizations to build transnational labor movements and alliances with progressive social movements by imagining the possibility of another, more just world. If the upsurge in global activism is to be relevant to women workers, worker organizations and social movements must develop the political discourses and spaces by which women can develop and engage as transnational political actors.

Our overall concern in this book is with the emergence of transnational feminist activism in trade unions and how feminists are using the resources of their union networks, feminist social movements, and the discourses of feminism to advocate for the labor rights of women in the global economy. We have selected sites of political activism that depend on diverse forms of networks and alliances in order to identify and explain what factors determine the impact of union women as transnational political actors. These sites include unions, international labor bodies, working-women's centers, conferences, campaigns, transnational advocacy networks, families and intimate relations, and the body.

We focus on strategies that develop where the women's movement and the labor movement come together at the level of discourses, practices, issues, and commitments, and at the level of individuals, organizations, and institutions. We ask how feminism circulates within labor networks and how the ideas of labor circulate within feminists' networks. Do their discourses reflect or transform each others' issues and ways of framing globalization?

Feminist literature on globalization and the struggles to create alternatives that are more humane is well developed (Basu 2005; Cohen and Brodie 2007; Conway 2008; Eschle 2001, 2002; Ferree and Tripp 2006; Gibson-Graham 1996, 2006; Hawkesworth 2006, 2009; Hawkesworth and Alexander 2008; Moghadam 2005; Naples and Desai 2002; Ong 1987, 2002; Sen 1997; Walby 2002). The hallmark issues of the global justice movement have been integral to feminist politics and theorizing for some time, in particular trade, debt, migration, taxes, structural adjustment programs, poverty, development, environment, health disparities, violence, and war (Bakker and Gill 2003; Bedford 2007; Benería 2003; Benería and Bisnath 2004; Hearn and Parkin 2001; Kay 2005; MacDonald 2002; Marchand and Runyan 2000; Quintero-

Ramírez 2002; Walby 2009). Feminists bring valuable insights to our understanding of the sexual politics of how globalization and global activism are gendered (Eschle 2005; Mohanty 2003). Such insights are important to finding solutions to some of the world's most pressing problems.

We argue that the task of making feminist politics in labor movements at local, national, and international levels has a notable and fine, if at times invisible, history. These efforts have not been an exercise in futility, even though labor movements and trade unions are often seen as male-dominated organizations in which gender issues are submerged by class politics and "bread-and-butter" issues of jobs and wages. Likewise, in the current context of globalizing economic, social, technological, and environmental issues, feminist politics can engage with labor movements to mobilize political action on behalf of women of different races, nationalities, and sexualities. Such mobilizing structures can be used to harness the resources for effective political campaigns and build transnational solidarity among women.[2]

Making feminist politics within and through the trade union movement involves challenging prevailing gender relations, gendered discourses, and gendered power. A small but critical mass of feminists active within and around labor movements confronts the task by utilizing prevailing discourses of the women's movement, the civil rights/human rights movement, and the global justice movement to forge a dynamic politics of transnational union feminism. Union feminists draw on historical strategies such as separate women's committees, forums, conferences, and courses, and on more recent technologies to create discursive alliances and political networks within and across labor movements and social movements.

Our central question is, How do union women make feminist politics within and through the trade union movement so that its complex structures and relations of power are reconfigured to achieve feminist goals? The particular focus is on how union feminists build transnational alliances and political campaigns across many lines of difference in the struggle for economic and social rights and global justice.

Why Unions?

In times of remarkable change, it is worth asking what is the value of focusing attention on trade unions and the transnational labor movement that appear conservative and out of date. Trade unions tend to be regarded as traditional institutions locked into relationships with states and capitalism that effectively impede economic and social progress for workers as well as the rest of society. By contrast, the women's movement is still categorized as a new social movement (although rapidly aging) and fits David Snow et alia's (2004) relatively inclusive definition of social movements as "collectivities acting with some degree of coordination and continuity" (11). As such, it has a more dynamic profile. Unions' declining membership in western and globalizing capitalist economies and lack of purchase in many developing economies could indicate that they are no longer relevant to contemporary societies (Erne 2008; Jose 2002; B. Silver 2003; Turner, Katz, and Hurd 2001; Western 1997). Certainly, the labor movement is being forced to stand on different legs from those on which it fought for workers' rights during industrialization and western empire-building: it can no longer rely on traditional labor movement politics.

Pressures exerted by neoliberal global capital are having varied effects on trade unions' support for their potentially diverse members, including women. When, however, the interests of labor overlap with other movements that focus on workers' rights, political spaces are expanding. Where there is increased hostility by the state, however, unions have reduced their support. In Australia, for example, where more than a decade of conservative neoliberal national government has actively destroyed its centralized industrial relations system, union support has contracted (Peetz 2006). Women's officers and training officers, both positions that provided useful resources to women workers and to building women's interests into trade union political agendas, have been cut, undermining the feminist strategy for change based on winning hierarchical positions of public power (Beccalli and Meardi 2002; Briskin 2009; Pocock 1997). Whatever gains were made for women workers in the past now seem quite tenuous. Such losses of specific women's positions and resources reveal the limits of a political strategy aimed at intervening in hierarchical structures of power, rather than transforming them. And yet progress is also being made, especially by those unions and peak bodies that are responding to feminist demands—for example, Nora Wintour (2006) documents the ways the international peak body, the Public Services International (PSI) has strategized to ensure that its affiliate unions meet the agreed gender equity targets for women in union leadership.

Threatened by pressure from neoliberal global capital to provide flexible labor, the trade union movement has adopted its own more flexible policies designed to include the needs and interests of the great variety of potential members. The foundational concept of the universal worker—that is, the full-time male industrial worker—has had to change in recognition of the complexity of what now constitutes workers (Walby 2009). In the same vein, it may be said that feminism has been enlivened by the need to include the diversities of global gender relations. We therefore suggest that these shifts and changes reveal new possibilities for progressive action.

Trade unions are formally structured to represent the economic and political interests of workers on the local, national, and international level, and thus connect workers organically to the multiple and contradictory processes and levels of globalization (Fonow and Franzway 2007). Unions link their members locally, regionally, and globally to the broader network of activists, social movements, and organizations concerned with similar issues—that is, labor rights and justice (Turner and Cornfield 2007). As sites of advocacy, unions bring workers together within and across workplaces, firms, and communities and within and across national borders.

At the international level, such networking occurs through a union's formal membership in international trade union secretariats and confederated labor bodies and, less formally, through strategic partnerships and alliances with transnational social movements, nongovernmental organizations (NGOs) and intergovernmental agencies. On the local level, unions connect workers within and across occupations and structure their collective relationship to regional labor bodies, to local governments and NGOs and to grassroots community organizations and campaigns.

Unions have always been involved in international labor networks, but tensions between nationalism and internationalism can be traced back to efforts by Marx and Engels to build international organizations of workers (Hanagan 2003; Lorwin 1929; Nimtz 2002; Pasture and Verberckmoes 1998; Waterman and Timms 2004). The U.S. labor movement, however, lost much of its credibility in international labor circles when cold war politics made it nearly impossible for labor to align with progressive or left-wing movements abroad. The American Federation of Labor and Congress of Industrial Organizations (AFL-CIO) not only expelled radicals in their own affiliates, but also cooperated with the Central Intelligence Agency (CIA) in undermining the influence of left-wing unions and parties in other parts of the world (Frutiger 2002; Scipes 2000; Stepan-Norris and Zeitlin 2002). The U.S. labor community still struggles with this legacy as it tries to sort out the type of international politics required by current forces of globalization.

However, not only is the international labor movement divided by barriers between states, but trade unions are also separated by borders of their own creation. A trade union that recruits members from areas outside its traditional coverage is seen as "poaching" and as hostile to other unions. This continues to be the case in countries like Australia despite the compression of hundreds of unions into a couple of dozen through amalgamations in the early 1990s, a process that was a calculated response to globalizing labor markets and to neoliberal hostility to unionization (Pocock 1997). In addition, the historically specific divisions created by industries, occupational hierarchies (managers, skilled, unskilled workers), gender, "race," public and private sectors, and "blue" and "white" collar stereotypes, differences, and boundaries are difficult to bridge let alone blur (Williams 1988). As a result, the potential effectiveness of united groups of unions, such as peak national and international trades and labor councils, can be limited.

One such limitation too often arises from the obstacles created by the persistence and ubiquity of unequal gender relations in the trade union movement. This common understanding of the trade union movement fails to evoke transformative possibilities. Overall, women make up 43 percent of trade union members in Australia, with similar proportions in Canada and the United States, but women remain underrepresented at almost all levels of union activity, especially at the more powerful levels of full-time and paid secretary and president positions (Cobble and Bielski Michal 2002; Colgan and Ledwith 2002; Mezinec 1999). Women have gained some leadership positions and made inroads into union agendas and resources. However, women's participation rates are disproportionate to their leadership rates and, on any measure, inequalities continue. As one woman union official in our research observed, "When I go to the national office I look around their walls and their photographs over years and years, and there is not one woman in sight, not one." This pattern is mirrored at the transnational level where women are underrepresented in international organizations of labor, including the International Labour Organization (ILO), the Global Union Federations (GUFs), the former International Confederation of Free Trade Unions (ICFTU), the European Trade Union Confederation (ETUC), and the newly formed International Trade Union Confederation (ITUC). Nevertheless, feminist politics aims for much more than winning leadership positions for women. It seeks to gain women's rights and social justice comprehensively and in all their necessarily diverse manifestations. Despite the obstacles, women's commitment to workplace and politics, activism, and militancy are significant. The minority positions of union women activists in trade unions together with their feminist politics give them strong incentives to work across state and union borders to make alliances that are creative and productive.

Political spaces for feminist activism have proliferated where the interests of labor overlap with other movements concerned about labor rights. This has become even more critical under current global conditions (Moghadam, Franzway, and Fonow forthcoming; Walby 2009). Increasingly, campaigns for labor rights are organized and funded not by the unions alone, but with support from religious organizations, foundations, universities, and in some instances from the state. Union issues are being defined in new ways, with many unions actively engaged in equity bargaining and family-friendly workplaces, as well as developing policies such as those opposing workplace bullying and those supporting international aid. New players from the nonprofit sector, such as the Women's International Coalition for Economic Justice, Women's Environment and Development Organization, and Women's Edge Coalition, and activists from other social movements, such as the Students against Sweatshops, are joining with unions as strategic partners in the growing transnational networks for labor rights (Liebowitz 2002; Moghadam 2005).

Trade unions and labor movements more broadly are valuable political resources, but more importantly, they embody basic principles endorsing workers' rights and social justice that are critical to feminism and the women's movement.

Gender and Sexual Politics

Our argument about making feminist politics in and through transnational labor movements is premised on the understanding that feminist politics hinges on the way gender is understood. Feminist theorizing of gender has become a highly sophisticated and nuanced field of debate and research. At the same time, gender has become code for women in popular culture as well as in too much scholarly work. In a discussion focused on the global and the international, we stress that gender cannot be understood in isolation from historically specific gender regimes or patterns of gender arrangements (Connell 2002). A set of gender arrangements are made up of the ways that people, groups, and organizations are connected and divided, often described as gender relations. If we define enduring patterns of gender relations as gender orders, then a global gender order is constituted by gender practices that are reshaped by global processes. Such practices may be local, but they "carry the impress of forces" that make a global society (Connell 2002, 111). It is this global/local gender order to which transnational feminist politics and women's movements are both a response and expression. Both loose and more formal organizations build alliances and campaigns within proximal and extended communities and organizations that extend across borders and boundaries.

Such politics and analysis suggest a complex notion of power that is not limited to a narrow focus on formal governance by nation-states or to hierarchical control (Armstrong and Bernstein 2008). Power may be understood as a productive network that reaches into every part of the social field and is woven into the fabric of everyday life (Foucault 1980). Social conflict and resistance, therefore, cannot be centralized. Political resistance must be heterogeneous as well as specific to the social logic of its particular sociopolitical field. Resistance continues to be possible if power is understood as potentially constructive, rather than always repressive. This understanding of power conceives globalization as "not a unified force rather it is constituted by diverse global processes" (Walby 2009, 444) involving transnational networks and flows of power (Gibson-Graham 1996). These transnational flows may give those on the periphery access to new technological, cultural, and economic resources that are open to adaptation and that connect local groups to transnational networks. Thus, power may be located in the production of global/local networks of activists.

Making feminist politics within the trade union movement involves contesting these explicit yet complex structures of power. Further, as we have discovered, women union activists use networks across and beyond trade unions. Their political strategies take diverse understandings of power into account to create a politics that confronts, resists, challenges, and transforms. These strategies likewise incorporate more fluid notions of gender that allow for the heterogeneity and diversity of women's experiences.

When women are absent from or insignificant to the central concerns of work, industrial relations, and social movements, it is not just a matter of ignorance or carelessness. Too often it is only women who are seen to be gendered; men are unmarked by gender. To label this as a problem of gender or a sexist gender order does little more than name it; we do recognize that to even achieve this degree of recognition of gender is a continuing struggle. However, the label fails to integrate the dynamic of gendered power, which the largely discarded concept, patriarchy, did imply at least.

We therefore propose a reworked version of the concept of "sexual politics" (discussed in more detail in chapter 2) originally developed by Kate Millet (1969), who broadened the definition of politics to refer to any relationships structured by power "whereby one group of persons is controlled by another" (23). Millet made what was a radical claim in its time, namely that the sexes as well as races, castes, and classes should be understood as well-defined and coherent groups and thus subject to politics (23–24). Sexual politics makes it possible to recognize that, under contemporary, globalized conditions as well as recent industrialized history, not only are men seen as the norm, but that men's power as men is invisible so that questions about how men achieve and maintain their dominance (for example, of trade unions) rarely arise.

It is central to our argument about making feminist politics that relations between the sexes are understood in terms of power and that feminist politics seeks to challenge the dominance of relationships by masculine and heteronormative power. However, we also argue that sexual politics encompasses complex gender relationships of power expressed as domination, resistance, alliances, and pleasures that are central to all social institutions, including the trade union movement (Franzway 2001). Sexual politics in its current and dominant form also contributes to the invisibility of social reproduction. Globalization has more than exposed the false dichotomy between public and private. It has transformed that dichotomy. For example, domestic work, childcare, sex work, and food production have been largely internationalized and outsourced. Private life merges with the public, and it becomes increasingly difficult to distinguish between work, family, and intimate spheres (Maher, Lindsay, and Franzway 2008). This has important implications for labor movement politics. It is essential for labor to recognize the challenge of the sexual politics of everyday life including family, intimate relations, social reproduction, sexualities, and self-care.

Gender and Globalization

Our focus on feminist politics and transnational labor movements points toward the interrelationships of gender and globalization. Women and feminism do not fare well in the broad narratives about globalization, which Catherine Eschle describes as "driven by economic forces, of social struggle as violent confrontations with the state, and of feminism as centering on identity and as universalizing and imperialist" (Eschle 2005, 1750; see also Walby 2009), thus producing a view of feminism as incompatible with antiglobalization movements. Typical of so much left and progressive politics of the last century, the struggle against globalization is framed as primarily class-based, rendering gender and feminism invisible. Eschle's evaluation of antiglobalization texts and their underpinning discourses substantiates widespread feminist critiques of the exclusion of gender from the dynamics of globalization or women's role in the resistance to its effects (Barker and Feiner 2005; Naples and Desai 2002; Odih 2007; Peterson 2003).

Feminist scholars have made us aware of the specific ways in which gender articulates with globalization, and their analyses have important implications for labor politics (Bakker and Gill 2003; Bergeron 2001; Brooks 2007; Caraway 2007; Gibson-Graham 2002; Moghadam 2005; Mohanty 2003; Sassen 1998; Wilson 2004). We summarize the gender dimension of globalization as follows:

- Women's labor force participation has increased worldwide because of the growth of the service sector and of the informal sector.
- Women are more likely than men to curtail consumption and to increase their domestic workload to compensate for household income loss.
- Women are more directly affected by a reduction in social welfare programs. The privatization of public services often means that these services are shifted from the paid work of women in the public sector to the unpaid labor of women in the domestic sphere.
- Labor flexibility has resulted in the proliferation of nonstandard jobs, which are more difficult to organize and are disproportionately filled by immigrants and women. They often disappear during periods of economic crisis.
- Millions of women migrate from poor countries to rich ones to perform "women's work" as domestics, health care workers, nannies, and sex workers. This "feminization of immigration" is encouraged by governments that have come to rely on the remittances women workers send home.
- Family and kinship relations have been reconfigured in ways that increase women's financial responsibilities. There are more female-headed families worldwide as men spend longer and longer periods of time working away from where their families live.

Feminist struggles to establish the significance of gender to the discourses and effects of globalization risk making universalizing claims of essentialized women, which has the effect of positioning feminism as part of the problem. By contrast, arguments produced by black and third-world feminist scholars that stress the intersectionality of diverse forms of power in different ways in different locations have been influential in opening up new spaces for recognizing the multiple axes of oppression and identity (Crenshaw 1989; James, Foster, and Guy-Sheftall 2009; Mohanty 2003; Yuval-Davis 2006). The longstanding feminist commitment to autonomous, democratic participation, in conjunction with black and third-world feminist insistence on the value of coalitions, constitutes what Eschle describes as a "discourse about feminist organizing" that would strengthen both antiglobalization movements and feminist activism (Eschle 2005, 1755). Yet little of this thinking is evident in movement texts or discourses, where a male-dominated sexual politics continues to marginalize feminism, the significance of gender, and the oppressive impact of globalized capital on women.

Global restructuring has increased gender divisions with the feminization of both the international workforce and of poverty (Chen et al. 2005; Wichterich 2000). The World Bank and the ILO acknowledge that unequal gender relations lead to women making up 70 percent of the world's poor (Mason and King 2001). The construction of women workers in the international division of labor as cheap labor, or as Jan Jindy Pettman (2001, 590) puts it, "labor made cheap" is worsening. Poorly paid women workers are gathered together to subsidize the operation of "free" trade zones created in deregulated labor markets; women domestic workers flow from poorer states to wealthier states; while sex workers are caught up in the international sex tourist industry, both within and across nation-states (Agustín 2007; Ehrenreich and Hochschild 2002; Parreñas 2001; Zheng 2009).

Discursive Frames and Alliances

Central to our question about making feminist politics in and through transnational labor movements is an understanding about the ways political opportunities need to be framed discursively as opportunities (Beckwith 2001a; Fonow 2003, 2005). A discursive frame interprets, simplifies, and condenses the world by selecting, punctuating, and encoding objects, situations, events, experiences, and sequences of actions in a way that makes sense within an individual's present or past environment (Snow and Benford 1992). To be successful, such frames must seek congruence and complementarity among the interests, values, and beliefs of the potential movement participants and the activities, goals, and ideologies of social movements (Gamson and Meyer 1996).

Discursive frames are important to social movement formation in three very specific ways: "First, discursive frames transform issues, problems and events into grievances and issues about which individuals believe something can and should be done. Secondly, discursive frames help to mobilize participants by identifying the formal and informal networks that organize a movement's resources. They help participants come to view particular mobilizing networks as places prepared for action. Finally, mobilization depends on the collective belief that action can make a difference, that there is something to be gained from becoming a part of a group. This collective or group identity is created and maintained as part of a movement's internal discourse and is constituted not only in the broader social movement, but also within specific organizations and solidarity groups constructed around particular social locations" (Fonow 2005, 222).

The women's movement and the labor movement use similar and divergent discourses to mobilize participants. Each movement has distinctive ways of speaking and writing that establish what makes sense. The choice of words, images, ideas, and symbols are deliberate and chosen to produce certain effects, including alliance building and better representation of the diversity of its membership. The discourse of rights has become increasingly more integral to the labor movement's fundamental role and to its campaigns (Heery and Conley 2007; Hunt 1999). Hyman identifies such campaigns as a response to the repressive transformations of global capital on workers (Hyman 2002).

The ILO adopted the Declaration on Fundamental Principles and Rights at Work in 1998, committing government, employer, and worker constituents to achieving universal workers' rights. The peak Australian body, the Australian Council of Trade Unions (ACTU), adopted the slogan "Rights at Work" for its campaign, running up to the 2007 national election against the proposal by Prime Minister John Howard's government to demolish the centralized industrial relations system, replacing enterprise collective agreements with individual contracts. By formulating human rights as workers' rights, labor utilizes the rights discourse to foster alliances and to limit employers' arbitrary authority (Muir 2008).

Women's rights have also been reframed as human rights in parallel with the civil rights movement, the disability rights movement, and the gay and lesbian movement, which have played important roles in expanding our notion of social rights and justice. Coupling the struggle for equity rights with the struggle for collective labor rights and resolving tensions between these struggles will open the way for a more radical approach to the question of workers' rights in the global economy (Clawson 2003; Compa and Diamond 1996; Elliott and Freeman 2003; Friedman and Wood 2001; Gross 2003; Lichtenstein 2003; Munck 2004; Smith, Sonnenfeld, and Pellow 2006).

Feminist writers and activists are generally skeptical of tendencies to universalize and naturalize rights discourse. Labor rights are only meaningful for women if women participate in the process of their formulation and enforcement. For feminists, the rhetoric of human rights as labor rights and as women's rights can be used to mobilize participants only if such discourse is connected to the local realities of women's lives. Similar concerns emerge when discourses of the family are used to counter global pressures and employer demands for intensified work practices. The family is discursively understood as a universal social institution in which care, intimate relations, morality, and social reproduction are highly valued (Barrett and McIntosh 1982; Folbre 2001). However, progressive gains are limited unless the sexual politics of the family is transformed so that women are no longer burdened by the family's discursive and material demands on them.

Unions connect their members to national politics and to transnational labor networks and alliances that are much broader than labor unions per se. It is within these networks that workers can find the political space to imagine a world different from the one we now have. It is here that workers find the discursive and political tools, including feminism, to fashion new ways to articulate their rights.

Furthermore, unions are creating their own labor NGOs like the Steelworkers Humanity Fund, which helps workers to see the international connections among workers (Fonow 2003). Through worker-to-worker exchanges, participation in international forums, and active engagement with various UN programs and activities, unions expand and deepen their transnational labor networks, engage with new ways of thinking about rights, and expand their repertoire of collective action. These growing external links between labor and NGOs are particularly beneficial for women and union feminists because feminism circulates more freely in these circles. This is particularly important for lesbian, gay, bisexual, and transgender (LGBT) workers, since gay rights are more likely to be addressed by NGOs than by labor. As one trade union feminist from Mexico asked at a small meeting of women activists at the International Metalworkers' Federation (IMF), "Don't we have to include the rights of homosexuals? The NGOs we wish to work with will require it" (author observation). Consequently, the women proposed that the union's discourse of rights needed to integrate LGBT rights. This illustrates what we have called discursive alliances in which social constructions of meanings are shared by political movements.

Political opportunities for social movements may be structured by possibilities configured by the state, including its gendered networks of power, but as Armstrong and Bernstein point out, "challenges to the state also involve challenges to meaning systems" (Armstrong and Bernstein 2008, 85). Thus, challenges to cultural discourses and practices, the location of collective identities such as the repression of gay identities, and to non-state institutions are also important to the politics of social change. Labor movements are located within state laws, with their practices and policies shaped by state agencies; the politics of women's movements likewise are cast in relation to the state and its sexual politics (Banaszak, Beckwith, and Rucht 2003; Franzway, Court, and Connell 1989; Hassim 2005). However, women's movements also find political opportunities within non-state institutions such as labor movements and religious groups (Katzenstein 1998). Political opportunity structures thus vary across the world as states, movements, and their interactions differ (Beckwith 2007). Nevertheless, patterns of gendered power are remarkably consistent at least at the broad level of male dominance. How that is played out is complex, unpredictable, and compounded by multiple factors (Mohanty 2003).

Although the state shapes political opportunity structures in important ways, other sites of political opportunity are available, particularly in the age of globalization, when new transnational locations for politics are emerging. Such sites are also essential as the state withdraws from its public roles in favor of "elite class power" (Harvey 2005, 188). Supranational, nongovernmental, private economic institutions and regulatory bodies, and transnational agreements are taking on state roles. International laws and courts, NGOs, social movement campaigns and conferences, UN programs, tribunals, and conferences as well as renewed international labor bodies provide increasingly transnational political opportunities for organized labor and the women's movement. Such opportunities are enhanced by mechanisms for transnational activism made available by growing Web access.

Transnational Networks

As a political environment, globalization has reconfigured the opportunities for politics and the repertoire for collective action available to labor and social movements. Emerging political opportunity structures, such as transnational labor networks, provide union women with the opportunity to participate in the ongoing construction of transnational labor solidarity. Keck and Sikkink (1998) identify such networks as transnational advocacy networks, defined as "those relevant actors working internationally on an issue who are bound together by shared values, a common discourse, and dense exchanges of information and services" (2). Networks serve as actors in politics and as a way to mobilize and structure the actions of participants, thus embodying elements of both agent and structure.

Discourses, information, and knowledge are at the core of exchanges in networks. Nontraditional actors within these networks can and do mobilize information strategically to help create new issues and categories, and to persuade, pressure, and gain leverage over much more powerful organizations and governments (Sikkink 2002a). Transnational labor networks have become mobilizing structures for feminists and labor activists, thus opening the way for union feminists to play an active role in shaping the discourses and mobilizing strategies of labor activism.

In their nongovernmental organizations, international conferences, and projects, union feminists struggle with differences among women while simultaneously campaigning for justice and equality for all women. Transnational networks connect actors across areas of concern as well as across national borders. For example, the World March of Women 2000, born out of the experience of a Women's March against Poverty held in Canada in 1996, brought women together from peace organizations, community groups, and trade unions in an explicitly global campaign for peace and equality (Conway 2008; World March of Women 2003). The Canadian Steelworkers were active in the coalition and mobilized one thousand of their members to participate in the march (Fonow 2003). The international network created by this action has developed further into an international network organization under the same name, with 5,500 women's groups from 163 countries. In 2005 it launched the Women's Global Charter for Humanity to reframe its international political campaign against poverty, violence, and war (World March of Women 2005).

Whether alliances are forged at local or at transnational levels, they are always at risk of breaking down over questions of strategy. Painful conflicts may occur over whether to focus on achieving consensus about the value of the principles at stake or on what can be done. In particular, feminist challenges to sexual politics are at risk of being weakened in the hope of making strategic gains. Issues around sexuality may be sanitized in exchange for human rights while queer organizing gives way to calls for same-sex pension rights, as we discuss in more detail in chapter 2. Here is the perennial dilemma for activists: "Focus on what we can organize," as one union woman said to us, "or stick to political principle." New alliances are formed although they are difficult to sustain, particularly when groups are under the pressure of competing interests and demands.

Transnational networks can be the vehicle through which working-class women are mobilized to struggle for economic justice and through which they forge collective identities as transnational feminist actors, but only if they are framed in a way that resonates with the realities of women's multiple and intersecting social locations and identities. Unions have the resources to bring together women from different countries and different sectors of the economy to exchange information about their experience of globalization and to build new forms of transnational labor solidarity. It must be a solidarity that does not ask women to repress the differences among themselves but rather encourages the productive use of these differences to expand ideas about democracy and human rights. Without the material resources, networks, and rhetorical tools of their unions, fewer working-class women from any part of the world would have the opportunity to participate in the debates and struggles concerning the politics of trade and globalization.

Union Feminists Mobilizing at Multiple Sites

Union feminists devise a range of political strategies to seize opportunities and possibilities available in trade unions for building progressive forms of transnational feminist mobilizations and contingent solidarities (Curtin 1999). Within transnational labor networks, union feminists come together with feminists from other social movements, with feminist NGOs, and with feminists at the ILO (ILO 2004a; Ledwith and Colgan 2002). Some of these are obvious sites that focus solely on unions, such as the ICFTU, and some are less obvious—for example, the regional feminist *encuentros* in Latin America. These *encuentros* bring together thousands of women from different countries who are active in a broad range of popular movements to exchange ideas and information. Union activists thus have the opportunity to meet with lesbian-feminist collectives, indigenous movements, landless movements, NGOs, academics, guerrilla organizations, and mainstream political parties. According to Alvarez (2000, 6), these gatherings "provided a unique space for activists to debate collectively the always contested meanings and goals of feminism and its relationship to other struggles for rights and social justice in the region." She believes that these spaces play a critically important role in fashioning common discourses and in providing activists in individual countries with tools of analysis and symbolic resources that they subsequently translate and redeploy locally. Union activists take back to their own movements and organizations new ways of thinking about and defining women's rights—ways that are decidedly more feminist. It is hard to imagine, for example, unions taking up the issue of violence against women on an international level without this input (Elger and Parker 2007; Urban and Wagner 2000).

In the context of intensified globalization, new interconnections of networks and communities reveal common needs and concerns and produce new alliances. We identify a number of sites where union feminists have mobilized resources and discourses to address the impact of globalization on women's labor rights and to forge collective identities as transnational activists. These sites can be sites of labor renewal and include formal organizations, networks and forums, less formal sites (such as international campaigns for pay equity or against sweatshops and unfair trade agreements), and even some surprising sites such as gay pride festivals. These are often overlapping sites whose participants come together on the basis of specific issues and campaigns.

One site of increasing importance to union feminists is the network of women's committees and equity offices within the Global Union Federations.[3] As we discuss in more detail in chapter 5, these federated international labor bodies originally came into being in the nineteenth and twentieth centuries to ameliorate the effects of economic competition on workers in different countries, to build international solidarity, and to facilitate the exchange of information and resources between unions in the same sector of the economy. They are organized regionally and by sector, representing millions of workers in transportation, public services, textiles, manufacturing, tourism, construction, education, media, chemical, metal, mining, electronics, agriculture, and food processing.

The women's committees of each federation are networked through the coordinating activities of the ITUC, formerly the ICFTU, which recently resolved to step up the organizing campaign "Unions for Women, Women for Unions," which aims to increase women's representation and participation in union programs, activities, and decision-making structures. The campaign targets specific groups of women workers including women working in the informal economy, young women, migrant women, women from ethnic minorities, and women employed in export processing zones. The ITUC has adopted the discourse developed by the ILO to frame these new initiatives, a discourse that links gender equality to issues of economic development and peace. Equality and nondiscrimination are at the core of a rights-based approach to economic development that links economic efficiency with social efficiency.

Union women and women from grassroots community organizations come together with the help of labor NGOs, such as the Canadian Steelworkers' Humanity Fund, to develop popular communication tools for organizing women, to discover how workplace rights are linked to social and political rights, and to develop the skills to produce, market, and manage their own economic activities. The Steelworkers' Humanity Fund was established to build global partnerships with local unions and community organizations. In 2008 it supported twenty-three major projects in ten countries including work with women's NGOs that emphasizes women's economic empowerment and struggle for labor rights (United Steelworkers Canada 2008). Such projects connect activists and are characterized by mutual support, worker-to-worker exchanges, and information and resource sharing. Women from the formal and the informal economy are brought together to discuss mutual concerns and issues and to develop strategies of organizing that are mutually beneficial.

Methodology

Transnational feminist activism in trade unions is an emergent, dynamic, and mobile phenomenon that changes across time, scale, and space and manifests itself at various sites ranging from large-scale international institutions like the ILO to the sexual politics of families and everyday life. This level of complexity requires a flexible methodological approach, and we employ three primary methods—historical, ethnographic (observation, participation and interviews), and discursive. We use feminist theory to guide our interpretation and analysis of the materials we have collected at various sites of activism. The sites, both real and virtual, include the World Social Forum (WSF); the ITUC; the IMF; the ILO; national peak union bodies; nongovernmental labor organizations, such as the Australian Working Women's Centres; and labor rights campaigns. Data draws on research we conducted that is extended and deepened by interviews with union women activists about their everyday lives, observations of relevant events and campaigns, and textual analysis of documents produced at these sites. The research is situated at the intersections of various disciplines, weaving together methodological strategies derived from sociology, women's studies, history, and labor studies.

Each of us had published extensively on the topic of women's labor activism in unions and over the years developed connections with labor activists and scholars in Australia, New Zealand, Canada, the United States, and the United Kingdom. Some of our insights are drawn from extensive field observations and interviews conducted for previous research projects and from our own involvement with specific unions. Mary Margaret Fonow has studied and worked extensively with the United Steelworkers in Canada and the United States. Suzanne Franzway is a longstanding activist in her own union, including stints as an elected official, as well as active membership of several local and national union women's networks. She was appointed to the executive board of the Working Women's Centre and served for ten years as its chair. Both are members of the Global Union Research Network (GURN) and the UNESCO Women's Studies/Gender Research network.

While we have drawn data from previous research projects, we have also collected new data specifically for this project. There are four primary sources of data including archival records, Web sites, interviews, and participant observations of events and activities.

Archival Records: We consulted records of the International Metalworkers' Federation women's activities from 1953 to 1980 housed at the International Institute of Social History (IISH) in Amsterdam and those covering women's activities between 1981 to 2003 at the IMF's headquarters in Geneva (which have since been moved to the Friedrich Ebert Stiftung Archive in Bonn). Records since 2003 are archived on the IMF Web site.

Interviews: We collected open-ended interviews with women union activists and delegates at the following sites: the World Social Forum, Porto Alegre, Brazil, January 26–31, 2005; the 31st World Congress of the International Metalworkers' Federation, Vienna, May 22–26, 2005; the Women in Male Dominated Occupations and Industry (WIMDOI) Conference endorsed by the ACTU in Adelaide Australia, November 10–13, 2003; and a women's committee meeting of the IMF held in Geneva in October 16–17, 2002. We also conducted interviews with select staff of the Gender Equity Office and the Office of International Labor Standards at the ILO, the Equality Office of the ICFTU and the ETUC, the officers of the national peak union body, the ACTU and the national Australian Manufacturing Workers Union (AMWU), Directors of Australian Working Women's Centres, and the president of the ICFTU. In addition, we have drawn on interview sets from research on Australian and Canadian women unionists conducted in the 1990s, published in Franzway (2001).

Participant-observation: Observations were made of the 31st IMF World Congress, the 2003 WIMDOI Conference, the 2005 World Social Forum, the 2004 ACTU Bread and Roses conference, and the regular meetings and conferences held by the Australian Working Women's Centres since 1993.

Web sites: Much of transnational labor activism is facilitated by the exchange of information, and the Internet has played an important role in spreading discourses and ideas and in mobilizing participants in various labor solidarity campaigns. The Internet not only allows for better coordination of campaigns across nations, unions, and organizations but also facilitates connections between local, national, regional, and international levels of participation. These sites contain research reports, newsletters, minutes of meetings and conferences, calls to action, training manuals, flyers and other campaign materials, position papers, discussion boards, blogs, and so forth. The sites are often linked to one another and serve as virtual mobilizing networks for transnational labor activism.[4]

Networks: We are members of two research networks that have provided us broader access to research on women and labor unions. GURN is a platform for trade unionists and researchers dealing with the challenges of globalization from a labor perspective. The network is a joint effort of the ILO, ITUC, the GUFs, and the Organisation for Economic Co-operation and Development (OECD) to provide union organizations with better access to the research being carried out within trade unions and allied institutions concerned with labor issues, including policy institutes, universities, foundations, and libraries. GURN holds conferences and workshops; publishes newsletters, journals, and books; and provides access to one of the world's largest databases of historical and contemporary source material on topics of interest to unions and those who study unions. Fonow participated in a GURN workshop on unions and globalization prior to the 2005 World Social Forum.

The second network is the Women's Studies/Gender Research (WS/GR) Network of UNESCO, which was launched from the Human Rights and Gender Equality Section, Social and Human Sciences Sector, at a meeting held in Manila in July 2007. Franzway also participated in the international meeting of the network held in Bangkok in February 2009, in conjunction with a meeting of the UNESCO Asia/Pacific Network. The WS/GR Network's objectives are to advance WS/GR by research and advocacy for women's rights; encourage capacity building for students, researchers, and WS programs and research centers; and encourage collaborations between UNESCO, NGOs, and inter-university partnerships.

Organization

In this chapter we present our analytic framework, rationale, and context for understanding feminist transnational activism in trade unions. We argue that despite setbacks trade unions remain relevant sites for making feminist politics on a global scale. Unions provide the activists within them with mobilizing structures and discourses that feminists use to build alliances with NGOs and grass roots activists, and with feminists outside of organized labor. These activists provide a feminist analysis of sexual politics that is helping unions to develop policies and politics more relevant to women in the global economy. Feminist discourses on gender, power, and globalization frame new political opportunities for union activists.

In chapter 2, "Sexual Politics, Activism, and Everyday Life," we contend that the politics of everyday life constitutes activism and that it is a site worth examining along with more institutional forms of political activism. We argue that successful strategies for making feminist politics at any level are subject to women's capacity to negotiate their own care in everyday life. Key to understanding the everyday as a site of activism is the concept of sexual politics, and here we define and elaborate why this concept is useful to our analysis. We theorize that the opportunities to practice politics depend in part on the gendered practices of everyday life. While feminists are more familiar with how women's responsibilities for social reproduction (the second shift) influence women's activism we rarely acknowledge the reproduction of women's own labor. We introduce the term "the laboring body" to define the body that requires care in order to work and to engage in activism in the context of the demands of everyday life. We found that women seek support (in a sense self-care) by creating separate spaces where women can come together to support one another, build alliances, and strategize for change. It is here that women often forge a collective political identity as union feminists. Other marginalized groups inside trade unions are using some of the same strategies adopted by feminists and we conclude this chapter with a discussion of queer organizing.

We turn our attention in chapter 3, "Sexual Politics, Labor, and the Family," to the family as a site for labor activism. It is significant for feminists that the trade union movement is taking up the family as a rallying point for labor campaigns, yet there are often hidden costs in doing so. Politics framed in terms of the family tend to rely on simplified definitions of the family and ignore the sexual politics within them or hold the dubious belief that the traditional nuclear family is the norm. When the family is used to frame the concerns of women workers, there is a strong risk that women will be seen only in relation to families and not as workers in their own right. We trouble the way family has been invoked historically to justify contradictory labor policies and practices—including those advocated by unions and feminists.

In chapter 4, "Political Spaces: Centers, Conferences, and Campaigns," we explore the material and discursive spaces created by feminists within unions for making feminist politics. These self-organizing spaces provided the opportunity for feminists to challenge the male-dominated sexual politics of unions and to advocate for the inclusion of women in all levels of union decision-making. These spaces help to integrate women into the life and politics of the union and to connect them to feminist activism in the broader community. We argue that the right to join the labor market is critical to achieving equality, but little is gained if women do not have the opportunity to shape the conditions of their labor. Without this capacity, the labor market becomes yet another site of discrimination and oppression of women. The same applies to unions. If women are left out, their issues and needs are overlooked or excluded, thus compounding the discrimination of markets. We explore a variety of self-organizing spaces for making feminist politics, including women's committees, women's conferences, women's leadership programs, working women's centers, and various campaigns for gender equity.

In the next two chapters we develop an analysis of feminist transnational labor activism within the international organizations and networks of organized labor. In chapter 5, "Feminist Politics in International Labor," we provide a brief historical overview of feminist activism within the institutions of international labor, the ILO, the International Trade Secretariats, GUFs, and International Trade Union Centers/Confederations. Both the women's movement and the labor movement have a long history of international activism, and here we trace how union feminism served as a bridge between these two movements. Feminists have used and continue to use these organizations and their networks to achieve feminist goals. By building and mobilizing transnational networks and alliances between movements, union feminists create political spaces for new workers and for a better understanding of workers' issues and concerns that arise out of the rapidly changing impacts of globalization on both workplaces and intimate lives.

In chapter 6, "Women's Activism in the International Metalworkers' Federation," we provide an in-depth case study of women's union activism in one of the most traditionally male-dominated sectors in one of the oldest Global Union Federations. The IMF is over a hundred years old and represents workers worldwide in the metal sector, including steel, auto, electronics, mining, and precision instruments. Women make up about one third of the workforce but are grossly underrepresented in the decision-making bodies of the IMF. We trace the efforts by women to gain visibility and voice in what was historically a very male dominated workforce. The campaign for greater representation provides a striking example of the ways union and feminist discourses have developed through persistent effort and the slow accretion of activist knowledge. Women held their first international conference in 1958, and over the course of many decades they were able to expand the opportunities to participate in union decision-making. By developing self-organizing spaces for feminist politics women are helping to make the IMF more relevant to the changing nature of the global economy. Feminists in the IMF are participating in feminist networks with women in other global union federations and with feminists at the ILO and other UN bodies in campaigns on pay equity, decent work, violence and sexual harassment, work/family balance, and so forth. Feminist discourses sharpened in these campaigns have become an important tool in campaigns against precarious work.

In chapter 7, "Another World Is Possible for Women, If . . .," we follow the activities of union feminists at the 2005 World Social Forum in Porto Alegre, Brazil. We had hoped to find spaces at the forum where activists from labor and the women's movements formed strategic alliances within the global justice movement. While activists from both movements were well represented, we found little evidence of material alliance building. However, we did find that discursive alliances between feminists and labor were produced, and some indications that such alliances provide opportunities for making feminist politics with and across transnational labor.

Overall, we conclude that union feminists create new political spaces that extend to transnational levels. Working as insiders, feminist union activists are challenging male-dominated sexual politics of labor movements and are able to develop union networks, alliances, and community organizations. Transnational union activism helps to mobilize women workers to reframe issues and tackle concerns that arise out of the rapidly changing impact of globalization.

2

Sexual Politics, Activism, and Everyday Life

> Can you be a union activist and still have a private life?
> —Judy Darcy, Canadian union leader (Darcy 1993)

How do individuals manage to come together to make politics? On the surface, it is a naïve question, but nevertheless, it lies at the heart of political theorizing and action. A related question of perpetual interest to scholars and activists alike is: What sustains their political activism? Political theorists and activists, union organizers, and social movement campaigners must confront these questions as they deal with ever-changing political conditions, as well as the political gains and losses. It is feminists, however, who bring questions about everyday life into the political domain, not only recognizing the central role it plays in women's lives, but also the complex and contradictory interactions between everyday life and public politics that is critical to understanding and political practice. In this book we bring the contradictions of everyday life to bear in our focus on the political activism of union feminists and the transnational alliances they create between women and labor.

Political activism arises out of a perceived need for change and the belief that taking action and making politics can make a difference. Activism requires spaces and structured opportunities in which activists "can meet, share experiences, receive affirmation and strategize for change" (Katzenstein 1998, 33). Working women who are union members become activists when they perceive the need to struggle for their rights and are able to engage in reflexive discussion over framing issues, means, and goals. Katzenstein (1998) proposes that this is a "politics of making meaning," which she calls discursive politics, involving "the effort to reinterpret, reformulate, rethink and rewrite the norms and practices of society and the state" (17). Its premise is that conceptual changes directly bear on material ones.

Feminist approaches to union activism define it as engaging in union activities, whether one is a rank-and-file member or has a formal, elected position. This activism involves "the capacity and willingness to act, and the practice of taking the initiative, of beginning new actions, of going on the offensive, of making things happen rather than waiting for them to happen" (Cuneo 1993, 111).

We agree that it is imperative to pay attention to women's and feminist activist practices (Eschle and Stammers 2004; Pratt 2004), which in union activism includes a wide range of activities from speaking up at meetings, to talking about an issue at work, to volunteering for routine tasks around the union hall, to participating in organizing drives. British researchers Fiona Colgan and Sue Ledwith (2002) identify the presence of "feminist lay activists and union officers" as a key factor in changing the structures, cultures, and agendas of trade unions in the UK (154). Altogether, activists play a significant role in creating political change.

In this chapter, we examine the ways that the politics of everyday life shapes political activism, and in particular, the activism of union feminists in making feminist politics within and through the trade union movement. Feminism has exposed the limitations on women's opportunities to make politics caused by the demands of the everyday life of home and family, and by widespread assumptions that public politics is a male domain. Feminists bring the sexual politics of everyday life, including women's needs and issues, into the political agenda. We argue that successful strategies for making feminist politics at any level are subject to the resources and capacities available to women in their everyday life. The issue of capacity is usually understood in terms of women's obligations and responsibilities for their care of the everyday lives of their families (Barrett and McIntosh 1982; Crain 2007; Folbre 2001). Although the family may be taken for granted in the West as normatively heterosexual and nuclear, an almost universal assumption is that women are central to family care, whether their families are extended, sexually diverse, or all of these. For working women, this responsibility has been characterized as women's "second shift" (Hochschild 1989), in recognition that women do a second round of work, in addition to their paid labor shift. We take the argument further to recognize that women themselves also need care, which they largely must do for themselves. We conceptualize the necessity for women to care for their own bodies in terms of "the laboring body." Thus, questions about the political opportunity structures available for women to make politics and become activists must also question the opportunities women have to take care of their own bodies, as well as care for their families.

The chapter goes on to argue that the capacity for activism depends on the resources available for women to negotiate the demands of their laboring bodies, and that this care constitutes an integral part of the workload of activism. This is an important, if mostly unseen, dimension of the work of making feminist politics. Grounded in this argument, we then examine the politics of feminist activism within the trade union movement and consider the value and necessity of the strategies of building political and discursive alliances and the equally important strategy of separate organizing. The issues at stake are exemplified in our discussion of the particular issues entailed in making feminist politics with lesbian, gay, bisexual, and transgender (LGBT) workers, or queer organizing.

Sexual Politics

As discussed in chapter 1, we have adopted and adapted Millet's term "sexual politics" to stress that gender is relational and ever-present, and that it always engages and challenges power (Franzway 2001). In this sense, sexual politics emphasizes that politics is intrinsic to the forms that gender relations take, and that gender relations are always being contested. Gender relations may be almost universally patriarchal (Connell 1987) but are always open to challenge from deeply ambivalent meanings of difference and power among women, including race, class, and sexuality.

Present-day usage of the term "sexual politics" tends toward a more direct emphasis on the politics of sexual identities and difference (Seidman 1997). Among the more influential is Judith Butler's work (2009) on sexual politics, which is closely associated with a focus on the politics of sexualities in contrast to the politics of gender relations. Her concern is to move sexual politics to the center of contemporary political life in a complex argument that links freedom and temporal progress. Butler points to political debates "which suggest that certain ideas concerning the progress of 'freedom' facilitate a political division between progressive sexual politics and the struggles against racism and religious discrimination" (Butler 2009, 104). Patricia Hill Collins moves somewhat closer to Millet's notion of the political with her definition of "black sexual politics" as a set of ideas and social practices situated at the intersection of "gender, race and sexuality" that are faced by African Americans (Collins 2004, 6). For Collins, the political is central to struggles around sexual identities so that black sexual politics frames how men and women treat each other. Collins argues that black sexual politics has largely silenced black women and marginalized black lesbian theorizing about sexuality.

In our argument, sexual politics are understood to incorporate the sexual and the political, and are always contested. The sexual politics of gender relations at any one time and place are characterized by the outcome of that contest (Cobble 2004; hooks 2000; Rowbotham 1973). With multiple possibilities in the configurations of gender relations, gender relations are not inevitably patriarchal (Connell 1987), although this is the usual assumption. Sexual politics are not static. The dominance of masculine heterosexuality and the resilience of men's power as men in much contemporary society, including the labor movement, is not inevitable. Rather, it is a continuing struggle that the lens of sexual politics makes it possible to see the ways male dominance and resilience are always being restated, reaffirmed, and reclaimed. Likewise, the stress on political contestation in sexual politics leads to multiple discursive meanings of gender and power, which allows for recognition of the diversity and difference of contested power among women.

In analyzing the sexual politics of the labor movement, we aim to sidestep the way that gender has become coded to refer almost exclusively to women. The conceptualization of the sexual politics of gender relations adopted in this book allows for the recognition, in the contemporary climate, of the centrality and dominance of masculine, heteronormative sexualities/identities, and reframes the analysis away from an arithmetical "gender inclusivity," which refers only to the category "women" and in which the intersections of sexualities, race, and class disappear (Franzway 2001). The concept of sexual politics avoids binary gender categories, thus opening up the complexities of power among women cast by sexualities, class, and race.

Sexual Politics and Activism

In these terms, we argue that activists and feminists, whether they are in trade unions, social movements, or other public organizations, face the difficult problem of sexual politics. Feminist unionists must deal with multiple forms of male heterosexual dominance as well as differences among women while, at the same time, working within union demands for tactical unity or solidarity that are critical to union survival and effectiveness (Briskin and McDermott 1993; Offe and Keane 1985). As a New Zealand union leader said of women in the trade union movement, "We do have a bigger battle, we have all the battles men have and then we have an additional battle, an added responsibility" (Nolan and Ryan 2003, 106). The political arena for feminist activism is much more complex than the clear-cut issue of tackling the apparently straightforward division between "the sexes" (so-called). The state of sexual politics influences political resources and therefore is intrinsic to political activism. Without access to relevant resources, activism becomes simply a matter of gestures. How much political activism women do depends on the power and resources available to them.

We argue that women's access to resources for political activism is conditioned by the dynamic and changing circumstances of sexual politics in which gender relations contest and shape political opportunities and social identities. Resources and capacities for political action are produced within sexual politics, but as feminists have long argued, the field of politics is not limited to the domain of certain public institutions (Butler and Scott 1992; Connell 1987; Millet 1969).

This argument is well demonstrated by the case of LGBT workers, who experience alarming rates of discrimination and prejudice in workplaces and organizations, as evidenced by the Australian study *The Pink Ceiling Is Too Low* (Irwin 1999). Over half of respondents said they suffered from homophobic behavior or harassment, and 11 percent experienced verbal abuse including threats of physical and sexual abuse.

Studies elsewhere also find that LGBT workers' careers are affected by the culture of work organizations and policies (Badgett 2001; Colgan et al. 2006). Where trade unions themselves have begun to collect data on the experiences of LGBT workers, they find that breaches of labor rights are common, as reported, for example, by the international peak body Education International at its Third World Congress in 2001 on behalf of gay and lesbian teaching and nonteaching staff and students (EI 2001).

Such efforts have led to greater awareness of the experiences, issues, and concerns of LGBT workers out of which two points emerge: first, this category of workers is no more homogenous than any other; and second, progressive gains can only be made with persistent and focused political activism. Blandford (2003) notes the limited available research on the economic effects of sexual orientation. He found in a study on the impact of sexual orientation on earnings that "open gay and bisexual men" earned up to 32 percent less than married heterosexual men, while "open lesbian and bisexual women" earned 17 to 38 percent more than married heterosexual women. He speculates that the labor market may penalize the non-marriage of male workers while it may treat the non-marriage of female workers more ambivalently. This differential effect may be a result of employers rewarding adherence to ideals of masculinity, while they penalize adherence to ideals of femininity.

In any case, Blandford argues that since sexual orientation has significant influence on income, its submergence within categories of married or unmarried serves to distort analysis of causes, and therefore the framing of political campaigns to achieve pay equity. Likewise, American research on heterosexism has found that studies on the impact of race and gender in the workplace that ignore sexual orientation tend to underestimate or misconstrue the effects of multiple identities on workers themselves, as well as on the value of antidiscrimination policies (Ragins, Cornwell, and Miller 2003).

The second point in relation to LGBT workers about the necessity for political activism must be stressed because to date little attention has been paid to issues of sexuality and sexual politics in the politics of any trade union movements, whether local or international, or in the research literature. Still less attention has been paid to the hegemonic or homophobic dimensions of sexuality (Genge 1983; Githens and Aragon 2009; Hunt and Bielski Boris 2007). The general silence on issues of sexuality among union activists stands in strong contrast with the clearly articulated view of feminist unionists that the male dominance of the labor movement can no longer be ignored or overlooked. For example, sexual harassment was identified in the 1980s as an objectionable aspect of hegemonic masculine culture in trade unions by union feminists challenging the widespread discursive acceptance that it is simply "what men do" (Attenborough 1983; Cunnison and Stageman 1995; Gutek 1985; Ledwith 2006). Meanwhile, considerable uncertainty and timidity remain about issues of LGBT identities, needs, and concerns in the labor movement.

Opportunities to practice politics and to engage in political activism depend in part on the gendered practices of everyday life. For women, everyday life centers both discursively and in practice on their commitments and obligations to the family. A European delegate to the International Metalworkers Federation (IMF) Congress put it this way: "The situation is quite conservative for the moment, you know. So if you would like to do some activities in the trade unions, ok, fulfill your household tasks, then take it as a hobby. . . . [T]his is not forced by the men, but it is especially the education, by the raising of the girls, so they feel it themselves" (Interview, IMF Congress, 2005).

Political activists, including heterosexual men, are situated within everyday life, a dimension of politics that is often overlooked by so-called gender-inclusive politics where women's interests are merely added on to the list. We propose that a focus on the sexual politics of everyday life and political activism turns attention to questions about the impact of gender relations on political opportunities and possibilities.

The Activist in Everyday Life

> So then we got to talking, I told him how I felt,
> How I keep him running just as smooth as some conveyor belt,
> For after all it's I'm the one provides the power supply,
> (He goes just like the clappers on my steak and kidney pie.)
> His fittings are all shining 'cos I keep them nice and clean,
> And he tells me his machine tool is the best I've ever seen.
> . . .
> So the truth began to dawn then how I keep him fit and trim
> So the boss can make a nice fat profit out of me and him.
> . . .
> I said "Don't jump the gun love, if you did your share at home,
> Perhaps I'd have some time to fight some battles of my own!"
> (Sandra Kerr, "The Maintenance Engineer" [quoted in Beale 1982])

The practices of everyday life are integral to political activism, yet they are rarely mentioned outside anecdotes and private conversations. Feminism's most influential move in the sexual politics of everyday life has been to identify the second shift and its massive impact on women's lives. Rooted in the 1970s campaigns on the politics and theory of housework and social reproduction (see, for example, Oakley 1974), the development of the notion of the second shift gained in credibility and public awareness. Hochschild's (1989) classic study, *The Second Shift*, as well as careful time budget surveys (Bianchi et al. 2000; Bittman 1991), the concept of "emotional labor" (Hochschild 1983), and the identification of care as caring labor (Finch and Groves 1983; Folbre and Nelson 2000), all provided keys to a more precise analysis of the second shift and the gendered division of labor.

Feminists have examined the opportunity costs of women's second shift, by which women provide the material and emotional back-up for men and children (Bittman and Wajcman 2004; Hochschild 1989; Ungerson 1997). The second shift identifies the necessary work women do to sustain families, households, and communities while it limits their participation in the paid workforce and in political activism. This pattern has been affected by the upheavals caused by the globalization of labor markets. Communities and essential support structures are often dislocated, leaving women increasingly responsible for the maintenance of community life (Ehrenreich and Hochschild 2002; Wichterich 2000).

The recognition of the second shift has been a theoretical and political advance for women. However, the issue of women's own needs and how they are met remains to be tackled. We develop a critique of these points in chapter 3. Here, we need to recognize that while women are taking care of others, they must also take care of themselves. It is widely accepted that women's care of others has a significant impact on their capacity and opportunities to participate in the public domain, which may include political activism. We argue that this situation is a matter of sexual politics, which can be and often is contested, although not always understood, in terms of gender. We do not take this interplay of gender relations for granted.

The notion of the second shift is constrained by its location within the heterosexual nuclear family of the Global North. It fails to offer theoretical insight into the everyday lives of queer activists and of those who live in the great variety of other family structures and cultures. At this point, we want to address an almost universally neglected dimension of this analysis, namely the question of women's need for care—that is, their need to utilize the products of this labor in the second shift.

Recognition and conceptualization of the second shift occurred when western feminists were grappling with domestic labor and the politics of housework within nuclear families and were trawling through Marx and Engels, deconstructing and reconstructing Marxist and sociological ideas about work, exchange value, use value, and surplus value (Dalla Costa and James 1974; Gardiner 1975; Molyneux 1979). In the domestic labor debate, feminists focused on the taken-for-granted aspects of housework, discussing examples such as the production of the family breakfast with its then-ubiquitous bowl of cornflakes. By tracing the housewife's labor that had gone into its appearance on the breakfast table, feminists argued the necessity of women's (invisible) labor in the social reproduction of the worker's labor (that is, the husband's labor).

However, what remained unseen was the question of the reproduction of the woman's own labor. We did not look to see whether or when the woman ate *her* cornflakes (Gardiner 1975; Seccombe 1974). As feminist research burgeoned, we learned that in highly gendered societies women usually ate last and ate least, that whole societies were founded on women's gathering labor, and that women were capable of exploiting other women to carry out the domestic labor (Bezuidenhout and Fakier 2006; Charles and Kerr 1987; Murcott 1983; Romero 1992).

Activism and the Laboring Body

We opened the chapter with a question about what sustains political activism, which has led to questions about the impact of everyday life on opportunities for political activism. The lens of sexual politics reveals that not only are women responsible for everyday life through their second shift with their families, but also that women must meet their own needs in everyday life. In the case of making politics, we ask: How do women activists take care of themselves? The sociologist Bryan Turner (1984) pointed toward this question with his notion of "bodily practices": "Bodies are objects over which we labour—eating, sleeping, cleaning, dieting, and exercising. These labours can be called bodily practices and they are both individual and collective.... We labour on, in and with our bodies" (159).

The problem is that women and men do not labor equally over their bodies; bodily practices are not gender neutral. Since women undertake a significant proportion of the bodily practices required by others' bodies, the question must be raised: What about the bodily practices required by the woman's body to undertake this work? How are *her* needs for food, clothing, cleaning, even health care to be met?

Building on rich insights gained from theoretical developments of Bourdieu's socialized subjectivities (1990) discursive constructions of subjectivity, Butler's performativity (1993), and Foucault's techniques of the self (1979), Baron and Boris (2007) identify the body as a work, "a product of human labor, and something that does work, masking the social power attached to bodily differences" (24). Their concern is to claim the body as a useful category for working-class history by exploring the bodily effects of discursive regimes, technologies of power and materiality. The question they pose is: How are bodies produced in ways that appear natural and thereby camouflage the social struggles that define them? Although Baron and Boris advance the argument for the recognition of the ways culture and work make and mark classed, gendered, and raced bodies, the material labor of women's reproduction is overlooked. The body is present, but the work entailed in its production is not.

Their work parallels that of Carol Wolkowitz, who found in her excellent survey of the field that the body at work remains invisible in the literature. Her particular concern is the body in paid work, and she proposes a concept of the body/work nexus that "takes the body as its immediate site of labor, involving intimate, messy contact with the (frequently supine or naked) body" that is the paid work on the body by occupations such as dentists, hairdressers, and undertakers (Wolkowitz 2006, 8). Wolkowitz addresses waged domestic labor, its contribution to reproductive work, and the increasing trend toward the transnationalization of such work with the rise in free and forced migration of body workers.

Yet the material unpaid work necessary to reproduce women is absent from these accounts. The unpaid work of care, emotional labor, and housework that women do for others is well recognized. But no attention is given to women's needs for the same care. We argue that it is overwhelmingly women who must do this work for themselves.

One way to bring women's own care needs and practices into the light is to focus attention on the body that women must work or labor on to enable them to undertake their other work. Despite the considerable attention paid to the regulation, consumerism, and anxiety associated with women's bodies (Weitz 2003; Wolf 1991), there is little recognition that women must supply most of their own bodies' needs for care, without being able to rely on others. A large part of the reproduction of the woman's body remains invisible; it is this body that is reproduced out of sight. Rather than limit our focus to women's need for care, we want to stress the work of care that women do in order to reproduce their own bodies and enable them to carry out their other work. We therefore use the term "the laboring body" to define "the body which requires care in order to work" (Franzway 2001, 32).

In this sense, the laboring body is generally invisible theoretically and in everyday life, but it is critical to women's capacity to work, is the basis of women's "freedom to act," and is central to women's everyday lives and their political activism (Gibson-Graham 2006, xxvi). In other words, the laboring body must be included with the second shift, emotional labor, and housework in our attempts to understand the conditions of women's opportunities for political activism.

In everyday life, women's production of the laboring body occurs in the space left by the second shift, and in the case of feminist and union activists must be squeezed in between their multiple activities and obligations. Women find very often that their bodily reproduction must be carefully calibrated so that they achieve what is normatively defined as appropriate for a working woman's body, at the same time as it aligns with the feminine body; a precarious balance as pregnant women discover in certain workplaces and public spaces (Vogel 1990): "My working pregnant body was constituted by others as transgressive in that it breached cultural norms about what a proper 'natural' mother should want to do before and after the birth of her child" (Dwyer 2006, 19).

Women's bodies can no longer be taken for granted as the result of nature or fate. Rather, discourses of the body have shifted so that the body must now be worked upon or self-managed (Giddens 1991). The feminine body does not simply develop of its own accord; it must be worked for and labored over. And so the production of the working woman's body, and the activist woman's body, must be contiguous with the discursively produced feminine body (Adkins and Lury 2000; Brewis 2000; Williams 1988).

Much greater ambivalence exists about ideal working women's bodies than about the feminine body. In so-called nontraditional fields of work and public life, it is men's rather than women's bodies that are the norm, while people in other occupations, such as flight attendants, find that their bodies are deployed to present a feminine aesthetic (Wolkowitz 2006) and to achieve the heteronormative definition of the sexually attractive body. Men's bodies likewise negotiate embodied demands of work, ranging from the embodied strength of miners and construction workers to the ubiquity of the collar and tie as an almost global representation of middle-class masculinity (Adkins 2002; Connell 2005; Holliday and Hassard 2001). Although the male body now has to be worked on with more attention than a fortnightly haircut and clothed in a slightly greater range of correct attire (made ready by a woman), nevertheless they are better rewarded in work, in leisure, and in status than are female bodies (McDowell 1997).

The notion of the laboring body with its attention to a critical third layer of work in women's everyday lives adds a significant dimension to Canadian union leader Judy Darcy's question at the beginning of this chapter: Can you be a union activist and still have a private life? It refers us not only to issues around the demands of normative family life (which includes the largely intransigent demands of children's care), but also to questions about what sustains a woman union activist? We have in mind two aspects: the material production of the body's capacity to work; and the aesthetic presentation of the body that is appropriate to the particular workplace—for example, the "healthy, fit, and attractive body" increasingly required of both men and women in professional and managerial work (Wolkowitz 2006). In addition to the kinds of services provided by body workers, such as hairdressers and physiotherapists as discussed by Wolkowitz, we stress that both aspects require women to engage in complex negotiations of discourses and practices as modes of bodily discipline (for example, through negotiating bodily fitness practices including exercise and vacations).

The physical activity of exercise, for example, has been privileged as a domain of individual responsibility, "which subordinates other ways of being that include relaxation, peacefulness, contemplation, ease of movement and awareness of the moment" (Fullagar 2003, 54). It has become a significant aspect of bodily self-care. More directly, the discursive imperative for women to manage their bodies is likely to produce a constantly dissatisfied self-scrutiny, while they experience their bodies as limited in their capacity to realize their potential. Women's fitness is limited by sexual politics of the gendered body. Yet, exercise has become essential to the production of the feminine body (Gimlin 2002), as well as to women's capacity to "work harder" and thus sustain the pressures of work intensification along with the demands of everyday life, as these women unionists remark: "Exercise? Well that's a problem. I really really tried to work fitness into my life but . . ." (Canadian union activist), and "Exercise? That's a little too structured so I don't do it much" (Australian union activist).

The benefits of exercise are well recognized, but for many women activists, finding the time for this form of self-care between the demands of work, activism, and everyday life, it is "not even on the list," as one Canadian expressed it. Any of the potential pleasure that might be gained from exercise and fitness is further undermined by fatigue, an important factor in women's generally low participation in exercise programs and in leisure activities.

Likewise, recreation in the form of vacations has become critical for the renewal of paid workers. But do activists go on holiday or take sabbaticals from their political commitments? They appear to have much difficulty in finding free time from the high demands and unpredictable nature of political life. Downturns and upswings are inevitable to social movements, and as one of the Australian activists interviewed by Sarah Maddison and Sean Scalmer (2006) said, "you'll be much more useful to people if you take time out and look after yourself a bit" (236). Several others mentioned burnout as a risk of long-term political commitment, particularly when defeats are more frequent than campaign victories. However, the difficulties are compounded by sexual politics, so that when women take holidays with their families there tends to be more work involved than if they stayed at home (Deem 1988). Women's recreation depends on the individual management of time, money "to really get away," and the necessity to fit in with other family members (Thomsson 1999). In addition, accumulating large amounts of annual leave has become a heroic and tangible demonstration of commitment to the greedy institution of the labor movement among women as well as men.

Doing Activism

> I was in a never-ending grind of work.
> —Canadian activist

As we observed at the beginning of this chapter, activism takes high levels of time and energy; it is an activity that typically has no limits. There is always more that could be done. Whether activists are unpaid participants in unions or social movements, or occupy elected or appointed paid positions, the work generally requires long, strenuous hours and great emotional resources. Ruth Needleman (1993), a labor scholar and unionist in the United States, notes that the ideal unionist resembles "a workaholic, eighteen-hour-a-day activist who always puts the union first. . . . Unions set high expectations for leadership and staff. Theirs is not an eight-hour job; the fight for justice is full-time" (410).

For women, this can mean that activism is the fourth level of their activity, following their paid work, the second shift of domestic labor, and the work of the laboring body. The reproduction of heterosexual men's working bodies is partly undertaken by women as their second shift, whereas the bodily practices of the laboring body to produce women's working bodies are placed firmly in the hands of women themselves. Women carry out much of their own bodily practices or pay other women to do it for them. They must cook or organize their own cornflakes, buy and wash their own clothes, manage their own health needs. In general, men can assume their mothers, daughters, or female partners will do at least some of these tasks for them; women cannot make this assumption. When activism takes place at the transnational level, the time and energy costs of travel, management of the second shift, and paid work (in addition to the financial costs) must be weighed. This is particularly the case for those whose home base is located on the global periphery.

The activist's workload in the greedy institution of the labor movement is intensified by a culture of masculine heroics that is common in trade unions as well as social movements, with their "[t]wenty-four-hours a day, seven-days-a-week commitment" (Cockburn 1991, 122). Such masculine heroics are not confined to trade unions. Discourses that value hard work and long hours have gained increasing prominence in the wider culture in parallel with the material reality of increasing work hours for full-time workers (Maher, Lindsay, and Franzway 2008; Pocock 2003; Presser 2003). The paradox is that very few unions have adopted the kind of flexible work arrangements for their own officials, delegates, and employees that they advocate for their members. While union feminists and officials are critical of heavy workloads and most decry the high personal costs, only mild attempts have been made to tackle the issue collectively and politically. Individual solutions to the demands of union workloads and to demands from women's domestic lives are far more common.

Perhaps even more ironically, feminist social movements face similar issues. Marusia López Cruz (2006), a feminist active in nongovernment organizations (NGOs), observed that "we have to rethink the conditions in which feminists are working, because many times we operate like maquila factories where basic labor rights are violated. In which if you are young you have to do voluntary work and if you are an adult you lack a minimal patrimony for retirement" (3).

Neither labor movements nor women's movements can claim consistent good practices around the work of making politics. Fatigue, burnout, and despair are too often part of the everyday life of making politics in trade union and social movements (Maddison and Scalmer 2006; Rooks 2003). Nevertheless, attempts are made to build their political resources and to find creative ways to enhance time and resources, and feminist activists look to the resources as well as the political goals of trade union movements for opportunities to make feminist politics.

Doing Activism in Trade Union Movements

Feminist activists, including those who focus on work issues along with union feminists, recognize the political opportunities available in the trade union movement. Or rather, feminists seek to create political opportunities and spaces out of what is at hand in trade unions (Conley 2005). As Maroney (1983) observed nearly thirty years ago, the labor movement has the capacity to provide "organizational continuity, material resources, and an established constituency in contrast with the more ephemeral, poorer, yet creative, self-directed and consciously holistic structures of the autonomous women's movement" (58). Labor's formal democratic structures provide "a means for trade union feminists to take advantage of the political and ideological space created by general feminist agitation, whether that be as a result of real sensitivity to women's needs or merely to their explosiveness" (58).

The development of feminist union activism requires the cultivation of political spaces for constructing feminist discursive politics, including agendas and strategies. As Curtin (1999) suggests, "separate spaces provide the opportunity for women to alter the discursive frameworks through which women's claims are constituted" (33). The creation of such spaces within unions and the international labor movement are a critical element of feminist union activism. As we show, however, these spaces are hard won and not easily retained, for example, in relation to alliances between LGBT social movements and labor movements (Colgan et al. 2006; Hunt and Bielski Boris 2007; Krupat and McCreery 2001).

To be effective, activists, particularly feminist activists in relatively marginal situations, engage in political alliances of the kind defined by Cynthia Cockburn (1998) as the "creative structuring of relational space between collectivities marked by problematic differences" (211). Cockburn (2000) identifies five principles that contribute to "a sustainable harmony" by creating "an optimal distance between differences, small enough for mutual knowledge, for dispelling myths, but big enough for comfort" (51). Briefly, these principles involve affirming difference, acknowledging identities and injustices done in the name of differentiated identities, taking care that political agendas avoid matters that would destroy the alliance, and an inclusive and transparent group process (2000, 51–53).

In this book, we discuss the new alliances that are being created by feminist and queer activists who are working at both transnational and local levels. Essential to this process of creating and building alliances is the social construction of meaning that we call discursive alliances—the terminology we adopt to stress the significance of shared discourse to political activism. Progressive union activists connect their experiences from within union hierarchies to the democratic ideals of unionism and of social movements, and reconcile the attitudes and interests of rank-and-file members with their own commitment to the trade union movement. The task for feminist union activists is further complicated by the need to negotiate tensions between women's interests and the hegemonic pressures of men's interests—that is, feminist activists must engage with the sexual politics of the labor movement, rather than a straightforward focus on mobilizing women themselves.

Union feminists who are committed to representing and advocating women's interests are assumed to represent all women and embody their needs, while many people, including other women, regard them as among the select few, the elite of the institution: "Trade union feminists are caught in a contradictory situation" (Maroney 1983, 58). If women are elected union officials, they are assumed to be able to exercise union power in a straightforward, uncontested way. Such expectations are heightened greatly when women become part of the union leadership.

Activism and Separate Organizing

Feminist politics within the labor movement calls for the equal representation of women's issues and thus poses a significant challenge to the trade union principle of solidarity and to its dominant heteronormative masculinity. A key, historical strategy for union activists is what Linda Briskin (1993) calls "separate organizing," or "self-organization" as it is termed in the UK. Briskin distinguishes separate organizing from separatism and its explicit refusal to work with men, as it reflects women's different experiences in the workplace and the domestic sphere.

Historically, women have organized separate women's unions in certain occupations and industries as a response to being largely excluded from mainstream "male" trade unionism (Brigden 2005; Elton 1976; Maroney 1983). For example, the United Bank Workers section of the Service, Office, Retail Workers Union of Canada (SORWUC), established in 1972, was a small, feminist independent union based in British Columbia that utilized feminist organizing strategies to encourage the participation of previously unorganized workers, mainly women. However, its isolation from mainstream labor and the hostility of some unions left it vulnerable to huge opposition from the banking industry and to reluctance of the union movement to support it. Although it collapsed after a few years, its initiative prodded the union movement to pay more attention to women workers (Baker 1993; Luxton 2001).

Small, women-only unions have also been organized in Japan (Broadbent 2008) and Korea (Lee 2003; Moon and Broadbent 2008), while a much larger organization, the Self-Employed Women's Association (SEWA), has had considerable success in addressing the needs of women workers in India, especially those in the informal economy (Hill 2008). Strategies that are more successful are possible where unions have a high proportion of women members combined with a progressive leadership. For one woman union leader, her female-dominated union "was a haven, it was a haven. . . . I don't think I would have survived if I'd been pushing up through a male-dominated union" (Franzway 2001). She went on to win the position of secretary, the most senior position of her union.

Separate organizing is an important mechanism designed to encourage active participation among the diverse memberships of the labor movement. It challenges the sexual politics of male domination of unions and "the domination of an organizational model based on bureaucratic, hierarchical, overly competitive and often undemocratic practices" (Briskin 1998, 7). Separate organizing has a long, complex, and often invisible history, some of which we explore in chapters 5 and 6. A multiplicity of forms have been devised, such as women's committees, caucuses, taskforces, conferences, and affirmative action to achieve reserved places on union governing bodies (Cook, Lorwin, and Daniels 1992).

Separate organizing allows women the space to identify and articulate their different needs, and it provides the means by which women can advocate change in the trade union movement. As a group of union women at a national conference for women in male-dominated occupations at which we were participant observers, said, "[The conference] is brilliant and I absolutely love it... everybody sticking together, the strength, the support and to give the support. I have got so much information, listening to other people's stories, what they do. It is actually great" (Interview, Adelaide, 2003).

Paradoxically, separate organizing appeared as an early strategy in the male-dominated metal trade unions in Italy and in Sweden, in part because these were the most politically militant sections of the labor movement. It was subsequently taken up in different ways by other groups marginalized within or by labor movements (Beccalli and Meardi 2002; Ledwith and Colgan 2002). Overall, its success is varied. In the UK, Colgan and Ledwith (2002) describe separate organizing as an "institutionalised faction, which union executives have felt constrained to accept" (159). Italian trade unions appeared to accept the strategy, but their leadership undermined it with effective passive resistance (Beccalli and Meardi 2002, 129).

Separate educational programs are among the more effective strategies, as Fonow's extended study of the Canadian and United States Women of Steel courses in the International Steelworkers' Union demonstrates (Fonow 2003). Women participants reported that they gained in knowledge, awareness, and confidence achieving an identity where they could become activists in their own unions and "join the table." In addition, our research has found that women unionists see women's groups, whether formal or informal, as very important to their own well-being as well as transformative of labor movement political agendas (Franzway 2001; Parker 2003): "Yeah, I got very tired but I drew tremendous strength and I kept my enthusiasm through those other activities and also I think the key was having a group of, a very, very cohesive network of women who were very close" (Interview, Canadian union official).

Helen Creed (1999), writing as secretary of a large Australian union, believes such groups are important to union women's survival in a broad political context that includes hostile politicians as much as other union officials. In an interview with us about the effects of losing a close union election, a

Canadian official said, "for me that [women's committee] was salvation. You could go and talk about what's going on, get support, learn about new ideas. Otherwise it would have been devastating."

This kind of support depends on much more than winning token numbers of women in formal positions. Many women union activists, as well as women outside the labor movement, have concluded that getting women into leadership positions is not sufficient to produce successful progressive politics. Targeting the top is, in some senses, an individualist strategy and, as has been argued elsewhere, it is a risky business for those in such positions who must negotiate dominant structures of power and cultures while championing feminist interests (Franzway, Court, and Connell 1989). Union activists have come to this view in the following terms: "I think it's hard for any woman in a difficult position in a male culture. There was a time when we considered that to get a woman in the position would change the culture of the organization.... We have changed dramatically from getting individuals into positions to trying to look at cultural change.... I would say we've got to do both" (Interview, Australian union official).

The shift to the recognition of the political value of changing culture has become an important dimension of union women's campaigns. Feminist unionists are engaging with sexual politics by naming and opposing a culture of masculinity in the trade union movement that includes a highly masculinized labor iconography, in which the symbolism of unionism romanticized violence, rooted solidarity in metaphors of struggle, and constructed work and the worker as male (Faue 1991; Muir 1997). Unless women's cultures, recognizing diversity (in whatever form), become integral to unionism then unions will continue to alienate and fail women.

Furthermore, by campaigning to change union culture with its male concepts of everyday life, family, and identity, feminists contribute to the ways women can negotiate the competing values and demands of the two greedy institutions in their lives, the family, and the union. However, as Janis Bailey points out in her study of a creative industrial campaign in Western Australia, framing a strategy around family, in particular "family work," may obscure issues of gender difference (Bailey 2005). We develop this theme in chapter 3.

In this chapter we have brought the sexual politics of everyday life onto the field of feminist activism in labor movements, whether they are local, national, or transnational. Such an approach directs our attention to relatively invisible dimensions of everyday life: sexualities and homophobia, which raise equally important issues for labor movements at local and transnational levels.

Alliances and Queer Organizing

"There's a lot of resonance with the union movement for gay men and lesbians. I mean, people work in fear of being known as a unionist in some work places and it's a double fear if you're a gay man or a lesbian, experiencing direct discrimination or harassment on the basis of sexuality" (Australian union activist). "The response to gay and lesbian issues has been to sanitize queer organizing and issues around sexuality" (Canadian union activist).

An exploration of the history of LGBT issues in the trade union movement reveals that, much like the engagement with race (particularly in the United States, Canada, and the UK), very little happens without alliances between the social movement and union members. Trade unions are dominated by masculine heterosexuality, reflecting repressive meanings of sexuality (including a lack of recognition and even hostility toward homosexuality and homosexual desire among men), which appear in the wider society.

Political campaigns have seen LGBT workers' issues framed as rights, based on the argument that equality would be more achievable if LGBT rights were successfully integrated into broader campaigns for labor rights at national, regional, and international levels. However, the politics are by no means straightforward: "This has been a major coup within labor [unions] to get a rights-based analysis incorporated into collective agreements so that you can actually file a grievance around sex-based or sexuality-based harassment. . . . I don't want to minimize that, but we've also paid a price because we don't want just to be regarded in the same way that heterosexual families are with the same rights to marry. . . . [W]e want to be able to in fact open up the family as an institution as well" (Canadian woman official). Nevertheless, the movement's responses to the needs of LGBT workers are relatively good by comparison with most public institutions and movements (Hunt and Haiven 2006; Ostenfeld 1998).

Perhaps unions have been motivated by the need to address criticisms that they are "male, pale and stale" as the UK peak union body, the Trades Union Congress (TUC), would have it (Barber 2005). Internal support structures and policies have been developed despite resistance from some union officials and members; unions do mount campaigns on explicit issues around sexuality, such as protection from homophobia in the workplace.

The first public endorsement of LGBT rights by an American labor union was in 1970 when the executive council of the American Federation of Teachers passed a resolution denouncing discrimination against teachers solely because the individual was a homosexual. In 1975, bus drivers in the Transport Employee Union (TEU) in Ann Arbor, Michigan, became the first union workers to have a sexual orientation nondiscrimination clause in their union contract. Some years later, in 1983, the American peak body, the American Federation of Labor and Congress of Industrial Organizations (AFL-CIO), condemned discrimination based on sexual orientation and called for federal and state legislation to ban such discrimination. In 1994, Pride At Work (PAW) affiliated with the AFL-CIO despite opposition from some members of the AFL-CIO's executive council. According to Holcomb and Wohlforth (2001), the affiliation was supported by union leaders, including the new AFL-CIO president, John Sweeney, who were motivated to halt a union membership decline. But unlike other constituent organizations, PAW was not given a budget to help fund its operations until 1999. Nevertheless, it gained access to other member organizations and unions, thus significantly enhancing its research and mobilization capacity.

The Canadian peak body, the Canadian Labour Congress (CLC), endorsed a policy on sexual orientation at its 1994 convention and held a national conference for gay and lesbian unionists in 1997, the first to be organized anywhere by official trade union structures (Genge 1998). The Canadian Auto Workers Union (CAW) was the first private sector union in that country to recognize "sexual preference" in its constitution and added transgender issues to its bargaining agenda in 1999 (Hunt and Haiven 2006). In the UK, a survey by Colgan and Ledwith (2002) identified eight out of the thirteen unions surveyed supported one or more relevant strategies. A few years later, an equality audit by the UK peak body, the TUC (2005), of its national affiliates found that twenty-two unions (46 percent) reported negotiating improvements in the position of LGBT workers.

These achievements are the result of LGBT labor activism that grew with the emergence of a broader social movement in the 1960s. Some political spaces were created within the labor movement. For example, the first Australian Gay and Lesbian Trade Unionists Group (GayTUG) was formed in 1978. Twenty years later, the Gay and Lesbian Australian Services Union Members (GLAM) was set up to articulate LGBT issues to the broad labor movement as well as within their own union. Similar separate organizing by networks of lesbians and gay men established internal structures such as the National Pink Triangle Committee of the Canadian Union of Public Employees (CUPE) in 1991 by convention resolution. This committee, composed of representatives from various regions of the country as well as staff, works toward eliminating homophobia and heterosexism and promoting the human rights of lesbian, gay, and bisexual members. In New Zealand, gay and lesbian unionists for equality formed Gay and Lesbian Unionists for Equality (GLUE) in Wellington to gain union recognition of the need to promote and protect the interests of lesbian and gay workers; later, the New Zealand Council of Trade Union's network (NZCTU), CTU Out@Work was set up for lesbian, gay, takataapui, bisexual, intersex, transgender, and fa'afafine union members.[1]

It is notable that these campaigns have been built with the kind of alliances with broader social movements that we have identified as critical to a new feminist politics. The famous campaign against Coors Beer in the United States resulted from an alliance—the LGBT–Labor Network—that led to a boycott of the company's products by all LGBT bars in San Francisco in the 1970s. However, more recently other LGBT organizations have accepted donations from Coors [Cohen 1999]), partly as a result of efforts by Coors to win back LGBT customers. Such alliances fuel internal union campaigns by feminist and LGBT activists to push unions and transnational peak bodies to address the issues and workers' concerns. As McCreery and Krupat (1999) argue, "the challenge for lesbian, gay, bisexual, and transgendered movements to confront elitism and inequalities in their own ranks, is to acknowledge common cause with other social movements, and to wage their struggles at the intersections of class, race, and gender" (5).

One of the more creative examples is that of a group of LGBT community activists, the Sisters of Perpetual Indulgence, who organized a gay contingent to participate in the 1981 Australian May Day parade, the annual celebration of workers' rights, although "it was not well received by some in the union hierarchy" (Towart 2002). Unions participate in the Sydney Gay and Lesbian Mardi Gras, a huge annual march through central Sydney streets, despite internal conflicts that have seen some union officials threatening to resign. Robyn Fortescue (2000) argues that events like Mardi Gras are not just about what happens on the night. Their impact derives from the organization, debates, and material support that must go on beforehand to enable the participation to occur. Such political and discursive alliances make Mardi Gras "the biggest labour festival of the year" (64).

Queer activism at the international level has emerged out of alliances of national and local unions, and social movements, producing a proliferation of political spaces. Local activists are able to engage in transnational alliances, such as the first International LGBT Forum, sponsored by the international union peak bodies, Education International (EI), and Public Services International (PSI). The forum was held prior to the EI World Congress in Porto Alegre, Brazil, in 2004. Its purpose was to develop a set of proposals for action on the rights for LGBT workers that would be presented to PSI and

EI. A declaration was produced, framed in terms of human rights, which recognized the diversity of the LGBT communities and lifestyles, asserted that the workplace must be a space free of discrimination of any kind, and urged that trade unions take the lead in eliminating discrimination. The declaration expressed the concern that "[t]he rights of sexual minorities are not explicitly recognized in most international and national standards and instruments; and that therefore discrimination and inequity based on sexual orientation and gender identity continue to persist at different levels. These include employment; access to public services; criminal and civil law; failure to recognize legally atypical personal relations such as same sex partnerships and de facto couples; lack of support for LGBT young workers and the specific needs of transgender people" (EI 2007).

The action plan developed from the forum called for establishing a sexual diversity network between PSI and EI that would facilitate the sharing of resources and coordinate national and international campaigns for LGBT labor and social rights; linking Web pages to provide a regular supply of news and updates about the work of the national networks; participation in a World Workers' Out conference; and holding an international forum on sexual diversity prior to the PSI World Congress in 2007.

The international Out at Work! conferences grew out of and extended global/local networks of gay, lesbian, and transgender workers. The first, held in Amsterdam in 1998, stressed the political value of global networks for campaigns on the rights of gay, lesbian, and transgender workers. Over 1,700 people from 113 countries participated in the 2006 Montreal World Workers' Out conference. Conference declarations and action plans stress the political necessity of global campaigns to tackle the appalling working conditions of those who, in the words of one delegate, "live in countries that still execute their homosexual citizens" (Workers Online 2002, 139).

Such transnational networks have the capacity to be effective when they draw on trade union resources to create forums and spaces for lesbian, gay, and transgender workers. But, as Carol Beaumont (2006), the NZCTU secretary, observed: "We are a long way from having stamped out homophobia—certainly in the community as a whole but also among unions—our officials, activists and members" (2). Mutual support across the trade union movement is both possible and necessary, but much needs to be done to create political opportunities, forums, and spaces for lesbian and gay workers in and around the trade union movement.

Networks and political and discursive alliances among union movements, feminist union activists, and LGBT activists are vital; complete consensus is unnecessary, but without such groupings, activists involved in queer organizing risk isolation and burnout, a significant factor in the everyday lives of activists more generally.

Conclusion

Making feminist politics takes time, emotions, thought, and energy, and no less so than when acting to achieve political goals through alliances with the labor movement. Such resources are difficult enough to find, organize, and sustain, but making transnational politics raises the bar even further. The flexibility, commitment, and focus of feminist activists bring vital resources of relevance, energy, and growth to the labor movement. However, there are difficulties, well summarized by a Canadian union feminist: "Activist women [in the Women's Movement] don't necessarily understand the Labor Movement; they come with the same kinds of misunderstandings hostilities even, and of course we come with our own prejudices, as far as racism and sexism. . . . It's a reality that we in the Women's Movement in the Labor movement live with, work with, and we've been able to because we feel it's really important [that] if we're going to get anywhere, our brothers are going to have to be supportive" (Interview, Canadian union official).

We argue that the potential of the political opportunities available from political and discursive alliances between women and labor cannot be realized without challenging the obstacles of sexual politics, such as the persistence of the second shift and the invisibility of women's laboring body, which are more complex than a rebalancing of the sexes. This is as critical to transnational politics as it is at the local, more visible level.

3

Sexual Politics, Labor, and the Family

> It rests with the unions to keep the woman in the home, while ensuring to the breadwinner the means necessary to maintain the family properly.
>
> —Male Italian delegate, International Metalworkers' Federation (IMF) 1958 conference

The Australian Labor Party won the 2007 federal election with a campaign paved by the endless repetition of the slogan "working families." It is a term that circumvents gender and class, refers to the core values of work and family, and invokes a social category of good citizenship. Those not included were clearly beyond the pale of the national agenda—too lazy, too marginal, even too rich. The Australian trade union movement's effective campaign, "Your Rights at Work," also addressed working families with media and organizational strategies that drew on concerns about so-called work/life issues as well as the erosion of workplace rights and conditions (Muir 2008).

This shift in focus from the working man as the male breadwinner who needed a "family wage" to support wife and family, toward workers and their families, or working families, is occurring across all levels of the labor movement, and has been in use for more than a decade (Masters 2004). For example, the American Federation of Labor and Congress of Industrial Organizations' (AFL-CIO) slogan "working together, working for families" is matched by the Trades Union Congress's (TUC) "time off for families" and the International Trade Union Confederation's (ITUC) focus on "working women and men and their families." The benchmark of union campaigns framed by family discourses is the International Labour Organization (ILO) Convention 156, Workers with Family Responsibilities, established in 1981 and subsequently modified. Convention 156 resulted from initiatives by international movements to reframe the concept of the worker from being produced by the invisible labor of their families to a more realistic and holistic notion of people with responsibilities that cannot be dealt with by the spending of wages alone. It broke with the public/private divisions. It required employers to recognize that the interests and needs of their employees extend beyond the workplace, acknowledging that barriers between the workplace and the rest of the society have never been completely impermeable.

Framing workers in terms of the family helps to identify the needs of the expanding female workforce, many of whom remain responsible for managing and nurturing everyday life, as we discussed in the previous chapter. Such a frame offers real gains for women and for labor and provides a basis for alliances between them. It is significant for new feminist politics that the trade union movement, at local and transnational levels, is taking up the family as a rallying point for labor campaigns.

New political discourses of the family are leading to new forms of politics, new possibilities, and new challenges for labor and feminist activists, while recognizing that the family and its relationship to work has always been a key issue for women and the labor movement. The family has become a site of political and discursive alliances between women and labor that extend from the local to the transnational level. However, family as a rallying point is neither as universal nor as reassuring as is often assumed.

In the discourses and practices of everyday life and politics, family has diverse meanings as well as various and changing normative structures, practices, and social locations. In the global Christian Right movement, a "natural family campaign" incorporates women's rights as part of its political agenda (Buss and Herman 2003, 305). Politics framed in terms of the family tends to rely on simplified definitions of the family in the pragmatics of political practice and can suggest that society exclusively comprises families. It may be said, nevertheless, that family is everywhere linked to women. Thus, when progressive labor embraces the family it appears to be placing women's interests and concerns on the union agenda (Bailey 2005).

However, what kind of equality for women can be achieved when the family is at the center of a political program? As Cobble and Michal (2002) warn, "the emphasis on 'family' rather than on women risks obscuring the still fundamental reality that these are issues that affect men and women *differently* and that women's needs are only *partially* met when they are defined as the same as men" (147, their emphasis). When family discourses have become the means to identify the needs of women workers, there is a strong risk of contradictory political consequences, since women may be seen only in relation to the family, rather than in their own right. In this chapter we contribute to the growing debates on the effects and effectiveness of union politics framed by family discourses by drawing together feminist understandings of the family and sexual politics with analyses of selected campaigns, including pay equity, childcare, and work/life balance, that have developed through alliances between women and labor.

Feminism and the Family

Behind the strategy to bring the family onto the political agenda of the trade union movement lies a history of women's struggles at all levels of the movement (Boston 1980; Milkman 1985). Family is a key institution in feminist politics and a central term in feminist theorizing because family is central to women's lives and identities (Calhoun 2000; Dalley 1996). More than a century of sustained activism by feminists has transformed assumptions that workers are male breadwinners and that women workers either threaten male pay and conditions or are no more than a reserve army of labor. But these gains can never be taken for granted. As the struggle moves back and forth over the decades and across the world, the politics of women and the family is always being contested, defined, and redefined.

Feminism has politicized the family, recognizing it as a site of sexual politics with its complex of gender relationships of power played out as domination, resistance, alliances, and pleasures. The family is theorized as constituted in historically specific ways through shifts and changes to sexual politics—for example, the history of the social and psychic construction of the "mother" identity as central to western women's perception of self challenges deeply held assumptions about the naturalness of familial roles and structures (Yeo 2005). Feminist critiques locate identity formation within the interplay of the sexual politics of the family, and thus family is a key site of contestation of the meaning, articulation, and embodiment of sexuality and of gender relations.

Feminism has been characterized as hostile to the family (Buss and Herman 2003; Hakim 2000), yet feminists themselves remain quite ambivalent. On the one hand, feminists see the family as a central social institution where women work and experience violence, their identities are concealed, and their exclusion from public life is justified. On the other hand, the family has become the premium site for discourses and practices of ideals surrounding intimacy, commitment, nurturance, collectivity, and individual autonomy, as well as the main base of women's material and potential power.

The problem, we believe, is located in the politics of the family. At local and international levels, feminist politics is making gains for women in relation to access to education and the labor market, and health and welfare support, but unless the sexual politics of the family is challenged, the result will be a limited and limiting political agenda that undermines any progressive potential to be won from bringing family into the public arena. If labor movements adopt a politics of the family that is reinscribed uncritically as the heterosexual couple and their dependent children (Nicholson 1997), all other forms of domestic relations and gender identities are not only excluded but also become invisible once again.

Modern political theory and practice suppress the sexual politics of family by defining it as "woman's place" in which she is "the centerpiece" (Goward 2006). When the sexual politics of the family is ignored or constrained, discursive and material male dominance within the family is submerged. By contrast, we characterize the family as the central "greedy institution" in women's lives. The family makes strong material, emotional, and discursive demands on women, but like any greedy institution, it evokes deep commitment and loyalty and offers meaning, identity, satisfaction, and pleasure (Franzway 2001). Women are not merely the oppressed and vulnerable subjects of the patriarchal family.

Although feminist theorists have persistently critiqued the ways political theory of the family limits or binds women, feminist advocacy of thoroughgoing transformation of the family itself has fallen silent over the last decade. It is something of a revelation to return to the highly influential British text *The Anti-social Family*, published nearly thirty years ago, and reread its clear indictment of what the authors call familialism, with its concomitant individualism and corrosive impact on the common good. The authors, Michèle Barrett and Mary McIntosh (1982), called for realistic alternatives to the attractions of family, which would lead to socialized public and private space: "We can at least be aware of the Scylla of home improvements, domestic comforts and security without getting psychologically wrecked by the Charybdis of squalor, isolation and impersonality" (147).

The size and shape of the family have undergone considerable change since then, and not only in the West. But a more egalitarian family is yet to be won, evidenced for example in the lack of significant change to gendered responsibility for housework, or in the rates of female victims of domestic violence. Men's resistance or, more precisely, the resistance of heterosexual masculinity to any curtailment of its dominance within the family is no less successful than the maintenance of that power in the public domain. No political party has confronted the issue of the sexual politics of the family in its political program, nor has feminist politics addressed it in any coherent fashion. Some piecemeal strategies have been developed, including the claiming of sexual and bodily rights and identities, wages for housework, community or state-based childcare, and public policies on domestic violence. In addition, feminists have helped to bring the family onto the political agenda of the trade union movement. Making headway on these issues demands vigorous political effort and activism as they constantly battle against prevailing notions about the sexual politics of the family. Thus, it is critical that union feminist campaigns be grounded in effective feminist analyses of the family.

Family Becomes the Center of Women's Work

> Woman's work, outside her home, is one of the sad novelties of the modern world; it is a true heresy. Woman, outside of her home appears to us as a being out of place, a woman without a country.
> —Chief factory inspector for Quebec 1922 (cited in Frager 1983, 47)

In the West, with emerging capitalist industrialization, the family became constituted as the central institution of women's lives. The point is an old one, but must still be made: women, whatever their class, were gradually excluded from the income and independence to be achieved with paid work in a capitalist economy, and were secluded within the family (McDowell 1999). This did not apply to all women. For example, women of color and immigrant women in the United States found they were left out of protective labor legislation because the main occupations to which they had access, domestic work, food-processing, and agricultural work were excluded from the legislation in the 1930s (Kessler-Harris 2001). Overall, the process was dynamic and chaotic, as preindustrial social structures, practices, and discourses were disrupted by powerful and unpredictable forces of political and economic capital accumulation. The impact on women was neither simple nor universal.

Over the course of the nineteenth century in industrializing countries, the emergence of class hegemony ensured that it became unwomanly to engage in paid work. Instead, middle-class women became organizers of consumption, class display, and social reproduction as they emulated the "lady" of the English aristocracy (Folbre 1991, 467), a role that depended on the labor of other women. Working-class women, together with their children, were drawn into new forms of work in factories and mines, and in service work in other women's homes. The convoluted changes to work that characterized the emerging sexual division of labor within industrial capitalism may be illustrated by women's relationship to mining. Images of women crawling through tunnels dragging carts of coal are among the most pitiful of early industrialization in Europe. But by the 1950s, women were so effectively excluded from underground mines (and other kinds of mines: see Eveline and Booth 2002) that Queen Elizabeth II (on her first royal tour) was not allowed to meet Australian miners at their workplaces. In certain towns, the exclusion extended to all married women working at any paid jobs, a ban that was not lifted in a few (admittedly notorious) cases until the late twentieth century (Williams 1981).

In tandem with the changes for women, men's connections to work and family also changed so that the ideal of the man as the family breadwinner came to dominate for men of all classes. This was a considerable break from the earlier period when all members were seen to contribute to the household. Statisticians gathering census data began to distinguish between male "breadwinners" and female "dependents" (Deacon 1985; Folbre 1991). This reclassification of women from domestic to dependent was an international phenomenon, which reflected a decision to ignore household production and to assume that the doctrine of separate spheres actually described the social order (Olssen 1996). The male breadwinner model was supported by skilled, white, male unionists in England who feared competition from cheaper female and immigrant labor (Seccombe 1986), a change that was doubtless appreciated by skilled male workers elsewhere. Over the same period, workers' guilds, associations, and trade unions had also become dominated by men for whom wages that could support a dependent family became a significant demand.

The family wage became an important barrier to women's participation in the paid workforce, and in the trade union movement. While men became breadwinners, women became mothers and housewives, and any wages they earned were deemed to be "pin money" (an allowance allotted by a husband to a wife for her personal expenses; a trivial sum of money). Class and race distinctions among women were obscured by the apparent similarities among housewives, whose work in the twentieth century combined service work, consumption, and reproduction (Hartmann 1987).

Ironically, the housewife role also masked race, class, and gender differences among men: if a man could earn, or be seen to earn, enough to sustain both himself and his housewife, he was the equal of any man. The capacity to support a full-time housewife signified successful masculinity and display of class, although this was severely limited in many societies by caste and race hierarchies. Part of a woman's attraction was her skill at keeping up appearances by managing limited budgets. As the sexual division of labor became more entrenched, the woman's direct contributions to the family budget had to be discreet (although not insignificant), while the man's contributions to household labor had to be imperceptible. And so it was.

However, the dominance of the male breadwinner/female housewife model has been eroded in the contemporary period so that the male breadwinner has ceased to be the employment norm (Fudge and Owens 2006, 15). But there is little to indicate that this is part of a broader reconfiguration of gender relations, which appear extraordinarily resilient. The feminization of labor, which began in the 1960s, has seen women's paid work become central to the market. No doubt the processes of globalization have contributed to the shift, but as Edwards and Wajcman argue, citing ethnographies that trace the different ways family structures mediate globalization, its effects are neither uniform nor inevitable (Edwards and Wajcman 2005, 253).

Globalization has recognizable affects on the family, which Bakker and Gill (2003) discuss in terms of three aspects of social reproduction: biological reproduction (the conditions and social constructions of motherhood in different societies); the reproduction of the labor force (subsistence, education, and training); and the reproduction of provisioning and caring needs. Or, to put it another way, they review the impact of globalization on the critical elements of life, labor, and love. Bakker and Gill take globalization to entail neoliberal restructuring of the market and the state in addition to the strengthening of individualism, resulting in the reprivatization of the demands of social reproduction.

The welfare state "melting under the withering sun of globalization" (Beck 2000, 1) has less capacity to meet care needs; the market breaks social contracts between workers and capital so that wages are insufficient to provide for dependents; while the family is compressed into smaller spaces and shapes. In addition, specific family forms and practices are subject to rapid changes from much increased worker mobility, including not only the highly visible international worker speeding across virtual global networks, but also the Zimbabwean women who travel long distances for trade (Mapedzahama 2008). The ILO estimates that over 86 million workers have moved countries to find work (ILO 2004b, 12; see also Ehrenreich and Hochschild 2002).

Feminist politics must therefore be clear that the family that remains at the center of women's lives is extremely diverse and plastic, its discourses and practices stretching to accommodate the long-term absence of family members in distant places, people who are perhaps tied to their work in free trade zones, on stringent contracts, or confined as live-in domestics, sex workers, or child laborers. And yet, despite these powerful structural and experiential changes, the work of life, labor, and love, the care work, housework, and emotional labor remain women's primary responsibility (ILO 2004a).

Family as Frame: Anatomy of Campaigns on the Family

During a lengthy industrial campaign in Western Australia that lasted for more than six months, the unions involved adopted a typical strategy of claiming a public space as a base for protest. The unions occupied a vacant block of land opposite the Western Australian Parliament House in Perth. The space was designed to be inclusive, comfortable, and friendly, "mirroring in many ways the activities of a suburban family home: cooking activities, areas for children, a garden and various rituals and ceremonies" (Bailey 2005, 114). Janis Bailey dubbed the strategy as "defiance via domesticity," which aimed to show that union resistance could be "a family thing" and could incorporate multiple identities and practices of everyday life and activism. However, framing the campaign around family effectively concealed issues of gender relations. Several years later, the political value or harm of this strategy continues to be debated.

We argue that the family is a key dimension of discursive alliances between women and labor even at the transnational level, but as Gerstel and Clawson (2001, 279) report, very little research examines the relationships between unions and work/family issues. Research has tended to overlook the substantial moves by unions and peak bodies to integrate gender issues into political agendas through family frames that perform several purposes. For example, at its Founding Congress in Vienna, November 2006, the ITUC called for measures that relied on assumptions about the value and universality of family to increase awareness among women as well as enable them to reconcile work with their personal and family life, while also allowing men to spend time with their families and share family responsibilities (ITUC 2006). Like many in the labor movement, the ITUC took the view that the future strength and vitality of the trade union movement depends on women joining its ranks and becoming leaders; it saw attention to issues around work and family as a key strategy to achieve this goal.

The success of this frame depends on the idea of the family evoking humane, universal values. No discussion needed. Campaigns framed by the family also allow unions to break through stereotypes of trade unions as organizations of blue-collar men concerned only with narrow, self-interested issues to the detriment of the economy and the rest of society. In addition, the family has the discursive capacity to counter the neoliberal push for individualism and to be a potent universal counterweight to the ills of globalization. This, in concert with longstanding feminist campaigns for gender equity that are gaining significance with women's increasing participation in paid work and women's potential as union members when union density is declining, has led to the family being scripted into campaigns up to and including the transnational level. Oddly enough, the family is the most local and intimate of social institutions, yet it plays major roles on the international stage. The family has become a cornerstone of union feminist politics.

Anyone—male or female—can work. The only requirement is that, as employees, they conform to the norm of the ideal worker. An ideal worker is a worker who behaves in the workplace as if he or she has a wife at home full time, performing all of the unpaid care work that families require. Personal problems do not belong in the workplace. Conflicting demands are expected to be resolved in favor of requirements of the job (Applebaum 2001, 29).

Feminist theories and politics have a substantial history of targeting the family and the sexual division of labor, aiming to change or at least modify the discourses and practices that create and reproduce this impediment to women's equality. Education and training, ideologies of femininity and masculinity, wages and conditions, and above all women's relationship to the family were identified and implicated in the barriers to women's equal participation in the labor market, in public life, and in the trade union movement.

Two feminist campaigns to remedy these conditions stand out: for wages for housework, which sought to value women's work in the family; and for equal pay, which sought equal value for women's work in the labor market. Neither has succeeded directly, but each has been influential in reshaping discourses on women's work.

The wages for housework campaign was intended to stress the oppressiveness of the apparent inevitability of women's family responsibilities. It was fueled by Marxist-feminist analyses of the place of domestic labor in the economy and by feminist social research on women's experience of housework (Kaluzynska 1980; McDowell 1999; Oakley 1974). Although the campaign itself largely faded by the early 1980s and direct wages were never won, modern economists now take "non-market household production" into account (Edwards and Wajcman 2005, 52).

The paradox of housework today is that neither new household technologies nor a widely held egalitarian view that housework should be shared has made much change to the household division of labor, which has "remained remarkably resilient'" (Walby 1986; see also Edwards and Wajcman

2005; Hochschild 1989; Schroedel 1990). The most common explanation of this phenomenon centers on women's role as mother, the carer of young children, who is discursively constructed as based in the family home. Part of the care that the "good mother" provides involves housework, cooking, cleaning, managing, and shopping, and so it is accepted that she performs this work for everyone in the household. However, when women move into the paid labor market, they continue to do the bulk of this work (Bittman and Wajcman 2004; Sayer 2005).

It is therefore quite realistic that union campaigns for family-friendly workplace policies, as currently developed, are assumed to apply mainly to women. As we show below, what is notable about such policies and relevant trade union campaigns is their central focus on care work, particularly care of children, in contrast to care for partners, emotional labor, or consumption. The rest of domestic labor—the housework—has once again become invisible, disguised by the rhetoric of equality that we are all equal now and should take equal share of the housework (a heteronormative claim that also overlooks able-bodied children). Rather, most evidence shows that the real changes are to women's practices (Evertsson and Nermo 2004). Middle-class women reduce their own housework time through outsourcing and buying in clothes, food, and care labor.

From Family Wage to Pay Equity

In contrast to debates about domestic labor, feminist politics has connected more directly with the labor movement around campaigns for equal pay, which also engaged with women's relationship with the family. Histories of these campaigns are complicated, with variations across the political opportunity structures in each country, including each country's different forms of relations among labor movements, feminism, and the state, as well as different industrial conditions and political agendas. Issues at stake range from the protection of women and children from harsh work conditions, the protection of men's wages from women's cheap labor, through to differences in employment conditions between married and single women and debates about the meanings and implications of "equality."

A key obstacle to be overcome by those framing equal pay campaigns was the deeply held view that women neither need nor want to provide economic support for families or dependents. Across the international movements, labor women and feminist activists drew together to call for equal pay and to defend married women's right to work (Cook, Lorwin, and Daniels 1992). An important part of the task for feminists and union women was to persuade the trade union movement that women do have economic needs of their own, which may include the support of dependents. A more difficult task has been to establish that women want to work in their own right, and, when they do, their work should have equal value, recognized with equal pay. Although the ILO charter adopted in 1919 called for equal pay for equal work, the arguments have continued throughout the last century as illustrated by Mary Turner of Britain's General Union (known as GMB) at the 1985 TUC Congress: "I tell you, I never went to work for pin money. I went to work because we have to go to work to provide the basic necessities of life. We go to work to give our kids food on the table, to give them clothes and shoes to wear to go to school. That is why we go to work" (cited in Heery and Conley 2007, 13).

Historically, the campaign has been reframed according to contemporary conditions and debates. Unions campaigned for a "family wage," or what became known as a living wage in Britain and the United States, from the 1870s (May 1985). Often narrowly defined, the broad consensus in the United States was that a living wage should provide "the ability to support families, to maintain self respect, and to have both the means and the leisure to participate in the civic life of the nation" (Glickman 1997, 3). With current neoliberal globalization and declines in real wages, a living wage campaign has been revived in industrialized and certain developing countries with local activists advocating public financial support and a minimum set of work conditions (Brenner 2002; Luce 2004).

In Australia the centralized industrial relations system, which set basic rates for all workers covered by industrial awards, established the concept of the "family wage" for working-class men in 1907 (known as the *Harvester* judgment). Since it was assumed that only men supported families, the female basic rate was fixed at 54 percent of the male basic rate (Ryan and Conlon 1989). The family wage or living wage came to dominate the industrial landscape worldwide, enhancing the notion of the normative worker as male and exacerbating inequalities and differences between and among women and men in workplaces and in unions.

During the depression years of the 1930s, which sharply increased the competition for jobs, women workers (especially married women) were targeted as a politically acceptable way to ease the problems of labor. For example, legislation was enacted to provide for the dismissal of married women from teaching and public sector jobs (Costa 2000; Lake 1999; Walby 1986). This debate was framed by the discourses of marriage and motherhood weakening women's right to work and questioning whether married women's participation in the public domain would debase their natural maternal wisdom. Feminists and socialists argued that the question about "good mothers" was based on "a nonsense" about mother love and motherhood in whose name "divorce reform is delayed beyond all reason, women are underpaid, the education of girls is crippled, women are denied the right of entry to posts which they could occupy with profit, or are forced to resign from work which they can do or needs doing" (Holtby 1935, 143).

The same debates were echoed in the United States in the 1940s when some claimed that raising women's wages would "destroy mother love" (Cobble 2004, 119). Working-class opinion was divided between those women who believed that men should have first claim on the limited jobs available (Cobble 2004, 71) and those who felt that a good mother would provide economic support for her family. The Australian unionist Muriel Heagney (1935) tackled the question directly in her book, *Are Women Taking Men's Jobs?* Using international comparisons, she made the case that women should have equal pay and the right to economic independence, whatever their family situation. Heagney, like other unionists, had moved away from protectionist arguments and reached the conclusion that women would only be accepted by trade unions if they could not be used as cheap labor (Lake 1999, 179). Interestingly, Caroline Davis, director of the Women's Department of the United Automobile, Aerospace and Agricultural Implement Workers of America (UAW), made a similar case against discrimination twenty years later at the 1957 IMF Women's Conference in Vienna: "There are still employers who attempt to use women wage-earners as a source of cheaper labor; there are still men workers and union members who fail to realize that the treatment of women workers as an inferior category merely weakens the union as a whole by creating a precedent for discriminatory treatment of other groups of workers who happen, in terms of their race, creed, color, age or national origin, to be members of some minority."[1]

Following the boost given to women's pay by the demands of World War II, when peace was declared many women were disappointed that their jobs were taken over by men, and their wages fell back to prewar levels (Fonow 2003, 40). However, the discursive value of the family wage also began to decline with the gradual increase of married women and single mothers in the labor force, albeit without permanency or other workplace benefits. Trade union movements began to support arguments for state-based provision of maternity leave and family allowances for children.

The family wage had already disappeared as a demand of French male workers before World War II (Susan Frader, cited in Cobble 2004, 267 n. 127). But the family wage remained as a touchstone in wages campaigns for trade unions in many constituencies. Differences were compounded around the question of how to define "equal," especially in contexts where the gendered categorization of jobs into "women's work" and "men's work" had become entrenched. The means to achieve equal pay were also disputed as different trade union movements took up different stances in relation to the state. In Australia the state was central to labor bargaining for the whole of the twentieth century, whereas in the United States some trade union bodies opposed what they saw as state interference in collective bargaining (Cobble 2004, 108).

By 1951 the ILO adopted Convention 100 for equal pay for equal work by men and women for work of equal value, which has since been ratified by most of the members of the ILO, an important advance that recognized the discriminatory impact of the sexual division of labor. The goals shifted to achieving "pay equity" between women's and men's work even when their jobs were not equal or even similar (Cook, Lorwin, and Daniels 1992), so that pay equity now refers to redressing the undervaluation of jobs typically performed by women and remunerating them according to their value (ILO 2007, 74).

The resurgent women's movement took up pay equity and began pushing trade unions to recognize that the sexual division of labor has far reaching consequences. The Working Women's Charters, discussed in chapter 7, were intended to articulate political agendas based on the case that equal pay for equal work is not enough. The campaigns often led to complex industrial and legal arguments, so that in 2007 the ILO was still reporting that the notion of equal pay for work of equal value is perhaps one of the least understood concepts in the antidiscrimination field (ILO 2007, 9). Nevertheless, we find that the following principles, adopted by the Global Union Federations (GUFs)—EI and PSI (EI 2007), generally underpin labor pay equity campaigns:

- Equal pay for the same work.
- Equal pay for jobs of an equal value or comparable value although they are different jobs.
- "Pay" includes base pay; bonuses or allowances; and benefits of cash (for example, superannuation contributions by an employer) and noncash value (paid and unpaid leave entitlements).
- Remove inequities and discrimination from pay systems and make them transparent and open to scrutiny.
- Gender is not a factor in determining pay levels.

Among union feminists, pay equity aroused debates about whether women in low-paid jobs would benefit, yet it became a rich terrain for union feminist political organizing, as one Canadian official said to us: "I love the pay equity work. Do you know there were spin-offs that none of us anticipated . . . ? You can get the women on the committee . . . and the men to argue for the women. So you have that kind of coming together and for the women, a lot of the women, it was the first time they'd ever been on a union committee" (Interview, Canadian woman official).

In a similar vein, an evaluation of the Public Service International (PSI) Pay Equity Campaign (2002–6) found it had been an effective mechanism in building women's union participation and leadership, and enhanced awareness of gender discrimination and international labor cooperation (Hegewisch, Hammond, and Valladares 2006). There is little evidence in the report of material, tangible pay equity for women workers: inadequate data is one problem that must be overcome, but this only partly explains the paucity of evidence. Significant gender inequalities in pay were among the most resilient features of labor markets across the world. Even though the gender pay gap narrowed in some places and stagnated in others, women continue to work, on average, for lower earnings than men (ILO 2007, 20; TUC 2005).

As these lengthy political and discursive campaigns show, alliances between feminists and labor movements are capable of mobilizing considerable efforts aimed at challenging gender inequalities that are complicated, not simply by gender differences, but also by the powerful complexities of sexual politics in trade unions, labor markets, and the family. These complexities are well to the fore in two further areas of political campaigning: childcare and policies for so-called work/life balance.

Childcare Campaigns

Childcare is a clear site where women and labor meet. Care is women's responsibility: mothers are the main organizers of the child's care and women are the main performers of the paid care work. The ILO identifies care as "the work of looking after the physical, psychological, emotional and developmental needs of one or more people" (Standing 2001, 17). Such a definition could include the care of healthy adult men, but most texts fail to mention this significant group of care recipients.

Public childcare is a basic tenet of contemporary feminism and an essential plank in women gaining equality in the labor market. Yet, the politics of childcare are fraught. Discursively, biological mothers care for children, for free and with love, in stark contrast to historical and contemporary practices. Thus, paid childcare is problematic for women, caught up in discourses of motherhood, in conflicts around the social and private responsibilities for care, and between the social benefits and private pleasures of child rearing. Consequently, paid care is undervalued and often is not formally recognized as labor. Or rather, it is trapped in an extremely complex jumble of legal, technical, and industrial practices and regulations. In the United States, for example, home-based childcare providers have no right to organize for the purpose of collective bargaining, and the state has no obligation to recognize or negotiate with the providers' representative without additional, specific legal authority (Chalfie, Blank, and Entmacher 2007, 9). At the same time, the cavalier neglect of the interests and needs of children (and their carers) certainly demonstrates that western societies have a large capacity for sustaining contradictory discourses and practices.

Although access to public childcare is a valuable political gain for women, present childcare policies do not challenge the sexual politics of the discursive dominance of family as the privileged place of care in society. The political and discursive stress on childcare, in particular, serves to minimize the value of other sites and forms of care. Yet western women are mothers of fewer than two dependent children, on average, for a relatively short period of their lifetimes. And in many societies, other family members undertake substantial unpaid care, although this is becoming less available even in many developing countries (Hein 2005, 76). Further, discourses of fatherhood now include care, even though men's care practice continues to lag.

The whole problem of gender, care, and the family is sidestepped with the employment of domestic care workers who are integral to "the global care chain" (Ehrenreich and Hochschild 2002). The class and race dimensions of women employing other women to do domestic labor and care work are contentious feminist issues (Duffy 2005; Romero 1992; Wolkowitz 2006).

What gets left out of this sexual politics of the family is husband care. Heidi Hartmann (1981) noted decades ago that men benefited from the resilience of housework as women's work, and they continue to do so, as is clear in much of the more recent research (Bowman 2007). Women's housework includes a large chunk of caring for men's everyday needs. When it comes to an egalitarian politics of childcare, feminist attempts to share care with men within the family require that the obstacle of men's resistance (whether caused by economic assumptions about male breadwinners or by discourses of heteronormative masculinity) be overcome, but it is a strategy that replaces the isolated mother with an equally isolated father (Franzway, Court and Connell 1989). This hardly seems like progress.

Union feminists and their feminist sisters have sought the social provisioning of childcare needs through much of the last century, persuading unions to include access to paid childcare, even work-based childcare in employment contracts and bargaining conditions. Women union leaders were persistent proponents of childcare programs through the crises of World War II and into the 1950s (Cobble 2004, 133). In the United States, working-class women turned to their unions to campaign for recognition that childcare was a necessary expense in paid work, equivalent to other business expenses.

Childcare work suffers from the conditions of highly feminized occupations, namely they are low paid, insecure, part time, and deemed to be "low-skilled" (Duffy 2005), much of it assigned to poor women from vulnerable ethnic minorities. Care work is also associated with labor shortages, the "care deficit," high rates of staff turnover, and high worker migration from Eastern Europe as well as the Global South (Ungerson 2003, 2006). Somewhat sardonically, feminist economists Paula England and Nancy Folbre (1999) suggest, "Workers who provide care must love their work, we tell ourselves (especially if they are cheap, convenient and polite to those paying the bill). Otherwise why would they do it for such low pay?" (5).

We argue from a different standpoint: that for care workers, care services are greedy institutions, similar to the family, to which they commit and in which they care for the clients of those services. Without their commitment, such services could not continue. At the same time, the exploitation of care workers pushes their commitment toward its limits.

The way care work is framed has significant political implications; framing care in terms of nurturance and relationships sees it as necessary, altruistic, informal, a social gift, and thus hard for economists to measure (Folbre 2001). And it excludes the reproductive care work of nonwhite workers (in jobs such as food preparation, laundry, and personal body care) (Duffy 2005). Framing access to childcare as a means of facilitating women's employment is far removed from the more radical discourse "which defined child care as a social right of citizenship and a means of transforming gender divisions of labor" (Charles 2004, 305).

How childcare work is framed also has implications for political and discursive alliances between women and labor that are critical to progress on issues for care workers and their work. Ferree and Roth's (1998) study of the sexual politics of a strike by women day care workers found that the workers were framed as different and difficult. Documenting the failure of the strike and its possibilities, they diagnose part of the problem as resulting from the simplistic and exclusionary frame and the related lack of organizational, communication, and personal links between feminist groups, the workers, and the unions. Ferree and Roth argue for a coalition politics in which solidarity is temporary, specific, and strategic (643).

In this book we argue making feminist politics within and through labor movements at local and international levels requires alliances. Such alliances depend on a politics that works to surmount these difficulties, both discursively and practically. As Marie Walker (2005), the executive vice president of the Canadian Labour Congress (CLC) said recently, progress on childcare has taken many years "of grassroots action, of lobbying, of organizing," but "we haven't done it alone. We've done it by working together with parents and grand-parents, with social activists, with rank and file child care workers. . . . In our unions we need to reach out to other progressive forces. Because collectively, we are much stronger than we are individually."

Childcare campaigns build on arguments about equality for women and for children, for disadvantaged communities and decent work for low paid, vulnerable workers. However, care workers are often at risk of losing their place, even in union agendas. The case for their improved wages and conditions is generally tied to the outcome of a "quality" service, one that must still be justified. Where unions and feminists advocate government funding for "the provision of decent wages and conditions of childcare professionals" the result will be "high quality, community based child care" that is regulated and accessible (see, for example, ACTU 2003).

The community childcare center has been an ideal of the women's movement, representing a material and discursive alternative to the limited patriarchal family and individualized care. Significantly, it fitted best between that same narrow concept of family and the modern, nine-to-five work regimen of western, white-collar workers; when that model gave way to the so-called "flexible workplace," the childcare center became yet another organization that women in particular had to negotiate.

Balancing Work and Life: Family Friendly? Woman Friendly?

Childcare and workplace flexibility are two dimensions that have been incorporated into the current version of the conflict between work and family. Work/life balance has become a critical discursive alliance between women and labor with far-reaching policy and political effects (Pocock 2003). Work/life balance recognizes that women work and that men have families. It is also a strategy that counters the push by globalized markets and capital for longer working hours and poorer conditions, unfettered by regulation and technical limitations.

Where neoliberal globalism holds sway, calls for the apparently essential "flexibility" required by the 24/7 global economy lead to unpredictable work hours that no longer mesh with the time of school days and many services. In those societies that had regularized work time, plumbers, churches, core business offices, and major entertainments continue to revolve around the nine-to-five, Monday to Friday working week. In effect, the cogs of social, institutional, and working life are running at different speeds: "The perception that life has become more rushed is due to the real increases in the combined work commitments of family members, rather than changes in the working time of individual workers" (Edwards and Wajcman 2005, 48). Women work more and men work fewer hours resulting in a dramatic redistribution of paid work between the sexes.

As a frame for making feminist politics with labor movements, work/life balance has brought women's issues onto union agendas. The ILO, which adopted the convention Workers with Family Responsibilities (No. 156) in 1981, argues for the recognition of conflict between work and family responsibilities, its implications for equality of opportunity in the labor market, and the necessity for reconciliation rather than the more prosaic balance (Hein 2005). Work/life balance "isn't just about juggling home and family" (Smithson and Stokoe 2005, 149) and has become a crucial vehicle for union campaigns on work conditions, particularly in the West. The union campaign is well summarized by CLC president Ken Georgetti:

> Unions have made a difference in people's lives by making it easier for workers to take care of the people who matter the most—their families—and work to their full potential without having to make a choice between one or the other. Whether it's paid vacations, maternity and parental leaves, compassionate leave, child care, elder care, taking time off to get married or cope with the loss of a loved one; unions are constantly working to find ways to help people work for a living rather than live for their jobs. (Atkinson 2005)

Such campaigns go well beyond traditional union demands for fair pay for a fair day's work, and as many in local and transnational labor movements are aware, campaigns centered on work/family issues are a major way to involve members and build a stronger labor movement (Firestein and Dones 2007).

However, the International Confederation of Free Trade Unions (ICFTU) was surprised to find from its Ask a Working Woman survey in 2001 that women workers' family responsibilities and family-related issues were relatively low priorities for the women who responded, as reported by the ACTU (ACTU 2001). The ICFTU survey was modeled after the AFL-CIO survey of the same name that, when run again in 2006 found that local conditions (for example, lack of universal health care in the United States) determine women's concerns. Nevertheless, it is possible to argue that work/family balance and work/life balance are terms that generally are understood to refer to women workers and their caring responsibilities.

The search for "balance" is about finding ways to synchronize work and life, work and family. The problem with this project is that the sexual politics of work and the heteronormative family are left out of the equation. Paid work is being redistributed between the sexes, but unpaid domestic work and care retains its gendered pattern, and the concept of the family in this discourse remains narrow and limited. As Raewyn Connell (2005) reminds us, "dropping dead from career-driven stress, or shriveling emotionally from never seeing one's children is a different issue from exhaustion because of the double shift, or not getting promotion because of career interruptions" (387). But she also observes that these are largely middle-class first world issues.

Poverty, the shortage of work, and the kinds of upheavals to communities already noted here cause different kinds of trouble for work and family life. Whether challenging the dichotomy between work and family is "the most difficult revolution facing women" (Cook, Lorwin, and Daniels 1992), maintaining both work and family has become a huge problem for many women. Confronted by massive changes to work patterns—specifically who works, when, and where—sustaining work and family has become women's responsibility.

Nevertheless, work/life balance in conjunction with discourses of choice, diversity, and flexibility are gender-blind in the early phases of political strategies in a bid to make feminist and workplace gains. Work/life balance has widespread and powerful appeal to progressive activists across many arenas, but feminists raise concerns similar to those around childcare: that the political benefits compromise feminist agendas and fail to advance gender equality (Smithson and Stokoe 2005). The idea of "work/life balance," as Connell (2005) argues, is a conservative expression of a radical impulse for justice, specifically gender justice. We propose that it has provided the political opportunity for discursive alliances between women and labor that enable political, material, and industrial claims to be made and won.

Conclusion

We began this chapter reflecting on the contradictory value of the term "working families" as a significant site for alliances between women and labor. Clearly, the family is essential, risky, and productive for union feminists and new feminist politics and has great value as a site in which women and labor can share political interests. It is widely understood as a central area of everyday life as we observed in the previous chapter. "Working families" has proved to be an attractive term in political campaigns with an appeal that extends across class, race, and gender. However, as we also show, the use of "family" as though it has shared universal meaning risks imposing assumptions that all families fit the definition of family that prevails in the West as nuclear, heteronormative, and middle class. Discursive and political alliances between women and labor that are premised on mainstream western definitions of family do produce tangible gains for women and workers more generally, such as publicly supported childcare and family-friendly workplace policies, and they even win political elections, as was the case in the recent Australian federal election. But such gains remain severely limited, even detrimental to feminist goals of gender equity, if the sexual politics of the family is not seriously challenged.

Feminists have long argued that the contemporary western family is implicated in the inequalities of the labor market and the public domain, but the gender relations of the family continue to be taken for granted. Campaigns for public childcare and work/life balance, for example, do very little to confront women's "second shift," the care demands of the laboring body, or the inequities of global care chains. We suggest that the challenge to the sexual politics of the family needs to be renewed in order to overcome the obstacles it presents to making feminist politics in the public spaces of the labor movement.

4

Political Spaces
Centers, Conferences, and Campaigns

> It's not good enough to be right. It's important to win something. In order to win something, we . . . need to agree on something. That something does not need to be an over-arching pre-ordained ideology into which we force-fit our delightfully fractious, argumentative selves. It does not need to be an unquestioning allegiance to one or another form of resistance to the exclusion of everything else.
> —Arundhati Roy 2004, World Social Forum

Arundhati Roy is talking in the terms of the new social movements that are open to making politics with adaptable strategies and limited objectives, in contrast to the constraints of an older politics that demanded adherence to an inflexible correctness. We recognize that making politics requires both material and discursive spaces, something feminism has been particularly creative in achieving. It has to be since women generally have to transcend the almost universal barriers against their entrance into the field of politics. Women need the kinds of political spaces that allow them to identify, articulate, and debate their needs, and thereby create feminist politics. However, making feminist politics within and through the trade union movement involves contesting explicit and complex structures and discourses of power.

Winning the right to join the labor market is critical to achieving women's equity, but little is gained unless women themselves can participate in the politics of social and economic justice. Without this capacity, the labor market becomes yet another site of discrimination and oppression of women. The same applies to workplace organizations: if women are left out, their issues and needs are overlooked or excluded, which results in skewed or discriminatory agendas. In all labor movements, women's participation rates are quite disproportionate to their low leadership rates and, on any measure, inequalities continue. Unions need to learn to "resonate more deeply with current and prospective members" (Cornfield and McCammon 2003, 37) in order to overcome the gendered impediments to women's participation.

Despite the obstacles of male-dominated sexual politics, women's workplaces, and political commitment, activism, and militancy are not insignificant (Briskin 2009; Foley and Baker 2009). The minority positions of union women activists in trade unions together with their feminist politics give them strong incentives to work across state and union borders to make alliances that are creative and productive (Hardy, Kozek, and Stenning 2008; Petrović 2000; Sayce, Greene, and Ackers 2006).

Contemporary union feminists are bringing their concerns into the traditional trade union movement and developing new and productive spaces for union women. Union feminists utilize political opportunity structures, what Frundt (2005) refers to as the "bones and sinews of struggle" (222). They are insiders having what Armstrong and Bernstein (2008) describe as the "best feel for the game" and thus able to initiate successful challenges to institutions (85). They have created gender-equity structures and discursive frames, and accessed resources to develop political spaces "where activists meet, share experiences, receive affirmation, and strategize for change" (Katzenstein 1998, 33). Brown (1995) argues that the development of feminist politics actually requires the cultivation of such spaces for constructing feminist political norms, strategies, and agendas. According to Curtin (1999, 33), "separate spaces provide the opportunity for women to alter the discursive frameworks through which women's claims are constituted." Material and discursive spaces serve as mobilizing structures, not ends in themselves, and they are useful not only for internal mobilization but also for building alliances with feminist supporters in other unions and with women's organizations in the community.

The move toward self-organizing groups has been a major structural change in trade unions. By creating women's committees, forums, and conferences and women's centers or units, women activists within the labor movement have developed effective mobilizing structures that can be used to harness the resources of their organizations to build solidarity among women (Healy, Hansen, and Ledwith 2006). Union feminists who participate in the networks, discourses, and campaigns of both the labor movement and the women's movement are creating overlapping spaces between movements for making feminist politics.

Unions have the resources to bring together women from different countries and different sectors of the economy to exchange information about their experience of globalization and to build new forms of labor solidarity. Feminists are constructing a solidarity that does not ask women to repress the differences among them, but rather encourages the productive use of these differences to expand ideas about democracy and human rights.

Creating Spaces, Frames, and Resources

Social movement theorists have debated at some length the relationship between structural inequality and collective action. While they differ from each other in significant ways, both the New Social Movement (NSM) theory and Resource Mobilization (RM) theory challenge the idea that there is a direct, unmediated relationship among structural conditions of exploitation, dissatisfaction, and collective action: they view the transition from conditions of inequality to action as a contingent and open process mediated by several factors (Snow, Soule, and Kriesi 2004). NSM theory places an emphasis on cultural factors (particularly expressive aspects) to explain social movements as struggles for control over the production of meaning and the constitution of new collective identities (Beckwith 2001b; Melucci 1994; Naples and Desai 2002). RM theory, in contrast, stresses the political nature of new movements and interprets them as conflicts over the allocation of goods in the political market—hence, focusing on the strategic-instrumental aspects of action (Canel 1997).

We integrate insights from both approaches as we examine the discourses, resources, and networks mobilized by feminists for collective action within male dominated unions. From RM theory we employ McCarthy's (1996) notion of mobilizing structures as "those collective vehicles, informal as well as formal through which people mobilize and engage in collective action" (149) to evaluate union gender-equity structures as both tools for and the outcome of mobilization. We see gender-equity mobilizing structures within unions as (potential) organizational mechanisms to collect and use the resources of both the labor and women's movements. However, if mobilizing structures are to be useful as tools for movement activity, they must be culturally framed as such, and here the emphasis in NSM theory on the relationship between structure, culture, and discourse is important (Rupp and Taylor 2003).

One example of such spaces for framing collective action on behalf of women's interests within the labor movement are the women's committees that predate second wave feminism and the contemporary period and have been established in local union branches as well as international peak bodies. The International Confederation of Free Trade Unions/International Trade Secretariat (ICFTU/ITS) set up its Consultative Committee on Women Workers in the late 1950s, while German unions had similar committees supported by branch offices and paid women officials. Without a clear feminist frame, there was some anxiety that "the local women's committees should not be separate entities: they were a means to an end, and should work alongside local branch officers."[1] Debate still continues over the extent to which women and men workers have the same or different priorities and needs (Foley 2000).

Dilemmas about which strategies are most effective have led to diverse responses by activists. One of the more common within trade unions, separate organizing, was discussed in chapter 2. This strategy may take the form of committees based on a particular aspect of worker identity, including gender, race, or sexuality, thus women's, black, or LGBT committees. (These can lead to problems of identification for workers who define themselves in terms of more than one identity, see, for example Colgan and Ledwith 2002). As feminist unionists became more politically experienced, they devised strategies that aimed at transforming labor movements rather than the separatism of women-only unions. Women's committees have become a route by which women become more active in the life of their union as the committees provide separate political space where women can strategically mobilize on behalf of their interests as women workers in a male-dominated union movement. In New Zealand, Melanie Nolan and Shaun Ryan (2003) are able to trace the rise of women into union leadership, despite a hostile external environment, which grew from their involvement in women's committees. These women's success depends on whether committee leaders can frame injustices of sexual politics in ways that engage women workers and union agendas. Other identity-based committees, such as those of LGBT workers, face similar problems in developing political frames that engage both potential members and the unions.

Success also depends on the structural location of the committee within the union and its relation to other union structures. If they are well located, they can be a conduit for women to become informed about internal debates, strategizing, and conflicts, which can enhance the development of women's own strategies and agendas. Whether these have an impact on union leadership depends in part on how essential equity advancement is seen to union survival and if that message can be made to resonate with a broad base of the membership (Briskin 2009).

Women's committees and the less common LGBT committees within unions and peak union bodies became strategic moves based on growing feminist recognition that the sexual politics in the labor movement needed to be confronted. The establishment of such committees is a tangible sign that issues of heterosexual, male-dominated sexual politics need to be addressed. However, making politics on the inside means that successful confrontation cannot be a simple matter of face-to-face conflict with male dominance in the union movement. Much else needed to be done for women to make any political gains as long as they remain unequal within the labor movement as well as the broader society.

Political and Discursive Alliances

While women remain in the minority in trade union leadership and have less access to union power than men generally, they must develop alternative strategies from those utilized in traditional union versions of winning and exercising power (see, for example, Moghadam, Franzway, and Fonow forthcoming). Women need to create and utilize alliances and networks that are capable of being extended across the labor movement and beyond in order to draw on the capacity and resources of other social movements and communities. They may be as constrained by factional and national conditions as their union brothers often are, but they have material and discursive motives to take up more flexible positions. There will be shifting alliances among women, and these will take various forms: "times when the unities of gender have brought women together; times when the pressures of class seem to drive them apart" (Phillips 1987, 28). And we would add that globalization has similar effects.

The intensification of globalization has not only produced issues that resonate for women across national and regional boundaries, such as precarious work, but it has also provided new means and technologies for political action. (However, it must be remembered that technology is not universally distributed and significant numbers of women, and men across the globe, have yet to make their first phone call.)

The growth of transnational networks among women's organizations has been valuable for union feminists, particularly as it is essential for women to join together to "act globally" (Sen 1997). As Domínguez (2002) observes, "women's transnational networking crosses more than national borders: it entails going beyond the workplace into communities and into the private sphere of the family" (222). We note that working women have a long history of organizing outside the workplace whenever the need and opportunity arose. During World War I, working-class women in Glasgow took successful collective action to freeze rents at prewar rates. Since their domestic concerns were central to their lives, they made the connection between the domestic and the political (Pyecroft 1994, 704).

Feminists, like unionists, have always incorporated international perspectives, but the increased globalization of capital, with its deleterious effects on the conditions of women workers, led to renewed efforts to go beyond their local communities and to forge transnational alliances between women's organizations, particularly feminist nongovernmental organizations (NGOs), and union women. Thus, union women joined with other women's groups at the 1995 UN Beijing women's conference to campaign for women workers' rights, with a strong focus on vulnerable workers in export processing zones (Moghadam 2005, 59). The shift of production work from countries of the North to the South also motivated international alliance building. For example, the Women Working Worldwide organization emerged in the UK in the early 1980s in support of networks of women workers' organizations in export processing zones in Asia (Hale and Wills 2007). It links women workers in different countries who work for the same multinationals, as well as fighting for women's rights in the informal sector in Asia and Central America (Hensmen 2002). Likewise, the Comité Fronterizo de Oberas (CFO; Border Committee of Women Workers) in the Americas started as a women's organization that aimed to "improve workers' conditions in the maquiladora [export processing plants] . . . specifically those of women workers and the protection of their health, life and welfare" (CFO, quoted in Domínguez 2002, 227).

These alliances strengthened the struggle by union feminists from different countries to claim political space for women within the labor movement. Women in the Authentic Labor Front (Frente Auténtico del Trabajo, or FAT, in Spanish), for example, view the labor movement as "a space in which women can discuss their problems and channel their demands." They believe it desirable "that men in the labor movement view the elimination of sex discrimination as their responsibility and not just the responsibility of the women" (Fonow 2003, 184). The women actively seek alliances with feminists in other unions in Mexico, as well as in the United States and Canada, and view the struggles around free-trade issues, such as the North American Free Trade Agreement (NAFTA), as an opportunity to form strategic alliances. They also participate in community coalitions concerned with broader economic issues and with border relations, such as the Southwest Network for Economic Justice and Mexican Network for Action on Free Trade. Active collaboration with the women of the FAT has broadened the understanding of feminists in the United Steelworkers about the value of building alliances across various sectors of political struggle, including grass-roots community groups and NGOs (Fonow 2003).

As we noted in chapter 1, alliances may also be difficult to sustain, particularly when groupings are under pressure from competing demands and interests, for example the agendas of individual organizations and male unionists. In addition, difficulties may arise if the constituents of women's organizations are perceived as middle-class women who want to compete with unionists in representing workers, an almost perennial problem with a history extending back to conflicts between first wave feminists and the labor movement in the nineteenth century (Rowbotham 1973; Tax 1980).

Women's organizations bring awareness of the significance of workers' everyday lives to the successful framing of alliances and union campaigns on women workers' issues. If campaigns focus only on economic questions of pay and working conditions, they fail to make headway with women workers. And both women's organizations and the labor movement need to recognize that where women are new to the labor market, they also have the capacity to create innovative forms of organizing (Hale and Wills 2007).

Conferences

Political spaces require resources that must be won through organizing within the labor movement around issues framed as legitimately deserving attention. The special or focused conference has long been such a space and a key strategy in making feminist politics around labor from local to international levels (Ferree and Mueller 2005; Rupp 1997). However, conferences, as any conference participant and conference organizer knows, have enormous potential that is difficult to realize; they can be tokenistic, ritualized events where everyone goes through the motions, or they can become historical moments of real shifts in policy, leadership, and political attitudes.

As we show in chapter 6, charting a series of such conferences reveals how union women have challenged sexual politics of labor movements to frame women's issues for effective collective action. The first women's conference held by the International Metalworkers' Federation (IMF) in 1957, discussed in chapter 6, generated a great deal of enthusiasm among women and the leadership who took the conference as an opportunity to develop and disseminate research on women members and to canvass the diverse ways that member unions saw and addressed the issues. It became a benchmark, which ironically could later be used as a barrier to further action and debate: at the first IMF commission on women workers some years later in 1963, discussion on women's specific recruitment problems were sidelined since they had already been "thoroughly dealt with" in 1957.[2]

The political space of the conference can be built from limited resources and still achieve a high level of visibility; the risk is that political commitment from the union may be only short lived if momentum cannot be sustained after the conference. Union feminists need to find ways to utilize the energy, ideas, and collective purpose generated by the focused conference to make an impact on the individual union or wider labor movement.

The case of the Australian biannual conference for women in male-dominated occupations and industries (WIMDOI) is typical.[3] It was initiated by women who had attended a national women's forum conducted by the peak union body, the Australian Council of Trade Unions (ACTU). They wanted a similar event for women in male-dominated unions who often felt marginalized by the men in their own unions as well as by women unionists from more feminized areas of work.

Tania Courtney, a union shop floor delegate who had attended the ACTU conference, approached Max Adlum, a women's officer in the Australian Manufacturing Workers Union (AMWU), to see if the union's women's committee could sponsor a conference. Max took the idea to her executive but it was rejected: the conference would be too costly, the women should be focusing on organizing and recruiting more women into the union, and women's issues were "not core union business" (interview with Max Adlum, 2007). The two women turned to the strategic potential of alliances with women in other unions where women were a minority so they could lobby the ACTU to sponsor a conference for the range of women unionists in male-dominated occupations.

The WIMDOI conference, first held in 1993, has become an intentional space for building solidarity among women across Australia that could focus some of their political energy on national and international campaigns. The women found that they could work together with other women from different unions and political factions. Influenced in part by feminist political strategies that encourage women to share experience and ideas, the conferences focus on how to survive in occupations that place them outside the social norms for their gender and isolate them in environments dominated by male culture.

Each conference typically includes a solidarity action with a local strike or labor campaign and group-building activities and workshops designed to build a collective identity among the participants, together with presentations by labor experts and activists. Much like the union courses, discussed below, the conferences aim to develop skills and confidence that will inspire participants to become activists in their local branches and beyond. Participation by local and national bodies, such as state peak union councils and Working Women's Centres (WWC), help to build alliances across the union movement, while transnational networks are also developed when WIMDOI delegates gain union support to attend International Labour Organization (ILO) meetings in the Asia–Pacific region.

At the 2003 WIMDOI conference in Adelaide, Australia, which we attended, delegates were sponsored by a wide range of unions that covered workers in prisons, policing, steel, auto, furniture-making, lumber and paper mills, construction, manufacturing, and the waterfront. The delegates argued that unions need to focus more on the ways unions provide a better life for workers, rather than only on the more traditional union issues of wages and conditions. They saw union renewal as an essential objective if women were to achieve their goals of gender equity and decent and just workplaces. Some believed that women are "natural organizers" who share and value one another's stories and develop creative and safe places to learn. But some of the younger women disagreed. They thought this was an old-fashioned view, preferring a more analytic, task-oriented model that focused on ways that women can be more effective in the union and on the job. They rejected essentialist ideas about women being natural allies and believed that "some women play power games just as well as men do" (Focus group interview, WIMDOI, 2003).

The special or focused conference is the result of successful union feminist campaigns to gain resources from their unions to be directed toward women's workplace issues. Although WIMDOI conferences are relatively small events, they constitute political space for the development of viable and effective alliances, something that feminists have attempted across movements, communities, and locations. Even where women are in the minority, as they are in male-dominated occupations and industries where a male culture is paramount, they are able to challenge sexual politics in both their own unions and their workplaces.

Courses

Many focused conferences call for specific training for women so they can become informed union participants, activists, and leaders. Since very few union women manage to accrue appropriate skills, experience, and knowledge in this male-dominated field, feminists generally are attracted to the political utility and feasibility of pedagogic projects, a strategy that union women have derived from other social movements as well as from trade union traditions. Or, as the ILO declares, "Educate, educate, educate" (ILO 2001). Women union activists have had some political success with pedagogic projects, which can be a valuable site of political challenge and transformation.

Trade unions themselves have a long history of providing educational programs for their members, but it is also the case that union officials, both women and men, are too often "thrown in at the deep end without being properly trained" (Berry and Kitchener 1989, 48). Some courses were designed to be vocational for workers who were prevented access to education by their economic circumstances; some were aimed at labor and union studies. Predictably, union courses did not include women until educational goals were reframed to allow recognition of the value of education for working women.

The Workers Education Association (WEA), for example, was set up in the UK in 1903 to bring trade unions together with universities as a strategy to achieve social change, and the association came to play a great part in educating many working-class women (Caldwell 1983). Its founder, Albert Mansbridge, who initially aimed the program at working men, was influenced by his mother (who was active in the Women's Co-operative Guild) to include women. By 1920 Barbara Drake (1984) was able to argue that "instruction in economics, industrial history and law," as well as practical experience, is essential for women officials (218). However, the question of how to educate women into trade unionism was still being discussed at the first UK Women's Trade Union Conference in 1926 (Kirton 2006, 33).

One of the first programs for working women in the United States was established by the Women's Trade Union League (WTUL), which was concerned that women should have access to the principles and practices of union organizing. It went on to set up the first residential school for women unionists in 1913 (Kirkby 1991). German delegates to the meeting of the IMF Women Workers' Committee in 1957 were able to report that their main task on behalf of women workers was the provision of training activities, including two training centers and three schools where courses are held for women.[4]

In the contemporary period beginning with the rise of second wave feminism, women's courses, intensive schools, and residential programs have become important sites for feminist politics. Unions have been persuaded to run their own courses—for example, the metalworkers union in Italy, the Federazione Lavoratori Metalmeccanici (FLM; Federation of Metalworkers), won paid educational leave as part of their annual contract in the early 1970s. Known as the 150 Hours Scheme, it initially aimed at giving workers access to school qualifications during the working day (Caldwell 1983). Similar courses elsewhere are often run by peak bodies—for example, the British Columbia Federation's Summer School. Such courses are likely to include a mix of feminists and other women who may be diffident at best about feminism and separate organizing. As a participant in a UK residential school said, "To be honest, I never thought you could have so many women together for a week without being bitchy" (Elliott 1984, 69). Kirton's (2006) recent study of women's courses in two UK unions twenty years later reports that some women were worried that "a crowd of women together" would soon start "insulting our brothers" (99). By contrast, Hazel Conley (2005) found that women delegates on residential courses also had to manage the concern of their male partners about the men participants.

With the growing influence of feminist demands, women-only courses were clearly not "remedial classes to give the ladies a chance to catch up" (Beale 1982, 104). Linda Briskin's (1993) influential analysis proposes they be classified as either based on the deficit model to address women's needs for specific skills and confidence, or proactive in developing transformative knowledge and practices. Kirton (2006) found that such courses are likely to be a mix of both, as women gain from overcoming the constraints on their confidence by the male-dominated labor movement while utilizing the political space of the course to develop useful political strategies.

Some courses aim directly at building women's leadership, since any improvement in women's conditions depends on leadership as well as activism to effectively challenge union sexual politics. Unions, in general, have turned to women's leadership training as part of a renewal strategy because they believe that women's increased activism will make unions more attentive to equity issues and therefore more attractive to women (Greene and Kirton 2002).

The Canadian Steelworkers Union developed such a course, interestingly enough with support and initial funding by a government equity office, the then–Ontario Women's Directorate in 1992. The Women of Steel course provides leadership training and brings together women who often work in isolation from one another to help them understand the systemic nature of gender inequality at work, in the union, and in society. It builds solidarity across social lines of division including race, ethnicity, language, and occupational categories. The course mobilizes rank-and-file members and is part of a broader process of acquiring and/or solidifying a sense of political efficacy, a sense of themselves as political actors, as citizens, as union members, and as women. The course has extended from its base in Canada and the United States to be adopted by women steelworkers in Mexico (Fonow 2003).

The feminist approach of the course opens out the definition of union activism to include a wide range of activities, from speaking up at meetings, to talking about an issue at work, to volunteering for routine tasks around the union hall, to participating in organizing drives. An evaluation of the course in 1999 found the most significant positive changes for participants were attending and speaking at meetings, and committee service. Before-and-after differences for voting in union elections, running for office, and being elected to office were not statistically significant, but women were running for and being elected to more influential positions on executive boards after taking the course (Fonow 2003, 164). These findings are not dissimilar to those in UK studies by Kirton (2006) and Conley (2005), where courses had strong positive influences on participants, showing greater confidence to pursue union careers, although the context of union structures and culture were more directly significant to their success.

Courses are also created with cross-union support. A modest example is the Anna Stewart Memorial Project, which was established in 1984 and continues to be run annually in several Australian states. It aims to increase women's union activism as well as the labor movement's recognition and understanding of women members. Anna Stewart herself was a union official in Australia who pioneered maternity leave campaigns in the 1980s and appeared to be successful and highly competent. Union women around the country were shocked when she committed suicide. It seemed that she had not felt able to call on her union sisters for support to help sustain both her family life and her union activism. The small national network of union feminists reverberated with discussion about how to overcome the isolation so many felt. Although strongly committed unionists, the women argued that the labor movement's blindness to women's concerns, combined with the boundaries imposed on them by union structures and membership demarcation disputes, was a great hindrance to mobilizing union potential for women.

The women determined to honor Anna Stewart and tackle union sexual politics by framing a program for union women as practical training and networking opportunities. By utilizing their networks, which included the few women in key positions with peak bodies and individual unions, the women won sufficient resources to allow twenty to thirty women to come off their jobs for the course. It has continued at the same rate each year since. Many of the women gained sufficient confidence and experience with union organizing and industrial work to become elected officials in their own state and national union branches. Similar programs are sponsored by national and international peak union bodies as well as by individual unions. The ILO, the International Trade Union Confederation (ITUC) (and its predecessor, the International Confederation of Free Trade Unions—ICFTU), and the Global Union Federations (GUFs) all endorse, develop, and provide varieties of educational programs aimed at social change for equality.

None of this would have occurred without considerable efforts from women themselves who are driven by the need to find ways to sustain themselves and their activism, and to confront sexual politics within the labor movement. It is doubtful that education and training programs alone will bring about changes in the opportunity structure within the labor movement. This will require more sustained forms of activism. What the programs do, however, is provide political spaces where participants can connect with networks within and beyond the labor movement to include feminist organizations and activists that strengthen alliances, feminist politics, and collective identity.

Centers

Women's centers constitute political spaces that are more stable, require larger resources, and are valuable and deliberate sites for alliances across unions or between the women's movement and the labor movement. The centers draw on strategies of the women's movement that created women's centers in India, Sri Lanka, Mexico, Peru, and the Philippines, as well as in the United States, Canada, and Europe (Rowbotham 1992), and on labor movement worker centers with their goals to support low-wage workers through advocacy, services, and organizing (Fine 2006; Hercus 2005; Weeks 1994). This reflects their origins in alliances of union and nonunion feminists working with unions, community groups, and state agencies.

In New Zealand, the Auckland Working Women's Resource Centre was set up in 1984 from an alliance of union women in clerical, hotel, and distribution work, along with woolen workers and early childhood workers. It began during the period when separate organizing was particularly energetic, as was the case in Australia. The Australian WWCs have been established by networks of union and nonunion feminists campaigning for state and union resources to support women in paid work. Centers generally employ several people with industrial relations expertise and are managed by boards drawing their membership from community, state, and union organizations.

The Australian WWCs also typify that country's feminist strategy of seeking and relying on state support for funding, legislative change, and policy to create gender equity (Franzway, Court, and Connell 1989; Sawer 1999). The South Australian center, which is also the longest standing, was established by feminists working within and around the state and the peak union body, the South Australian United Trades and Labor Council. It is mainly funded by an annual grant from the South Australian state government plus small labor movement grants, and supplemented in recent years by smaller, more conditional grants from the federal government.

Such a strategy has often caused difficult and knotty problems for feminists around roles, alliances, and political autonomy, and the WWCs have been no exception. All centers have experienced conflicts over the politics of funding that have been intensified by increased controls imposed by funding bodies, particularly at the federal government level. Many felt cautious about funding from the patriarchal state, and this feeling was exacerbated when a conservative federal government was elected in 1996. As it introduced legislation and policies that limited union power, undermined workers' conditions, and cut funding to welfare and nongovernment services, fierce debates arose over questions of defense and strategy. As a result, two centers (out of five) were forced to close in 2006 (one in Tasmania and the other in New South Wales). The recent change to a federal Labor Party government (2008) was expected to provide some ease and opportunities to rebuild this resource, as has been the case.

As the Australian industrial landscape has become increasingly harsh, the main focus of activity and casework has become vulnerable working women, including those who work in precarious and/or low status employment, Aboriginal and Torres Strait Islander women, women from non–English speaking backgrounds, women in regional or remote areas, women with disabilities, and women with family responsibilities (Working Women's Centres 2010). The WWCs frame their goals from feminist perspectives on women's work, and on economic and social justice. As the South Australian WWC states, it campaigns for the achievement of access to work, fair pay, and conditions for all working women, so that they may enjoy a balanced and quality life. Issues of equity, education, and opportunities are translated into tangible goals and campaigns to gain access to the political agendas of unions, the state, and even some areas of the women's movement.

The WWCs are sites of advocacy and empowerment for women. They build knowledge resources gained from their educational work, advocacy, and casework; from action research projects; and from alliances with union and feminist activists at local and international levels. The centers have created spaces in which such major issues as outwork (also known as piecework or homework), sexual harassment, homophobia, workplace bullying, and the impact of domestic violence on women's work are identified and debated among unions and other feminists (Working Women's Centre 1994; Franzway 2001).

The service focus of the WWC has a double edge to it: individual casework and broader campaigns for change. Responding to individual women's work problems and taking up specific cases of workplace discrimination provides centers with obvious and tangible evidence of continuing need. These cases also provide grounds for continued funding to support campaigns for change in policies and practices by unions and the state. However, casework is voracious and almost infinite, so that centers always struggle to balance the needs of clients with their advocacy and policy work (see also Fine 2006). The challenge is how to measure and maintain an appropriate level of casework as well as meet other priorities, particularly in an increasingly difficult industrial climate. Nevertheless, centers continue to participate in advocacy and campaigns with union feminists. Such work contributes to the larger political and discursive alliances between feminists and union movements, and their campaigns to confront the difficult political and strategic issues that are relevant to working women.

Campaigns

Campaigns are critical to making politics. They are, by definition, instances of collective action and aimed at effecting change to specific areas and conditions, or to internal agendas and structures of organizations. Campaigns are a series of coordinated activities and are not spontaneous, but require a degree of focus on specific goals, planning, organization, and responsiveness to changing conditions. They also need material and discursive resources, as well as capacity to frame issues; campaigns may aim at achieving effective frames that resonate with a specific target audience, such as the transnational labor movement. Campaigns are important activities for the women's movement and the labor movement. They can focus on local issues, such as legislative change, or international goals, such as the eradication of human trafficking. Campaigns are key sites for alliances between women and labor, and this has been the case throughout the last century. One of the earliest examples in the contemporary period saw women's liberation groups in the UK participate in a major campaign in the early 1970s aimed at persuading office cleaners, mainly women, to join a union (Coote and Campbell 1982, 37).

A campaign that spread through international feminist networks as a challenge to the sexual politics of the labor movement was focused around the development and implementation of the Working Women's Charter (Rowbotham 1989). With its roots in national communist parties and socialist feminist groups, the charter was a site of feminist campaigns in several countries from the late 1960s until the early 1990s. Jenny Wolmark (2003) claims that it was feminists in the UK Communist Party who were instrumental in drafting the original charter of ten demands from which the Working Women's Charter campaign developed. Ruth Elliott (1984) describes the charter, launched in 1972, as an initiative of feminists in what was then the London Trades Council (union peak body).

The demands contained within the charter generated enormous popular support and led to the formation of a network of charter groups that organized with the trade union movement to campaign for policy changes that would benefit women, although Coote and Campbell (1982, 38) observe that the campaign tended to be viewed with suspicion in the higher quarters of the labor movement. The UK Trades Union Congress (TUC) responded by publishing its own charter, Aims for Women at Work, in 1975, which included most of the demands from the original charter. The campaign was also taken up as a focus for feminist activism in labor movements in Australia and New Zealand.

The inclusion of the demand for free, safe, and legal abortion was the most contentious issue and delayed adoption of the charter by peak bodies and local unions. It was positively divisive in New Zealand (Nolan and Ryan 2003), where the peak Federation of Labour only adopted it at the third time it was proposed, while the primary school teachers union (predominately women members) refused outright. In Australia a charter, influenced by the UK campaign, was produced by the first WWC working with a union women's committee and endorsed by peak bodies, including the ACTU, in 1977 (Owen and Shaw 1979).

By this point, the charter had grown to eighteen demands and therein was the problem: although the charter campaign created a structure through which feminists could participate in trade unions, it suffered from a lack of focus. The issues surrounding women's work were so numerous and diverse, it was difficult to agree on what was the best strategy (Rowbotham 1989). Furthermore, union feminists were not well placed to ensure that the unions worked to implement the charter in their own organizations or in the workplace. They occupied few formal positions or were unable to make successful claims for union resources. Nevertheless, the charter, in its various forms, proved to be a viable answer to the question: What do women want in their work and in their unions?

Where the charter campaign focused on union agendas, other campaigns were framed by feminist challenges to women's work conditions and became the grounds for strong alliances between labor and women's movements. Sexual harassment is the most visible and painfully contested evidence of sexual politics in the labor movement. The term was coined in the early 1970s, although women workers were protesting against violence at the hands of male employers as early as 1734. Engels recognized it as a problem a century later: "If the master (employer) is mean enough, and the official reports mentions such cases, his mill is also his harem" (cited in Hadjifotiou 1983, 5). It only became possible to name women's lack of sexual safety at work with the emergence of the contemporary women's movement, which theorizes sexual harassment as an exercise of heterosexual male power that excludes and controls women and reinforces homosocial masculinity (Connell 1987; MacKinnon 1979; Williams 2002).

Sexual harassment for (mainly) women workers and (less visibly) for LGBT workers raised questions about gendered and unequal relationships of power, the discursive dominance of masculine heterosexuality, and practices of invisibility, none of which were easily resolved by the application of feminist or union principles. These issues have particular bite in male-dominated occupations and industries where women are in the minority and so struggle to have their concerns recognized in workplaces and their relevant unions. Recognition of women's agency and capacity to resist is critical, but to be effective, women's resistance needs to be connected through organizational and collective power. The recognition of sexual harassment enabled feminists to claim that male dominance in the workplace extended beyond the discrimination of the sexual division of labor to the complexities and hostilities of sexual dominance.

Union women and men regard sexual harassment as a clear site of feminist politics (Ledwith 2006). But it remains a vexed and complex issue for women and unionists to tackle, in part because it depends on the subjective interpretation of verbal and physical behaviors as harassment by the victim herself. This means that the victim's interpretation of the situation must hold against all others, which is very difficult in the context of patriarchal sexual politics. At the same time, feminists were concerned that women would be seen as victims or worse, that their sexuality was causing trouble in the workplace.

In addition, sexual harassment proved to be a critical issue for union feminists especially when both perpetrator and victim were union members: How could the union represent the interests of both? Unions are often confronted by members' conflicting interests, yet when sexual harassment was recognized as a critical issue for working women (through the efforts of feminist activists), the sexual politics of both workplaces *and* unions were thrown into sharp relief.

As discussed earlier, union feminists are able to access the organizational power and resources of the labor movement, although under variously limiting conditions. As mentioned above, coworker harassment has proved to be a source of conflict among unionists committed to worker solidarity. Field (1983) warns that "mass culture portrays working class men as uncouth animals ready to molest women at the drop of a hat," while economically more powerful harassers are overlooked (153). However, class analysis does not resolve the dilemma of coworker harassment. Taken up early by some unions, it was addressed as a problem of conflict of interest. An early policy recognized the likelihood that the situation of one member making a complaint against another member will arise. It was determined that both members are rightfully entitled to union representation (ACOA 1982, 61).

Others argue that "unions cannot represent members clearly guilty of harassment" (Lawrence 1994, 139). The issue is complicated by difficulties surrounding the legal principles of innocence and guilt, and the union's commitment to all members. If a union determines not to represent the accused, it may be appearing to assume guilt; if it does represent the accused, it may appear to minimize the seriousness of the issue.

Campaigns have been built on political and discursive alliances between women and labor and achieved some success, but not without conflict among the women and between women and men unionists. Rachel Brickner (2006) reports from her study of a Mexican union that it took women's leadership and three years of campaigning for the union formally to oppose sexual harassment. The women were reluctant to speak out for fear of reprisals from kin in their workplaces, and the men resisted out of fear of being accused of harassment. Sue Ledwith (2006) found similar responses at a recent workshop for Ukrainian women and men union officials but, over the course of the project, the dominant discourse of the denial of sexual harassment was "spectacularly unsettled," allowing the issue to be moved into the mainstream of the public agenda. Ledwith is cautious about long-term effects but was able to demonstrate that adequate resources and the appropriate framing of sexual harassment as relevant to union women has helped to make a start in transforming gender relations.

However, as women officials well know, the complexities involved in the sexual politics of sexual harassment means that while unions may adopt the appropriate policy they often fail to act appropriately. An essential aspect of the politics of sexual harassment is the framing of it as an industrial matter and as a question of equity in the workplace (including educational situations). A union campaign on sexual harassment depends on winning the union leadership's agreement that it is an issue of industrial relevance to their members, something that is not gained without overcoming a deal of opposition. The value of alliances, resources, and framing for successful campaigns was described to us in this way: "Do you know the [campaign] that I most remember that was great? . . . I organized the phone-in on sexual harassment. The [union] and the Working Women's Centre did it. . . . It had interpreters from non–English speaking backgrounds (Interview, union official)." The official's satisfaction rested on two key points: the issue was framed successfully so that it won support of members who were mobilized to respond with sufficient enthusiasm, and second, their response persuaded the male-dominated leadership of the union that this was a significant issue. Union leaders may be persuaded about the importance of issues by the weight of numbers concerned about them. In addition, the alliance with the NGO Working Women's Centre was central to the overall success (Franzway 2001).

The definition of sexual harassment, together with the development and implementation of relevant legislation and policies, is both a stage of women's challenge to male domination of the public domain and a site of contest over discourses and practices of sexual politics. In a relatively short space of time, sexual harassment has become an issue about which union feminists agree: it must be challenged in workplaces and in the unions. The campaign has successfully moved it from being contained as a "women's issue" to being recognized as an industrial issue and thus has a place on union agendas.

Conclusion

Each of the examples discussed above is a form of feminist organizing constituted by the ongoing and shifting forms of interactions between women and labor. This kind of activism is crucial if women are to play their part in revitalizing trade unions and to achieve gender equity. Despite the considerable obstacles they face from the sexual politics in workplaces and labor movements, women's political commitment and activism are making significant impacts. Union feminists in alliances with the women's movement are creating and using political spaces, national and international networks, and community organizations to mobilize women's participation to address workers' issues and concerns arising from the rapid changes of globalization.

Union feminists' activism contests the sexual politics of the labor movement from the local to the international level. In doing so, they win something that, in Arundhati Roy's terms in the epigraph that opens this chapter, enables their feminist politics to change the cultures and structures of the labor movement, and to contest the new demands on workers and everyday life imposed by globalizing capitalism.

5

Feminist Politics in International Labor

> For every famous speaker or writer or delegate to an international congress, there was at least one woman, sometimes several, who shopped for and cooked three meals a day for that speaker, made his bed, cleaned his toilet, raised his kids, and tended to his ailing mother and father. Men's work of labor internationalism rested on women's work of reproductive labor—which didn't qualify them to be "cool" proletarians.
> —Frank 2004, 106

The activism needed to revitalize labor takes many shapes and forms and emerges at different but interconnected levels of organization—local, national, regional, and international. In this chapter, we focus our attention on the history of feminist activism within three international labor bodies—the International Labour Organizations (ILO), the Global Union Federations (GUFs), and the International Trade Union Confederation (ITUC).[1] Much like women in the past, feminists in these organizations are using self-organizing and discursive alliances with the global women's movement to contest and refashion the sexual, racial, and heteronormative politics of their unions and of the labor movement more generally; and it is within this struggle that resources and capacities for political action are produced. By building alliances with activists in other organizations, networks, movements, and campaigns concerned with labor rights, they are opening up new spaces for feminist activism and new ways of doing labor politics.

Union women are connected to these transnational sites for labor activism by virtue of their membership in their local union and their union's membership in a broader network of national and international organizations, including national peak labor bodies, international labor federations, and the ILO. For example, a woman working in an automobile factory in Adelaide, Australia, joins her local branch of the Australian Manufacturers Workers Union (AMWU), which is an affiliate of the peak labor body, the Australian Council of Trade Unions (ACTU), connecting her to workers in other unions within her city, state, and nation. The ACTU, in turn, is a national affiliate of the ITUC, which connects her to a variety of peak labor bodies from around the world, such as the American Federation of Labor and Congress of Industrial Organizations (AFL-CIO), the Congress of South African Trade Unions, the Canadian Labour Congress (CLC), and the Japanese Trade Union Confederation.

In addition, her specific union, the AMWU, is affiliated with the International Metalworkers' Federation (IMF), one of the sector/trade specific GUFs representing the metalworkers unions worldwide. This affiliation connects her to women who work in steel, auto manufacturing, electronics, and mining. The IMF and the ITUC have official standing at the ILO, and participate in ILO programs and activities sponsored by the Workers Bureau and the Gender Equity Office. The ILO also facilitates connections between these labor bodies and a wide variety of nongovernmental organizations (NGOs) and governmental agencies with responsibility for labor relations.

Individual workers are often unaware of how they are embedded in these structures and networks or the opportunities they present for labor activism. It is the work of the union leadership and activists to help workers understand their value as sites for mobilization and politics. Feminists are well aware of the value of these organizations and networks for building solidarity among women for making feminist politics. As we discuss in chapter 4, feminists working on the inside have conducted studies; written policy reports and action plans; held conferences, workshops, and seminars; formed women's committees and equity offices; and organized women's participation in transnational labor campaigns. They have traveled to international meetings, forums, and congresses to make the case for women's rights. They have lobbied, marched, and rallied to support economic justice for women and men around the world, often at great personal cost.

As Fonow (2003, 2005) has argued elsewhere, union feminism is both discursive practice and goal-oriented collective action. Activists use discursive tools (such as conference resolutions, policy statements, newsletters, Web sites, and education programs) as well as institutionally sanctioned spaces (such as conventions, workshops, labor schools, and committee structures) to create a network of resources that can be called into action to mobilize members and potential supporters at strategically important moments. Women forge a collective sense of themselves as political actors through the day-to-day activities of building and sustaining these networks. The point of their activism is to make their unions and the labor movement more responsive to the concerns of women workers, and increasingly this involves a global approach.

To achieve their goals, feminists have had to become adept at negotiating alliances across various factions within their own unions as well as forging links across the often contentious divide among unions. Such negotiations become even more complex at the transnational level when political, social, and cultural differences and inequalities between and within nations make cooperation a challenge. In this chapter, we explore the sexual politics of working from within these institutions and evaluate the efforts of union feminists to create mobilizing networks and discourses for women's transnational labor activism. We approach each institution through a historical lens.

Labor Internationalism

The institutions and organizations we examine as sites for making feminist politics have their roots in the nineteenth century, when the idea that workers in different parts of the world held common interests was part of the "teeming mass of ideas" associated with the French and American Revolution, with solving the social and economic problems of the Industrial Revolution in England, and with the principles and ideals of socialism (Lorwin 1929, 11). Intellectuals and activists of the day condemned the ruthlessness and competitiveness of unrestrained capital and proposed new ways of reorganizing society that ignored political boundaries and national differences. By 1840 activists began to think it might be possible to establish international labor legislation and an international labor movement (Lorwin 1929).

London and Paris became the centers of activism where socialists, Chartists, social democrats, communists, revolutionists, and nationalists met and planned and schemed (Lorwin 1929). Among them was the French feminist and socialist Flora Tristan. In her treatise *L'Union Ouvrière,* translated into English as *The Workers' Union* (1843), which sold over twenty thousand copies, she presented the first concrete plan to create an international labor organization. Tristan called on workers to form themselves into a class and to unite without regard to sex, politics, religion, or national boundaries to obtain a share in political and economic power. She proposed the formation of the Workers Union with committees of correspondence in all the capitals of Europe. Five years before the *Communist Manifesto* was written, Tristan called upon the working class to emancipate itself and wrote, "isolated you are weak and fall under the weight of all kinds of distress!—Well then, leave your isolation: Unite! Union creates strength" (Moses 1984, 108).

Flora Tristan's feminism, according to Moses (1984), was an integral part of her socialist beliefs, and she viewed gender through the prism of class. She believed that workers' organization had a role to play in the liberation of women and framed her reasoning for women's rights around the benefits that free, educated women would bring to men and children of the working class: "It is on behalf of your own interest, men; it is for your betterment, you men, finally, it is for the universal well-being of all men and women that I enlist you to demand rights for women, and while waiting, to acknowledge them at least in principle" (20).

Tristan was remarkable but not particularly representative of women's influence on the construction of labor internationalism (Anderson 2000; Cross 2004; Tristan 2007). According to Frank (2004), women's labor activism was largely invisible because the theories and historical accounts of the international labor movement did not capture the less glamorous roles of women, nor did they provide an understanding of the gender dynamics of labor internationalism. Most accounts of labor internationalism focused on the formal institutions of labor and of the Left where the most visible actors were men. The movement these men participated in tended to replicate the sexual division of labor (and, we would add, sexual politics) within the home. Women did the reproductive labor that made it possible for men to participate in labor politics.

Efforts, however, to build international labor solidarity were not only distributed from the top down through formal labor organizations and across national borders, but also through the more diffuse flow of ideas and resources carried back and forth by immigrants, radicals, and labor activists. Yet, when you look closer at the exciting movement of people, institutions, ideas, and resources—what Frank (2004) characterizes as a "moveable feast"—you discover that women made the feast possible. Men did most of the imagining, writing, debating, and traveling, while women did the cleaning, cooking, and fundraising that made it possible for men to participate. "The story is gendered. Who immigrates? Who gets to talk during meetings at which an international workers' movement is debated? Who counts as a worker in that conversation? Who washes the dishes afterward?" (Frank 2004, 96).

International Trade Secretariats

As the labor movement grew stronger within specific countries, efforts to build cooperation between unions from different nations emerged within specific industrial sectors. The first of these organizations, known as Trade Secretariats, was established in 1889 by printers. By the outbreak of World War I, there were thirty-three such secretariats, mostly headquartered in Germany. These federated bodies were organized along trade lines and became autonomous associations of individual trade unions of workers in specific industries, occupations, and sectors of employment—mostly industrial and thus mostly male. Their main goal was to create and maintain worker solidarity, and their principal activities included information sharing about trade conditions in different countries, strike support and the promotion of trade unions in less organized countries (Bendt 2003; Lorwin 1929; Stevis and Boswell 2008). Motivations for forming such organizations included the desire to prevent workers in one country from acting as strikebreakers in another.

The task of building cooperation among workers from different nations proved formidable, and international solidarity was hard to maintain in the face of a worldwide depression and the rise of fascism during the 1930s. Secretariats headquartered in Germany, Italy, Austria, Spain, and Czechoslovakia were destroyed, discredited, or forced to move to other countries. This reduced their overall number and forced some of the smaller ones to merge. Immediately after World War II, there was a period of optimism about rebuilding Europe: cooperation among allied nations produced a period of renewal for the international labor movement. Within a few short years, however, cold war tensions would divide the labor movement into Christian, social democratic, and communist factions that would make the achievement of a unified international labor movement more difficult (Bendt 2003; Waterman and Timms 2004).

Decolonization and the formation of new states brought real and potential growth in the membership and activities of the Secretariats. Between 1950 and 1980 the secretariats pursued a strategy that was less burdened by ideology and more pragmatic. At a time of high-stakes ideology, taking this approach made the secretariats more attractive to trade unions from the third world who wanted to hold themselves apart from East–West controversy (Bendt 2003; Windmuller 1995). The eventual collapse of communist rule in Central and Eastern Europe created a new opportunity for growth and expansion of labor internationalism as the secretariats opened their doors to independent unions from this region. In an effort to understand what these changes mean for women, in chapter 6 we take a closer look at women's activism in one of the secretariats, the IMF.

Global Union Federations

The challenges of globalization have created renewed political opportunities for organizations to work together across the boundaries of one industry or sector. Today, there are ten different International Trade Secretariats (ITSs), now known as GUFs, representing millions of workers in almost every country in the world. Each has an active women's committee and sponsors gender specific events and activities designed to increase the participation of women in the affiliated unions.

Union feminists have been at the forefront of creating equity structures, projects, and discourses within the GUFs to address discrimination in the workplace and in the union. All maintain Web pages devoted to women and gender equity issues; eight have developed women's committees to specifically address women's issues; five hold women's conferences; and four have formal women's leadership programs. Less common are equity offices and affirmative action quotas. The most common activities taken on behalf of women include campaigns, research and publications, seminars, and International Women's Day celebrations. Campaigns are sometimes coordinated across the GUFs, such as the ILO's Decent Work for Women campaign and the ITUC's Organizing Women Workers campaign. Other campaigns are sector specific, such as the Public Service International's (PSI) Water Women and Workers campaign, while some focus more on the social rights of women and the prevention of violence against women. The GUFs conduct surveys of women members, publish reports on the status of women, and produce handbooks and videos on gender awareness, diversity, and equity bargaining.

Feminists often use these structures as staging areas for much broader campaigns including organizing women in the informal sector and in export processing zones; building alliances with feminists working in NGOs (such as Oxfam) to prevent the exploitation of workers in sweatshops; joining forces with feminists at the World Social Forum to address the gendered inequities associated with globalization; joining the World March of Women against poverty and violence; and passing antiwar resolutions at international conferences. While attention has been paid to women in the past, with some organizations holding women's conferences since the 1940s and 1950s, the

Table 1. GUF Equity Initiatives for Women 2008

GUF	% Female	Activities for Women	Gender Equity Structures	LGBTQ Support/Endorsement
Education International (EI) www.ei-ie.org (26 million)	65.4	Campaigns against sex discrimination and in support of various UN/ILO initiatives for gender equality and human rights	Women's Committee	Publication of a report on the rights of lesbian and gay teachers and education personnel
		Publishes report on women's educational status globally every three years for EI World Congress	Women's Conference	Created with PSI an LGBT Forum, LGBT Web page, and training guide on LGBT issues
			Working group on violence against women	
		International and regional roundtables and seminars	Pan-European Standing Committee on Gender Equality	Held two-day workshop on LGBT issues
			Women's Web page	
		Celebration of International Women's Day with thematic emphasis on violence against women, child labor, freedom from sweatshops, poverty, and peace	Equity Office	
			Leadership Program	
International Federation of Building and Wood Workers (IFBWW) (12 million)	15	Publications on women worker's rights and health; guidelines for trade unions on equal pay for equal work, daycare centers, and measures to stop sexual harassment at work	Working groups for women	
			Women's Committee	
			Women's Web page	
		Campaign to address women's rights and to increase female membership in Africa and Asia	Leadership Program	
			Action Program	
		Gender awareness campaign and equality training		

Table 1. Cont.

GUF	% Female	Activities for Women	Gender Equity Structures	LGBTQ Support/Endorsement
International Federation of Chemical, Energy, Mine and General Workers' Unions (ICEM) www.icem.org (20 million)	>30	Special conferences, workshops, and educational seminars for women Publishes a monthly e-mail bulletin on gender issues and HIV/AIDS Supports the ILO "Decent Work" Campaign Sponsors regional women's meetings that focus on work–life balance, the pharmaceuticals industry, maternity protection, and various other issues that affect women workers	Working groups for women Women's Committee Women's Conference Women's Web page Action Agenda	Women's forums on LGBT rights Facilitation of LGBT exchange
International Federation of Journalists (IF) www.ifj.org (600,000)	17	Conducted a study on the contribution made by women journalists in the trade union and press freedom movements Campaigns, protests, and other forms of activism to display resistance to events like women journalists' arrests (Iran) and suppression of women and their voices in the media culture Conducted a survey of regional women journalists to pinpoint the causes of their leaving the profession Campaign for equal rights for women journalists	Gender equality (LOTCO) trade union development program Maintains a Web page on gender issues	Supports conference of LGBT trade unionists Places the issue of LGBT rights within broader human rights issues

Table 1. Cont.

GUF	% Female	Activities for Women	Gender Equity Structures	LGBTQ Support/Endorsement
International Metal-workers' Federation (IMF) www.imfmetal.org (25 million)	30	Special seminars for women Campaign to recruit more women in trade unions Workshop on precarious work	Women's Conference Women's Committee Women's Web page Set aside seats for women on executive body Office for Equal Rights	Supports and endorses the Workers Out! Conference
Public Service International (PSI) www.world-psi.org (20 million)	65	Produced resource package and video on pay equity with ILO collaboration Campaigns for maternity protection, pay equity, ending violence against women, and the rights of migrant and women health workers Publishes a monthly newsletter Celebration of International Women's day marked by a "Water Women and Workers" campaign	Women's Committee Equity Office Women's Web page	Created LGBT Forum with EI Publications on equal rights of LGBT workers Condemns discrimination based on sexual orientation
International Textile, Garment and Leather Workers' Federation (ITGLWF) www.itglwf.org		Organizing for Equality Campaign Improvement of statistical information collected about women Educational campaigns on sexual harassment and maternity protection Celebration of International Women's Day	Women's Committees Women's Web page Campaign to make half of all members of governing bodies to be female Leadership Program	

Table 1. Cont.

GUF	% Female	Activities for Women	Gender Equity Structures	LGBTQ Support/Endorsement
International Transport Workers' Federation (ITF) www.itfglobal.org (4.5 million)	13–17	Campaign "Mobilizing Solidarity Strategy" for gender justice Publications on women transport workers Produces resource packets and films	Women's Committee Women's Conference Women's coordination network One of the five vice presidents is designated as the Women's Vice President Five seats are reserved for women on the executive board Women's Web page	Articulates support for lesbian and gay trade unionists
International Union of Food, Agricultural, Hotel, Restaurant, Catering, Tobacco and Allied Workers' Association (IUF) www.iuf.org (12 million)		Published a Gender Equality Guide Seminars on problems of women workers Publication of a training handbook for women in the Asia–Pacific region Detailed policy on sexual harassment Celebration of International Women's Day	A Web page dedicated to news items all over the world focused on women and work	
Union Network International (UNI) www.union-network.org (15.5 million)		Promotes integration of women in trade union structures and activities Project Global Equality Campaign to help women organize at work—in both the formal and informal economies—and supports the ILO decent work initiative Creates strategies to improve the gender balance in knowledge-intensive service companies and promote diversity management Celebration of International Women's Day	Women's Committee Women's Conference Women's Web page	Committed to a notion of solidarity that encompasses the fight against discrimination that affects young people, black citizens, and indigenous groups and gay and lesbian workers

pace of change has picked up considerably with the renewed energy of the international women's movement.

Queer activists, many of whom are feminist, are borrowing and expanding the strategy of self-organizing to build political spaces from which to make claims for representation and participation of lesbian, gay, bisexual, and transgender (LGBT) workers. As we discussed in chapter 2, two of the GUFs—PSI and Education International (EI)—are playing a lead role in articulating the social and economic rights of LGBT workers within the network of global union federations.[2] In 2007 they held a two-day workshop at the PSI World Congress that drew over three hundred participants and covered a range of topics, including collective bargaining for LGBT equity issues, diversity and antidiscrimination training, bullying and workplace climate, building alliances, and protecting and expanding quality public services like free education for all.

Individual GUFs are formally connected to other international organizations concerned about labor standards, practices and rights. These include the ILO and various UN suborganizations, employer organizations, and more recent financial institutions like the World Trade Organization. Increasingly, GUFs have become more involved with building alliances with NGOs in international campaigns for workers rights. According to Bendt (2003), joining forces with activists from women's, environmental, and social work associations enables achievements that would not be possible without a cooperative approach. But, more importantly, such activism helps forge closer alliances within the GUF network itself.

International Secretariat of Trade Union Centers

Developing alongside the industry-specific international secretariats (see discussion of International Trade Secretariats above) was the International Secretariat of Trade Union Centers. Between 1890 and 1920 federated or peak labor bodies consolidated within specific countries called national trade union centers—that is, the British Trade Union Congress, the American Federation of Labor, the CLC, and the ACTU. These national centers brought workers from different unions together to address national concerns of their respective labor movements, and by 1901 they were sufficiently stable to hold international conferences.

To build a broad base of support for the International Secretariat of Trade Union Centers, many political differences had to be broached, and much of this occurred at biennial conferences. There were clashes among very different types of trade unionism, from the highly centralized, industrial prosocialist, class-oriented (German), to the decentralized wage-conscious craft, nonsocialist (England/United States), to syndicalism with its revolutionary vision and more militant tactics (France). In order to cast the broadest net possible, it was decided in 1905 that the International Secretariat should exclude "all theoretical questions and questions affecting the tendencies and tactics of the trade union movement in the various countries" and limit its concerns to "the promotion of closer association between the trade unions of all countries, the collection of uniform trade union statistics, the provision of mutual support in industrial conflicts, and all other questions directly relating to the trade union organization of the working class" (Lorwin 1929, 104).

By 1913 the International Secretariat had a bureau with paid staff and attracted a stable core of nineteen Trade Union Centers from fourteen different countries (primarily European) with a total membership of 7,394,461. Germany, the United States, and England had the largest representation. It changed its name in 1914 to the International Federation of Trade Unions (IFTU) to indicate its expanding organizational base and began to establish contact with workers in Argentina, South Africa, and Australia. It is at this time that the IFTU began to regularize contact with the ITSs and thus became a conduit for exchanges between federations (Lorwin 1929, 112). While there were periods of cooperation, the cold war antagonisms would prevent the national peak labor bodies from sustaining a united approach, and in 1949 the noncommunist camp broke away to form the International Confederation of Free Trade Unions (ICFTU).

While not much is known about the history of women's activism within this organization, feminist scholars of the international women's movement and of the international labor movement are unearthing documentation that will allow us to piece together an account of women's activism. Most recently, Cobble (2008) has told the story of labor feminists and social democrats who were active in transnational reform networks, including the IFTU/ICFTU and the ILO. She traces their agenda over time, their personal and political relationships, and the formation of their collective identity as transnational political actors.[3]

According to Cobble, the first attempt by women trade unionists to forge an international movement occurred in 1919 at the International Congress of Working Women where women from nineteen different countries established the International Federation of Working Women (IFWW), one of the first experiments by labor women with transnational policy-setting. The IFWW was short lived and dissolved in 1924. While delegates agreed on the goals of the organization—the need to organize women into unions, to promote international labor standards, and to integrate women into the governance structures of international labor bodies—they disagreed over how to achieve them (Cobble 2008, 16).

Points of contention concerned who was eligible to join, which unions would be involved, which labor standards were important, and how and if to include men. There were political, cultural, and racial tensions and debates about autonomy: would the IFWW be an autonomous labor women's organization separate from the male-dominated labor movement, or would it be included within the IFTU? There were disagreements among feminists about the need for special protective labor legislation for women workers (Rupp 1997). In the end, according to Cobble, the organization opted to merge in 1924 with the IFTU, thus making it harder to include women outside of Europe and harder to build separate women's committees or programs. In fact, the women's movement within the IFTU fared poorly over the next two decades, and women's committees only met sporadically after 1924 and stopped entirely after 1938.

After World War II the political tensions within the IFTU forced a permanent split, and the IFTU broke away from the socialist and communist factions to form the ICFTU. Feminists affiliated with the ICFTU undertook a campaign to reform the organization by bringing forward a feminist agenda that included immigration rights, paid maternity leave, regulation of child labor, rights of domestic workers, and multinational standards for work hours (Cobble 2008, 20). Feminists continued "to put great weight on helping women balance market work and family and on formulating policies to upgrade the work traditionally done by women, including household labor, paid and unpaid" (Cobble 2008, 23).

Yevette Richards Jordan discovered that despite cold war tensions in the 1950s and 1960s, the ICFTU Women's Committee was engaged in alliance building with women workers in Africa. The Women's Committee pressed the ICFTU male leadership to use its African Labor College in Kampala, Uganda, as a vehicle for incorporating African women into the labor movement. According to Jordan (forthcoming), the leadership's unwillingness to take seriously the committee's campaign to organize and develop female leaders at Kampala was a misstep that served to "highlight their myopia in not foreseeing the impact of the feminization of labor for organized labor and the global economy" (2). She further argues that the ICFTU Women's Committee did not act in the same paternalistic manner as their male counterparts toward male workers in Africa. She attributes the difference to the fact that the members of the women's committee had already experienced the resistance of the men in their unions when they pressed for women's rights and when they pressed to open formal membership in the ICFTU to non-Europeans. African women could not join the ICFTU Women's Committee until the rule could be changed. The sexual and racial politics of the ICFTU in this period made it nearly impossible for African women to take advantage of trade union training opportunities, and the Kampala college closed rather than deal with the tensions. It would not be until 1985 that the ICFTU would set aside two seats on its executive board for representatives of the Women's Committee and to hold regular World Women's Conferences. In the next chapter, on the International Metalworkers' Federation, we provide a more detailed history of women's international labor activism.

In February 2003 the ICFTU brought women union leaders from 225 unions and 148 countries to Melbourne, Australia, for the 8th World Women's Conference. The event was hosted by the ACTU, and delegates participated in workshops and panels on a wide range of topics, from those more narrowly associated with trade unions, such as collective bargaining, to more pressing political issues, such as the upcoming war in Iraq. Delegates passed a strong feminist antiwar measure that spelled out the specific ways war affects women and girls.

Included on the program was Elmira Nazombe of the Women's International Coalition for Economic Justice (WICEJ), a prominent feminist leader from the nonprofit development sector. She addressed the delegates about the importance of building alliances between labor and transnational NGOs. The WICEJ, founded in 2000, is a transnational network of forty-five women's economic and human rights organizations from every region of the world that focuses on the link between gender, race, and macroeconomic policy within international intergovernmental policy circles. The coalition works with labor bodies, such as the ICFTU, the AFL-CIO, and the PSI, to get governments to pay greater attention to ILO core labor standards. The coalition is actively involved in the World Social Forum, the UN Commission of the Status of Women, and the UN Financing for Development process. Their primary activities are policy advocacy, education, and the development and distribution of popular tools for economic analysis. WICEJ has developed a methodology that allows activists, unions, and NGOs to conduct an analysis of the way gender and race intersect with globalization (Fonow and Franzway 2007).

In 2006 the ICFTU merged with the World Federation of Labour (WFL) to form the ITUC. At the time of the merger, the ICFTU was the largest international labor federation with a worldwide membership of 158 million workers from 150 different countries. It has three major regional offices in Africa with 13 million members, in Asia and the Pacific with 30 million workers, and in the Americas with 44 million workers. The WFL, a much smaller organization with a membership of 26 million workers, was created in 1968 and descends from the International Federation of Christian Trade Unions, which was inspired by the social-Catholic movement in Latin America.

While state-controlled unions in China and in remaining socialist states are not included in the new organization, the end of the cold war has meant an end to almost a century of division and conflict within the international trade union movement. Enormous debates remain, but unity is being driven by the question of how to combat global capital. According to Traub-Merz and Eckl (2007), the new merger represents for the first time a united international body of national trade union centers.[4] According to the constitution of the newly created ITUC, the organization is nonpartisan, "Unitary and pluralist the Confederation is open to affiliation by democratic, independent and representative trade union centres, respecting their autonomy and the diversity of their sources of inspiration and their organizational forms" (Traub-Merz and Eckl 2007, 2).

Both the ICFTU and WCL had women's committees, and programs and activities for women so it is not surprising that the new ITUC would expand these efforts. In fact, Sharan Burrow, one of Australia's leading labor feminists, president of the ACTU, and former president of the ICFTU/ITUC, was elected on June 25, 2010 as the first female general secretary of the ITUC. Often referring to herself as a feisty feminist and woman warrior, Burrow is a strong advocate of moving unions beyond traditional notions of labor politics. In an interview, she told us that union feminists play an important role in helping unions understand how to close the gap between the organization of women and the low labor standards underpinning women's work (Interview with Fonow, May 24, 2005, Vienna, tape recorded).

The ITUC has an Equality Department that coordinates antidiscrimination activities and campaigns. It produces and disseminates policy reports, training manuals, fact sheets, newsletters, and brochures, and it coordinates with the ILO's and the GUFs' various transnational campaigns for women's rights, including campaigns to end violence against women and girls, for maternity protection, and for pay equity. Union feminists within the ITUC recognize that sexism within organized labor makes it difficult to organize women workers and to create strategies that will make the labor movement more relevant to women and strong enough to achieve social and economic rights for women. They are aware that if unions are to work for women, "Organising and representing women working in the formal, traditional sectors should extend to women in the informal economy, export processing zones, young women, migrant women, women from ethnic minorities, women in rural and urban areas, teleworking and home-based workers, domestic workers, single working mothers, and women in short-term employment, temporary, casual, low paid jobs and other workers vulnerable to exploitation, by helping them to identify and meet their own needs through solidarity action" (ITUC 2006, 3).

This ITUC Action Programme for Achieving Gender Equity in Trade Unions has been actively encouraging the adoption of similar programs at regional and local levels. For example, there is a new initiative to organize women in the Maghreb region (five-state trading region in North Africa), and women's committees, conferences, training seminars, and organizing campaigns have been established in affiliated unions in Morocco, Algeria, and Mauritania. High-quality campaign materials produced in Arabic are being used to raise awareness about the rights of women. The action plans at all levels call for introducing targets (30–40 percent) for women's representation and participation in all union decision-making bodies and leadership and training opportunities. They also call for the inclusion of women in negotiating committees and for the expansion of collective bargaining agreements to include equity issues.

International Labor Organization

The final pillar in the organizational infrastructure of labor internationalism is the ILO, established in 1919. Although the labor movement had lobbied for an international labor parliament with the power to pass laws regarding labor standards that would be binding on all nations, the most they achieved was an institution that was halfway between a parliament and an advisory body designed to reconcile the ideas and purposes of governments, employers, and labor unions (Lorwin 1929, 478). The original role of the ILO was to draft universal conventions regarding labor standards, monitor compliance, conduct research, publish information, and facilitate cooperation among labor, government, and employers. The establishment of the ILO afforded the international secretariats new opportunities to expand their activities and to participate in setting minimum standards and norms at work.

The formation of the ILO provided labor with a much broader range of international contacts than was possible before: through its annual conference, it provided representatives from South America, Asia, and Africa a place to meet on a regular basis with representatives from Europe and North America. The tripartite structure of the ILO created spaces where representatives (including feminists) from labor, employers, and government could meet, debate, and exchange ideas and information. The ILO also created a consulting process that incorporated civil society, an arrangement that would hold up well as the network of International NGOs grew and included many more transnational feminist organizations (Hawkesworth 2006; Lubin and Winslow 1990; Moghadam 2005; Waterman 1998).

It was through their membership in the ILO that the ITSs and the IFTU gained official access to the League of Nations and eventually to the UN. According to Berkovitch (1999), the establishment of the League of Nations and the ILO in 1919 ushered in a new phase of world polity that made possible more permanent cooperation between nations, and feminists took full advantage of the opportunity: "They opened a new arena for women's mobilization by offering a central world focal point that theretofore had been lacking. In so doing, they changed the context in which women's organizations operated, consequently provoking changes in their modes of operation as well" (109).

The parameters of the ILO and the League of Nations were laid out in discussions at the 1919 Peace Conference in Paris, and representatives of the international labor movement and the international women's movement insisted that the voice of labor women be heard. To mobilize and maximize their influence, both movements held meetings and conferences leading up to the peace conference. From these emerged an agenda of labor rights for women. The British trade union leader Margret Bondfield, a seasoned participant in the international labor movement and a feminist, lobbied successfully for the inclusion of two amendments in the constitution of the ILO. These required the ILO to consult with women when any question concerning women's labor was under consideration and to employ a certain number of women on the ILO staff (Lubin and Winslow 1990, 21).

Union women from other countries, including the United States, France, and Belgium, added their own more specific concerns, as did representatives from the growing network of international women's organizations (Rupp 1997). The International Council of Women (ICW) demanded equality of opportunity for men and women, including equal pay for equal work, participation of women in the deliberations of all international commissions concerned with labor organization, support for an eight-hour day and a working week of forty-four hours, an end to child labor, and suppression of night work for women, where possible, "without creating a situation unfavorable to women" (Lubin and Winslow 1990, 21). Other women's organizations and reform movements lobbied for a wide range of economic issues, including paid maternity leave, vocational training for girls, minimum wage, and social insurance for women. While the more general Bondfield proposals represented what was achievable in 1919, the other demands (while not specifically incorporated in the original charter of the ILO or the League of Nations) would set the agenda for the ILO for years to come. The very idea of an international body establishing labor standards separate from what nations established was controversial, even without the feminist demands.

The establishment of the UN in 1949 opened additional avenues of transnational activism for labor feminists and an opportunity to reinforce some of the successes feminists had accomplished at the ILO, as well as stimulate new directions. By establishing a dense and complicated network of governmental and nongovernmental organizations and mechanisms to facilitate cooperation between them, the UN provided women's organizations with greater access to governments and to the world of intergovernmental relations (Gelb 2002; Prügl 2004). Feminists from Latin America and Australia took advantage of the opening and helped to spearhead a campaign to inject gender into the founding documents of the UN, but to do so they had to challenge the gender neutral approach favored by the men who prepared the documents. They created a woman's caucus consisting of the few women who were included in their country's delegation to the 1945 UN Conference on International Organization; launched a successful campaign to secure an affirmation of the equal rights of women and men in the preamble of the UN Charter; and managed to get approval for nondiscriminating clauses in four other clauses of the charter (Hawkesworth 2006, 88).

Although it would take decades, feminist activism inside the UN created a women's policy machinery—offices, bureaus, and ministries spread throughout the divisions and activities of the UN, including the ILO. According to Hawkesworth (2006, 91), creating such machinery was seen as a tactic for change and something that could be done at the international level. These units provide research on the status of women, provide equity training, promote gender mainstreaming, publish educational materials, and stage conferences, forums, campaigns, and so forth. The machinery created and maintained a network of experts and resources that could be mobilized for women's rights. The discourse and symbols they created became part of a larger transnational women's movement. Feminists within organized labor who were working at the transnational level borrowed freely from the UN machinery.

The influence of international NGOs continued to expand in this period with numbers increasing from twenty-five organizations at the founding of the UN to fifty by 1975—the International Women's Year. Numbers of international feminist NGOs continued to grow with each successive UN forum or conference on women (1985, 1995, and 2005). According to Hawkesworth (2006), feminist NGOs were not only constitutive of, but also gave birth to, an increasingly vibrant transnational feminist civil society. They played key lobbying and monitoring roles—pressuring for UN conferences, then pressuring intergovernmental conference participation to produce concrete programs for action, and then using these platforms to leverage nations to change their laws and structures to conform to the UN platforms (Hawkesworth 2006, 105). Union feminists were connected to these circuits at the UN through the affiliation of their unions and peak labor bodies with the International Secretariats and the ICFTU, which had standing at the ILO (Lenz 2003; Moghadam 2005).

As the result of feminist activism, and particularly since the election of Chilean diplomat Juan Somovia in 1999 to head the ILO, gender mainstreaming has become ILO policy, and its Bureau of Gender Equality monitors the progress of women's equality in all programs and projects of the ILO. About 50 percent of the ILO's budget now goes toward providing technical assistance to the developing world and includes many special projects for women and girls that cover vocational training, job creation, labor relations, and improving work–life balance.

The bureau monitors compliance with gender mainstreaming directives of the ILO leadership and facilitates the development of institutional mechanisms for incorporating a gender perspective throughout all of the ILO's sectors, departments, programs, and field offices as they plan, implement, monitor, and evaluate their work. The bureau also disseminates information and research about gender issues in the world of work to ILO staff, its constituencies, and the international community. It acts as a liaison with the UN system, NGOs, and academic and women's organizations, and it is consulted by the ILO governing body about gender concerns within the organization itself.

Out of this activism, in 2003 the ILO governing body adopted the Action Plan on Gender Equality and Gender Mainstreaming, which serves as an instrument to institutionalize gender mainstreaming within the work of the ILO office. The action plan provides a gender sensitive methodology, a uniquely feminist invention, to measure the inclusion of gender concerns in planning, programming, implementation, monitoring, and evaluation of all activities and policies of the ILO. The ILO has instituted gender audits to assess whether internal practices and related support systems for gender mainstreaming are effective. The audit conducted by the Gender Equity Office employs a participatory methodology with an emphasis on team building, information sharing, and reflection on gender. The purpose of the audit methodology is to help the individual units develop the capacity to conduct a gender analysis of their programs, policies, and activities. Units must own the process if they are to scale up their activities on behalf of women.

Finally, equity became a key component of the ILO Declaration on Fundamental Principles and Rights at Work and one of four core labor rights spelled out in the declaration. They are: 1) freedom of association and the effective recognition of the right to collective bargaining; 2) the elimination of all forms of forced or compulsory labor; 3) the effective abolition of child labor; and 4) the elimination of discrimination in respect of employment and occupations. Whether they have ratified the declaration or not, each member state of the ILO has the obligation to respect, to promote, and to realize, in good faith, these core labor rights. Feminists use the declaration on the ground in specific countries to frame campaigns for women's economic rights.

Union feminists have been at the forefront of creating equity structures within unions at every level to address discrimination in the workplace and sexual politics in the labor movement. They use the structures in the unions, peak bodies, the ITUC, GUFs, and ILOs to urge the labor movement to act more broadly to achieve feminist goals. Because these institutions are organized transnationally and regionally, the activism of union feminists can spread well beyond the unions and labor networks of Europe and North America to include Africa, Asia, and Latin America. This has allowed for better coordination of activities and greater opportunities for feminists to share ideas, discourses, and strategies within and across regions and nations. For example, the ITUC and the GUFs have taken up the ILO global campaign for decent work and have modified it for women as the Global Campaign for Decent Work, Decent Life for Women. The campaign focuses on upgrading the conditions of labor for women by strengthening women's recruitment, representation, and participation in unions. The ITUC and the GUFs have agreed to focus their activities on the sectors of work where women workers are most vulnerable, such as export processing zones, domestic work, part-time work, migrant work, and work in the informal economy.

Conclusion

Union feminists weave together strategies that emerge from the labor movement and the women's movements—each with its own history of international activism stretching back to the nineteenth century. By building alliances with activists in other organizations, networks, movements, and campaigns concerned with labor rights, union feminists have opened new spaces for feminist activism and have developed new ways of doing labor politics. Through self-organizing, women have challenged the sexual politics of three venerable institutions of labor internationalism. By mobilizing the discourses and networks of global feminism and leveraging the gender equity machinery of the UN, union women are making labor more responsive to the equity concerns for working women.

Today all three of these organizations have institutionalized equity structures and leadership activities for women. The most common activities include organizing campaigns, conferences, seminars, Web sites, and women's committees. For example all three are involved in a worldwide campaign for Decent Work for Women and have agreed to focus their attention and activities on those sectors of work where women workers are most vulnerable, such as export processing zones, domestic work, and various forms of precarious work. While attention has been paid to women's issues in the past, with some organizations holding women's conferences in the 1940s and 1950s, the pace of change has picked up considerably in the past ten years.

After decades of struggle to make unions more representative and more democratic, union feminists are revitalizing the labor movement and helping to make unions more responsive to the challenges of globalization. However, for labor to benefit from the work of union feminists, unions must increase and enhance the participation of women within their ranks. This requires a rethinking of structures and practices that perpetuate male dominance in the labor movement. In the next chapter we provide an in-depth analysis of how women in one of the GUFs, the International Metalworkers' Federation, have become transnational labor activists.

6

Women's Activism in the International Metalworkers' Federation

> Decisions are taken without consulting women and without considering them. Yet the world run by men alone is not so good that it can be said to be the best of all possible worlds.
> —Ilda Simona, IMF Women Workers' Conference, Geneva, April 17 and 18, 1975

We extend our analysis of the sexual politics of labor internationalism in this chapter by offering a case study of women's transnational labor activism in the International Metalworkers' Federation (IMF), which is a Global Union Federation (GUF). Over the course of its history, metalwork and related occupations have had a strong male tradition, and so have its industrial organizations. But there have always been women metalworkers, even if their numbers have been small at times. Their campaigns to win space in the workplace and the union for their interests and issues provide a striking example of the ways union and feminist discourses have developed through persistent effort and the slow accretion of activist knowledge.

As the union feminists under discussion in this chapter work to challenge the sexual politics of the labor movement, at transnational levels in this case, just as elsewhere, they are confronted by debates familiar to feminists everywhere. Questions about strategies based on the meaning of equality, pay equity, protectionism, and separate organizing surface frequently. What follows in this chapter is a discussion of the IMF as a site of women's political activism and transnational union feminism.

Structure, Organization, and Mission of the IMF

According to its Web site, the IMF is a worldwide federation of two hundred national unions—a union of unions—representing about one third or 25 million of the world's metalworkers in one hundred countries.[1] Women are estimated to be about one third of the membership, with about half of that membership located in Europe. The IMF represents workers in blue-collar and white-collar occupations in a range of industries, including iron and steel production, electronics, engineering, shipbuilding, automobile production, precision instruments, and tool making.

The IMF was initiated at a meeting in 1893 in Zurich, Switzerland, when a small group of metalworkers from Europe and the United States came together in the spirit of solidarity and was formally established in 1904. After World War II, the IMF grew beyond the borders of Western Europe and began to open regional offices, from Tokyo in 1957, to Chile in 1960, to New Delhi in 1969, Johannesburg in 1984, and in Kuala Lumpur in 1998. Unions in Central and Eastern Europe were able to become affiliates following the collapse of the Soviet Union.[2]

The IMF, like all GUFs and peak union bodies, does not decide the policies of its affiliated unions, but rather coordinates their international activities. The IMF provides national unions with technical assistance, with an international forum to develop and exchange ideas, and with research and published reports, and it develops programs and activities designed to build international solidarity. It is represented at the International Labour Organization (ILO) and is networked with other GUFs, and through these links it provides another way to embed its affiliates in transnational circuits of labor activism. The IMF participates in the World Social Forum, discussed in chapter 7, and is building alliances with transnational nongovernmental organizations (NGOs) and a number of popular social movements.

The original purpose of the organization was to improve wages and working conditions, to promote international solidarity, and to secure collective bargaining and trade union rights. Unions in countries with stronger labor movements and organizations could offer assistance to workers struggling under regimes that are more repressive. It was also the hope of the IMF that fostering international solidarity would help reduce international competition for cheap labor. Explicit attention to the rights and concerns of women workers by the IMF and its affiliates began early in its history, but has required great efforts on the part of active women unionists (Downs 1995; Fonow 2003; Gabin 1990; Milkman 1987; Sugiman 1994).

First IMF Women's Conference 1957

Sexual politics has always been integral to how the metal trades are organized. Women needed to struggle against sex discrimination in the workplace as well as for greater representation within their unions for more than a century. Following World War II, women worked to regain some standing in their unions, including those of the metal trades. A significant breakthrough occurred when the electronics division sponsored the IMF Women's Conference in Vienna in 1957. The metal unions sent twenty-three delegates, seven of whom were men, from ten countries (United States, Great Britain, Italy, Germany, Denmark, Belgium, Netherlands, Norway, Sweden, and Austria) to the first conference. Other participants included five invited guests (all women) from the ILO and peak labor bodies, including the Austrian Trade Union Federation, the British Trade Union Congress, the Vienna Chamber of Labor, and the top two leaders of the IMF, both men. Before the conference, the IMF conducted an extensive survey, the first of many, on the status of women, their wages, working conditions, rates of unionization, and participation. Data gathering has since become an important plank in endeavors to enhance women's union rights and mobilization.[3]

With the cold war at its peak, the conference was also framed by claims for democracy in opposition to communism. What we would now refer to as the equality/difference question was cast as the critical value of women's working conditions in democracies. Does equality mean that women have to be treated exactly the same as men, as in the Soviet Union, or do the presumed differences between women and men mean that women need to be protected from hard work, as in the industrialized democracy? In the Soviet bloc, women may have had the same working conditions as men, but these were described as "the hardest, heaviest and most disagreeable jobs."[4]

Adolphe Graedel, the general secretary of the IMF, equated the protection of women from masculine forms of hard labor as one of the hallmarks of democracy. He offered a protectionist argument as the preferred path to equality: "In our view, equality between men and women should not be expressed by the possibility or necessity for women to do navvying work, to handle pick and shovel or move heavy wheelbarrows loaded with building material. . . . That is not the kind of equality we want in democratic countries."[5]

Caroline Davis Head of the Women's Department of the United Automobile, Aerospace and Agricultural Implement Workers of America (UAW) likewise appealed to the principles of democracy to advocate for economic justice, reminding unions of their obligation to struggle on behalf of women's rights in the workplace. But democracy without equality for women would be "a fundamental contradiction, to say nothing about hypocrisy." However, women's family responsibilities were not under challenge, but rather should be supported: "This is as it should be."[6]

Enabling women's participation in the workplace, the union, and the community would benefit their families as well as women themselves. Davis proposed that mainstreaming the so-called special interests of all workers would strengthen the broader labor movement. It was folly to do otherwise. Miss W. Baddeley, representing the Amalgamated Engineering Union of Great Britain, took a more direct feminist line, declaring "to some extent, the men are at fault" for the marginal numbers and status of women. It was men's responsibility to make unions hospitable to women, as well as to encourage the women in their own families to become union members.[7]

A second familiar debate surfaced over the question of the "family wage" in contrast to equal pay. Which was better, an adequate family wage so that women did not need to work, or equal pay so that all women, whether or not they were married, had the right to be financially independent of men? The principle of equal pay for equal work was an issue of long-standing concern to women in the labor movement. Despite the 1951 ILO Equal Remuneration Convention (C100) on equal pay, little progress had been made to close the wage gap between men and women in the metal trades at the time of the conference. Even though there was a developing body of law to regulate wages in a more equitable manner, there was no apparatus to implement such measures in most countries. Equal pay would not be achieved without the active support of unions and peak labor bodies like the IMF, thus the importance of this debate at the Women's Conference. Not surprisingly, the IMF welcomed the view that equal pay would depend on increasing women's unionization.

Reports from delegates on the efforts of their unions to address women's issues revealed the diversity of conditions, arguments, and strategies developed by each affiliate. In the United States, the UAW had adopted separate organizing strategies and established a women's department. Davis reported that its purpose was to mainstream women's union activity, interests, and treatment. The women's department would then be no longer needed. Baddeley reported that her union had created a women's division in 1943 that held women's conferences, collected data on women's progress, and published a monthly women's journal. The Industrial Union of Metalworkers from West Germany offered and financed courses for women to build confidence in participation. Branches of the union also held special women's meetings, films, discussions and "mannequin parades" (fashion shows) made popular in the 1930s.

Only Denmark reported on a separate women's union, the Danish Women Workers' Union established in 1885 by washerwomen who faced the hostility of employers and skepticism of other working women.[8] According to Dan Gallin (2000), it was established because the General Workers' Union at that time "refused to admit women into membership" (4). In 1958, the Women Workers' Union believed it was the world's only all-female union, run by female officers for its 42,000 members over 130 local branches. The union experienced a degree of cooperation that surpassed their expectations: it did not disband, unlike some of the smaller women's-only unions discussed in chapter 2.

The Netherlands and Italy reported the most difficulties organizing and representing women workers, in part due to broad opposition to married women participating in the workforce. Ironically, the married delegate, Mrs. Weidma from the Netherlands, noted that the government as well as many companies had instituted marriage bans so that women could be dismissed when they married. Nevertheless, her union established a committee on women's questions. It was headed by a man because "we believe that the question of female labour is not merely a matter for women, but is a question as a whole, for both sexes."[9] The Italian delegation felt that married women should not be employed in times of high unemployment. The male breadwinner's wage was paramount, while women's proper place was in the home.[10]

Belgian unions had established a women's department but had not succeeded in eliminating contractual wage differentials between women and men in the engineering divisions. Union caution led them to argue that women's minimum wage be raised to 85 percent of men's as a first step. A kind of class bias seemed to be in play, since it was felt that there was a "certain mentality among the working classes, which induces them to accept this tradition of different rates of pay for the two sexes too easily."[11]

The range of debate at the conference on why little progress had been made in achieving equal pay for women has since become familiar to campaigners for pay equity. Some delegates believed that because wages are tied to skill levels and women are segregated in those specializations within the metal trades that require less skill, they are paid less than the men who are located in the more highly skilled sectors of the industry. In Norway, for example, a sexual division of labor saw women and men in very different jobs, even within the same factories. Women's "nimble fingers" were still worth 25 percent less on average than men's capacity for heavy work.[12] For this reason, some delegates argued for equal pay for work of equal value and not just equal pay. Others argued that prejudice played its part, and that unions as well as employers were at fault. Yet, these union women were prepared to argue that women should be recruited and encouraged to be active in their unions.

The ILO conventions on women and work were brought to the discussion, and we see that a discourse of rights begins to make some headway, although it remained embedded in a framework of protectionism, based on women's so-called "*natural* handicap due to child-bearing and her lesser physical strength." Hence, women can have no real equality of rights with men unless there is special protection for women.[13]

The IMF (male) leadership expressed some surprise at the level of debate and agreement reached at this first women's conference: "This proves that, from the point of view of expressing their thoughts, women are not inferior to men—far from it! It demonstrates strikingly that women can play a leading part in the battle for trade unionism and for the improvement of workers' conditions. But women must also shoulder responsibilities within their union, workplace and wider society. Only then will they be treated as equals."[14]

Transitional Discourses and Structures

By the early 1960s, support for protective social legislation for working women and thus for women's difference was changing. Restrictions against night work for women were beginning to weaken, and the emphasis shifted to protecting women's reproductive health against workplace hazards. There was no widespread questioning of the biological differences between men and women but rather a questioning of the value being ascribed to those differences. As a German delegate to an IMF meeting said, "The Germans were conscious of the differences in the sexes; they did not wish the difference to lead to any differentiation in value."[15]

Although the IMF was prepared to hold women's conferences, it rejected any additional activities, preferring to rely on individual affiliates and the International Confederation of Free Trade Unions (ICFTU). In addition, the IMF leadership was reluctant to support women delegates in activities that would go beyond the orbit of IMF affiliates, such as the problems of women workers in developing countries. The achievement of the second IMF women's conference in 1961 was to establish a formal commission for women workers. Its role was to develop plans to improve women's rights at work and to recruit and organize more women into unions. At the initial meeting in 1963, the mainly European delegates continued to ponder the problem of women's lack of equality, and this was despite instances of women's activism such as a three-day strike by Austrian women on pay issues. By 1964 the commission had become a committee with Ilda Simona appointed as the director, a position she held for more than twenty years. Non-European affiliates began to attend and included delegates from Japan, the United States, Columbia, Israel, and Mauritius.

Debates continued among affiliates over whether to develop special structures in the unions and whether to advocate protective measures for women workers, a particular concern for the IMF, which had coverage of a wide range of nontraditional women's occupations. Influenced by the debates taking shape at the UN, the IMF had begun to seriously question protective labor legislation. According to a letter from Simona to the participants of the fifth annual meeting of the IMF's Women Workers Committee held in Geneva on April 29 and 30, 1969, "These measures are more and more controversial within affiliated unions and international organizations. Some people are of the opinion that the special protection of women should be reduced to a minimum or even eliminated in order to increase their employment possibilities and to guarantee equality in respect of employment and occupation. Others take medical and sociological research into account and insist on the necessity to maintain a special protection for women."[16]

Before the 1970s few women unionists in the IMF had any alliances with women's organizations and institutions concerned with women's problems. In general, they preferred to work with the then ICFTU, women's sections of other unions, and with political parties—that is, labor, socialists, and communists—on issues of concern to women. Some of their female members also belonged to the Housewives Federation because of the organization's opposition to increased prices of consumer goods.

The 1970s marked an important decade for women's activism in the IMF. The third Women's Conference on Women Workers was held in 1970, the activities of the IMF Women's Committee were regularized with annual meetings held throughout the first half of the decade in preparation for the UN International Conference on Women in 1975, and finally, activities were expanded beyond Europe to Latin America and Asia.

Despite a general decline in manufacturing jobs, women's employment in the metal trades increased throughout the 1960s. The most spectacular growth in women's employment occurred in Japan, where there was an increase of 64 percent between 1960 and 1966.[17] It became apparent to the IMF that women were here to stay. The wage gap between men and women in the metal trades showed signs of decreasing and the category of "women's jobs" disappeared from most collective agreements. While a single system of job classifications applying to both women and men became the norm, progress was deceptive. According to Simona, employers found ways around the principle of equal pay, including arbitrarily designating some jobs light or heavy depending on the gender of who does the work.[18]

The trade unions began to become aware of the deleterious impact of sex discrimination on the workplace and on their women members. For example, as the Italian delegate told the audience at the third IMF women's conference in 1970, "The particular problems of female labour are the direct product of the concept even more wide-spread in our society that women are above all housekeepers who accidentally go to work at the factory or the office."[19] Importantly, it was also recognized that reasons for the low level of women's participation in union life, even as they were joining unions at higher rates than men, "must be sought in the very structure of the union."[20]

Debates among delegates to the IMF's women's forums began to be framed in feminist terms. They challenged the unmarked gender of the universal trade unionist: "In most cases the trade union structures still bear the mark of the traditional model—the union of manual, adult, male workers."[21] Delegates raised questions of power and women's lack of role in decision making. It was observed that even where women were progressing satisfactorily as far as their social status is concerned, they were conspicuous by their absence from the decision-making organs of trade unions. Thus it was noted that there were only 5 women out of 264 delegates at the IMF World Congress held in Lausanne in 1971. Simona tells the 32 delegates from Europe and Japan who attended the 1972 Women's Committee meeting in Vienna: "Decisions are taken without consulting women and without considering them. Yet the world run by men alone is not so good that it can be said to be the best of all possible worlds."[22]

Union women's concerns about access to decision making broadened to include decisions a woman might make about her body, and so questions about women's bodily integrity were brought to the table. Thus, the frame of equal rights extended beyond equal pay to include reproductive rights. Equal rights for men and women were seen as a "burning political question, a pressing need which must be dealt with urgently and rapidly. More liberal legislation on contraception and stopping abortion being treated as a crime are equally imperious needs."[23] The Women's Committee's proposed resolution on reproductive rights was taken up at the next IMF Congress: "Congress asks affiliated unions to demand of their respective governments the necessary legislative measures to avoid the moral conflicts of conscience and the social problems posed by the birth of unwanted children and by the lack of child-care facilities."[24]

As the IMF expanded its activities for women beyond Europe, it held a series of seminars for women and youth in Asia and Latin America. These seminars fueled arguments for attention to women's specific needs in recognition of women's differences. For example, the first symposium held for women in India on January 26–27, 1973, reported back from the field that women wanted women's committees and wanted unions to pay particular attention to women's problems and to draw up continuous programs for organizing women workers. Participants also recognized other inequalities based on social and cultural differences, arguing that trade unions should organize all workers irrespective of caste, sex, creed, or color.[25]

Notes from these meetings indicate that equal rights are being framed as human rights. For example, the minutes of the Hong Kong meeting in 1975 state, "No substantial progress can be achieved in the field of equal rights for women at work without radical reform in the social status of women," and urges that "women be recognized and treated as full human beings with full human rights."[26] At this point, universal human rights appeared to be a valuable frame for campaigns for women's equality. Critics observed that human rights have too often been constructed with the male citizen as the normative subject, and that differences among women were also obscured (Crenshaw 2000; Fonow 2005; Hutchings 2002).

Women's rights campaigns were boosted by the UN's International Women's Year (IWY) proclaimed for 1975, providing union feminists in the IMF and elsewhere with leverage to secure more resources: "One might say that for an International such as ours, which has been fighting for many years to achieve equal rights for women, every year is an international women's year; but this would be failing to recognize the importance of the United Nations' decision."[27] The IWY was seen as a turning point and a catalyst in the adoption of new measures to improve women's status. The speech that Simona prepared for the IMF's 1975 Women's Conference reflected the traction of feminist discourses, which had grown with the emergence of second wave feminism and transnational activism focused on women's issues within the labor movement. Simona recognized that international solidarity among women is difficult to achieve unless national variations and diversity are taken into account. She expressed the classic feminist dilemma: "The basic problems women face are often identical in all countries, but each group may experience these problems in their own particular way."[28] The sexual politics of the family, the workplace, and the wider society are framed as problems of human rights, which are interconnected.

Within the space of twenty years, the IMF had moved from an agenda limited by traditional issues to one that advocated for the rights of women workers across the globe. Between 1963 and 1983, the IMF created a women's committee and a department, and held forty meetings, seminars, and conferences (an average of two meetings a year) in Europe, Asia, Africa, and Latin America. By 1979 the Women's Committee developed an action program, Equal Rights and a Better Status for Women, that incorporated discourses of the UN's Declaration of Human Rights and of the Declaration of the Elimination of Discrimination against Women (CEDAW).

The first IMF African Women Workers' Conference was held in Nairobi on May 20, 1981, with thirty women from eight African countries, discussing economic and social development, health, childcare, the status of women in the family and society, education, and trade union training, as well as wages and conditions. It must be noted that delegates were deeply concerned about the huge number of refugees on the African continent and appealed to the IMF and its affiliated unions to call on governments and international organizations to put an end to wars and guerrilla actions as well as all other causes of tremendous suffering and starvation of people, in particular of women and children. These participants saw women's work as not only undervalued, but also as invisible within the family, where women do the bulk of the work. Equality was viewed as impossible unless men and women shared domestic and family responsibilities. "Our societies must recognize the right of women to work just as they recognize that of men and must act in such a way that this right can be exercised in practice."[29]

At the same time, those women involved at transnational levels of the IMF became more engaged with other parallel organizations, such as the UN and its specialized agencies; the ILO and United Nations Educational, Scientific and Cultural Organization (UNESCO); and European Union agencies and the Organisation for Economic Co-operation and Development (OECD). Nongovernmental women's organizations and the broader women's movements also became part of their political landscape.[30]

Yet for all these efforts and diverse strategies, it remained abundantly clear that women continued to be underrepresented at all levels of the labor movement, including the IMF. In the broad metalworkers' industry, women made up 21 percent of the workforce and 14 percent of union membership, yet only 6.3 percent were on a bargaining committee.[31] Similar situations could be found across national labor movements as well. In Japan, for example, women constituted more than a quarter of union membership, but very few were active even at local levels. In a survey conducted by the union on rates of union participation, 60 percent of married women cited housekeeping and child rearing as keeping them away, while 40.7 percent said they were too fatigued to participate after work.[32] We discuss the effects of fatigue on women's activism in chapter 2. In Australia during the 1980s, women constituted 33 percent of the union workforce, but their influence within unions remained minimal, and they were not represented in union leadership in proportion to their membership numbers (Mezinec 1999). Australian metal unions addressed women's equality issues by relying on their affiliation with the national peak body, the Australian Council of Trade Unions (ACTU), with its Working Women's Committee and Working Women's Charter, a strategy not dissimilar from that of the IMF during the postwar period.

Strategy Changes

Women activists in the IMF took the view that different strategies were needed if progress for women were to be made beyond the limited gains achieved over the preceding decades. As separate organizing (Briskin 1993) became a more widely understood, if not accepted, strategy in the international labor movement, union women became more confident in identifying women-only activities as resources for union women. In the IMF, this took the form of women's workshops rather than the large, international meetings and Women's Committee meetings. Workshop themes focused more on skills and less on abstract principles of women's rights. They covered a mix of union and women's issues, such as comparative analysis of collective agreements, women's participation in negotiations, women shop stewards' education needs, and building negotiation skills.[33] The target countries of India, Japan, Malaysia, South Korea, and Thailand believed that women still remained outside the power structures of their unions and needed to be brought into the more central functions of unions such as collective bargaining. IMF activists felt that "The time has come to go beyond the mere statement of principles in support of women workers' rights, without any impact on the core activity of organized labor, that is, collective bargaining—women's voices are still almost ignored."[34]

The problem was characterized as a vicious circle whereby women's low participation rates preclude them from gaining sufficient experience and skills to become negotiators at the bargaining table. The combination of women's lack of confidence with men's reluctance, even resistance, to sharing power needed to be tackled more directly. However, it was decided to persist with the focused activities of workshops, and proposed that women's self-confidence and skills as union activists could best be addressed by exchanges across national borders through a series of workshops. This kind of separate organizing was strongly promoted by the international union movement, which provided a range of support, particularly in the Asian region (Broadbent and Ford 2008, 5).

The tenor of these workshops held over the next five years in Africa, South America, and Asia can be seen at the Bangkok meeting of November 1995:

"We all know that this is not the time any more for theoretical conferences on equality issues: women have to be given the tools and encouragement they need as workers and union activists in an effective and practical way."[35] Pragmatism was taken to mean building skills and understanding of the processes of collective bargaining, finding ways to guarantee women's participation as delegates to the IMF World Congress as well as at regional meetings, and identifying women's unequal power in their union as well as their workplace.

The issue of differences among women was approached with the view that women's situation in the metalworkers unions was similar in all regions, and their different conditions in different unions and countries could be utilized as a resource.[36] As a U.S. delegate observed at a later workshop, "The participants had determined their common problems as women metalworking unionists, and the course of action they had together determined was necessary to address those problems were more important than their political differences."[37]

At the same time, some (such as the workshop in Thailand) reported a gloomy resignation on the part of the women participants who felt that male dominance is universal and impossible to break, with the equal rights question having become a kind of unachievable utopia.[38] The manifestation of neoliberal economic policies in concert with globalization created further doubt for those women who felt that individualization, flexibility, new forms of work, and the spread of insecure employment would only undermine women's industrial conditions. For others, the deteriorating economic and political environment was even stronger ground to argue for gender equality within the labor movement, and for the development of resilient transnational alliances. As workshops were open to suggestions to campaign on issues such as child labor, sex tourism, and prostitution, such alliances could also extend to NGOs and feminist organizations.

Modern Times

Perhaps the pessimism among the women metalworkers in the 1990s was well founded: the 2001 World Congress in Sydney found that the IMF was the only GUF that still had no women in its executive body. Women delegates to the congress issued a challenge to the male leadership about its poor record of increasing women's leadership and organization. The action program for 2002–5 endorsed by congress stated, "The plight of women rightly deserves special emphasis" (International Metalworkers' Federation 2005, 69). Shortly after the 2001 congress, Jenny Holdcroft was appointed director of the Equal Rights Department and convened an advisory group to begin discussions on rejuvenating women's representation and participation across all IMF structures and activities and its affiliated unions.[39] In 2002 the advisory group proposed that at least six seats specifically for women be added to the IMF executive—one from each of the six regions of the IMF. They also proposed establishing women's structures at world, regional, and subregional levels, setting a 20 percent target for women's participation at meetings of the Central Committee and Congress, and holding women's conferences. The Report to the 31st World Congress noted that while some increases had been made, the figures mask the fact that only a few affiliates had actually made the necessary changes (International Metalworkers' Federation 2005, 70).

As an outcome of women's activism and women's demands for greater representation within the IMF and its affiliated unions, the IMF recently added eight women to serve on its highest executive body. The eight women from Brazil, South Africa, Canada, Czech Republic, Macedonia, Singapore, and Sweden were officially introduced with much fanfare at the 31st World Congress in Vienna in 2005. In addition, each affiliate was required to include a section in its activity report that detailed efforts to increase the membership and participation of women within their unions. These efforts to increase the representation and voice of women are viewed by activists in the IMF as a necessary condition for developing the mobilizing structures within unions that can be used by feminists to organize for women's rights on and off the job.

Women's Conference 2005

A further outcome of the action Program was the Women's Conference held on the day before the opening of the 2005 World Congress.[40] One hundred and twenty-six of the women delegates to the congress came together to strategize about how to increase their visibility and effectiveness at the congress. The women discussed and approved two resolutions on women's rights to be introduced and discussed at the larger congress. The first resolution, Women's Work under Globalization, called for the IMF affiliates to take a stand against inferior forms of employment for women by researching the impact of gender segmentation and to work with other women's organizations to improve the lives of working women. It was clear from the language of the proposal and the tenor of the debate that the delegates were as concerned about the extension of labor rights to women outside organized labor as they were with their own rights inside the union movement.[41]

A second resolution supported the premise of separate organizing and reaffirmed the need for the IMF and its affiliate unions to support women's committees, to recruit new women members, and to take up the unique needs of women through collective bargaining. Separate structures and campaigns for women provide feminists with a staging area from which to build alliances and coalitions with women in other unions and with women at the ILO and NGOs.[42]

The discourse framing the resolutions reflected a feminist understanding of the sexual politics of globalization and its damaging impact on women workers: "Women's employment under globalization is precarious. Millions of young women throughout the world are hired at minimal wages, only to be laid off when they get married or start a family. Women's jobs are the first to be lost, often forcing them into even more marginal and potentially dangerous means to earn a living, or to migrate in search of work."[43] Union feminists argued that unions will need to be part of a much larger movement for global justice.

Additional profile was given to the IMF's commitment to women's issues when a congress keynote address was given by Sharan Burrow, President of the ACTU and the first woman elected to the presidency of the ICFTU. She argued for the value of building stronger alliances with NGOs and the rest of civil society. Burrow elaborated in an interview that union feminists play an important role in helping unions understand how to close the gap between the organization of women and the low labor standards underpinning women's work (Interview with Fonow, May 24, 2005, Vienna, tape recorded).

Adrie Papma, Director of Alliance Building at Oxfam-Netherlands, also addressed the IMF Congress about her experience of working with unions on various campaigns dealing with fair trade and labor rights. Oxfam had shifted from being a humanitarian organization to one that recognized the value of alliances with organized labor. She told the audience, "It is our strong belief at Oxfam that we stand a far better chance of building a global campaigning force capable of making trade fair and enduring sustainable livelihoods for people in all corners of the world, if we work, among others, with the largest, best organized and most democratically legitimate consistency of global civil society—the global union movement."[44]

As Papma made clear, NGOs and unions need to be wary that employers and companies may seek to play them against each other. After years of skepticism on both sides, unions and NGOs are reaching out to each other through alliances and networks, assisted by feminists playing active roles in shaping an approach to labor advocacy that reflects an understanding of the interplay among gender, globalization, and resistance.

Women and Precarious Work

The IMF views precarious work as forms of labor that exclude workers from positions of permanent employment and from jobs governed by decent labor standards. Precarious work includes labor practices such as outsourcing, subcontracting, homework, and use of private employment agencies, labor brokers, personal contracts, and daily hire. The insecurity of not knowing how much work will be available is exacerbated by the erosion of labor standards and social protections. Precarious conditions disproportionately affect young workers, women workers, those with limited skills, and migrant workers. Wages are lower for precarious workers, in some cases 50 to 62 percent lower, and as the proportion of precarious work spreads within an industry or sector, those with more secure jobs feel threatened.[45] The IMF places the blame for the rapid growth in precarious work on transnational companies seeking to cut costs by reducing their permanent workforces and on government policies, such as trade agreements, lower taxes, and deregulation, that encourage such practices.

The key strategy of organized labor is to recruit these workers into existing unions. In addition to challenging national labor statutes, the unions, with the help of the IMF, are educating their members about the plight of precarious workers and creating opportunities for precarious workers to participate in union activities.

Women activists in the IMF have been a catalyst in helping the organization to reach out to unorganized precarious workers. In November 2007, more than fifty women activists participated in an IMF women's workshop on precarious work held in Salvador de Bahia, Brazil—one day before the central committee meeting of the IMF. Participants from around the world discussed why women are more likely to be in precarious work and possible union approaches to improve the working conditions of women in precarious jobs. Hyewon Chong of the Korean Metal Workers Union told the gathering, "Once you fall in, it's almost impossible to climb out and get permanent work."[46] She noted that precarious workers are by definition robbed of the tools to change their lot: the right to strike and the right to collectively bargain.

Delegates put forth a list of proposals for the central committee to consider. The activists believed that women are forced to take precarious work as a way to reduce women's dual burden of paid work and domestic labor, and they called on the IMF to improve the work–life balance in regular employment so that women do not have to depend on less secure work. Then too, because violence against women may increase when "lives are made more precarious by insecure and precarious work,"[47] union feminists demanded that the IMF's campaign against precarious work incorporate attention to domestic violence.

Conclusion

For the IMF to benefit from the activism of union feminists within its ranks, the IMF must increase and enhance the participation of women in the organization—a long-time demand of union feminists. This requires rethinking the structures and practices that perpetuate male dominance within the IMF and within the labor movement more generally. Marcello Malentacchi, the president of the IMF, recognized the importance of increasing women's participation in the IMF when on International Women's Day 2007 he said,

> Incorporating more women into union structures is essential if unions are to be able to present themselves as organizations worth joining to a female workforce. Organizing women will require different strategies than the ones used in the past to organize men. Women workers want and need unions that can fight for their rights just as much as for male workers, yet they will not be attracted to joining organizations that present a predominately male profile and culture. They need to be convinced that unions do understand their needs and are prepared to accept women in to their leadership as equal partners.[48]

As a consequence of women's activism, the IMF added women to its executive body, established gender quotas for conference delegations, and reconstituted its equity office. It is taking seriously the mandate to organize women, particularly in export processing zones, and has added equity bargaining and violence prevention to its agenda.

The character and scope of women's activism in the IMF has changed since the first women's conference in Vienna in 1958. The early debates focused on the meaning of equity and the question of special protective labor legislation for women. With the rise of the women's movement, women could no longer be viewed as "'housekeepers' who accidentally go to work at the factory or office." Women's activism in the IMF accelerated, and during this period there was a flurry of activities for women members and new structures to promote women's activism. Some of this was spurred on by the UN's IWY and conference in 1975. Feminists brought new issues to the union table, including the sexual politics of the family, bodily integrity, and reproductive rights. Feminist discourse expanded beyond equal rights to include human rights, and the cultural differences among women was beginning to be recognized.

New partnerships were forged with NGOs concerned with poverty reduction and development. The emphasis has shifted from large conferences that focused on abstract universal rights for women to workshops and seminars with a more pragmatic emphasis on building skills that would allow women to participate in collective bargaining.

The rapid acceleration of globalization has proven to be a challenging environment for organized labor. With the growth of more precarious forms of labor in the metal trades and the decline of industry-wide collective bargaining agreements, the landscape for unions in the metal trades has changed dramatically. By 2005 we saw an upsurge of women's activism and the rapid expansion of their participation in all levels of decision making within the IMF.

7

Another World Is Possible for Women, If . . .

> Another world will not be possible without another conception of democracy. And another democracy is only possible through a process of personal and subjective revolutions, of men and women, with an active recognition of diversity, taking on the intersectionalities of struggles as a collective challenge.
> —Feminist Dialogues, 2007

On a hot January day in 2005, we joined the huge march through the streets of Porto Alegre, Brazil, that opened the 5th World Social Forum (WSF). In the custom of such events, we first gathered with a like-minded group. We met in a shady side street with a small group of women who were dressed in white wedding dresses and faces painted white protesting violence against women. They distributed cardboard fans in the shape of lips with the slogan, "your mouth is fundamental against fundamentalism," first used at the 2002 forum by the Latin American group Articulación Feminista Mercosur, in English Mercosur Feminist Articulation (Conway 2007). The march of a multitude of activist groups, nongovernmental organizations (NGOs), trade unions, political parties, religious organizations, banners, and bands took many hours to arrive at the forum site. It epitomized the WSF as public space, performance, and spectacle; to rephrase John Berger (1968) on the street march as practice for revolution, the march was indeed a demonstration that "an alternative world is possible."

We traveled to participate in the forum since it had become a highly visible space for new processes of transnational politics opposed to the dominant and oppressive forms of globalization. As Jackie Smith and her collaborators (2008) observe, what is innovative about the World Social Forum is that it does not develop strategies and politics itself, but rather "it provides an infrastructure within which groups, movements, and networks of like mind can come together, share ideas and experiences and build their own proposals or platforms for action" (32). We were keen to observe how the potential for new political and discursive alliances might play out for the more traditional politics of feminism and labor movements. And, alerted by feminist commentators who had participated in earlier forums, we were looking to see just how "like-minded" groups at the forum were about issues of sexual politics (Alvarez, Faria, and Nobre 2004; Duddy 2003; World March of Women 2004).

In this chapter, we examine the deliberate global site of the World Social Forum for its potential in making transnational feminist labor politics. We investigate processes for building alliances across the many lines of difference and fragmentation associated with globalization. During our participation in the 2005 forum, we observed events, collected documents, participated in Forum sessions and activities, and conducted interviews with union feminists. Fonow also participated in a pre-forum workshop on trade union responses to globalization organized by the Global Union Research Network (GURN), a project housed in the Workers Activities Division of the International Labour Organization (ILO) (papers published in Schmidt 2007). In addition, we consulted the extensive array of documents on the Web produced by and about the WSF as a way to better understand the broader "alternative-globalization" movement and the role of unions and feminists within it.

World Social Forum

According to its Web site, "The World Social Forum is an open meeting place where social movements, networks, NGOs and other civil society organizations opposed to neo-liberalism and a world dominated by capital or by any form of imperialism come together to pursue their thinking, to debate ideas democratically, to formulate proposals, share their experiences freely and network for effective action."[1] Forums have taken place annually since 2001, in venues in the South (Brazil, India, Africa), different regions (for example, Europe, the United States and Australia), and local sites (individual cities), attracting many thousands of people who have organized hundreds of workshops, panels, marches and meetings (della Porta 2005, Leite 2005). The extensive diversity of these events means that the World Social Forum is, in the words of Michael Hardt (2004), "unknowable, chaotic, dispersive" (231). Nor is there one World Social Forum; it has grown to become "a space of spaces, a network of networks" (Conway 2007, 51) and moved out from its annual meeting into a multiscale and multisited process. Likewise, feminist participation is expressed across a great diversity of issues and sectors, and in a vast array of grassroots, institutional, local, and transnational forms, which are not equally visible. We focus on those spaces at the forum where the interests of feminists and labor overlap.

The World Social Forum did not spring up overnight. Rather, it emerged from the convergence of a number of factors, including the growth and maturation of various strands of the global justice movement, particularly those in the global South who protested against international institutions like the International Monetary Fund, the World Bank, the World Trade Organization (WTO), and the World Economic Forum (Hintjens 2006; Juris 2005, 2008). The World Social Forum was designed as both a strategic and symbolic counterweight to the World Economic Forum, an annual meeting of the world's economic and political elites held each year since 1971 in Davos, Switzerland, to discuss economic globalization (Smith et al. 2008).

At first, there was little room in Davos for civil society, although in more recent years NGOs, left governments, and celebrities (such as the singer Bono) have attended as a way to influence talks. Pressing social issues like AIDS, debt reduction, poverty, and hunger began to appear on the agendas as progressive organizations and activists increasingly targeted the World Economic Forum (WEF) as representing the global dominance of corporate interests. By 2002 the International Metalworkers' Federation (IMF) had decided that its participation in the WEF was counterproductive and withdrew. Marcello Malentacchi, IMF general secretary, said, "Despite the fact that many prestigious politicians and scientists have been speaking at the Davos Forum, the outcome of these discussions is very poor in terms of concrete measures to improve the working and living conditions of workers and their families" (Malentacchi 2003).

Many others, including many feminists, had also grown disaffected with the UN, another potential key site for progressive global politics with its various conferences, forums, and commissions. Nonetheless, the UN had created an organizational infrastructure that made it possible for feminist, NGO, and grassroots activists to engage with one another across national borders and movement sectors in order to create common ground (Harcourt 2006; Hawkesworth 2006; Moghadam 2005). Campaigns against free-trade agreements like the North American Free Trade Agreement (NAFTA); sweatshop labor; structural adjustment policies that reduced public services; and rising debt in developing nations were increasingly being connected to campaigns for indigenous rights and women's rights, sustainable development, peace, and decent jobs. Today, these are no longer viewed as simply oppositional movements to neoliberal globalization, but as catalysts for a new political dynamic within the global landscape capable of proposing alternatives and new ways to achieve them (Smith et al. 2008).

The World Social Forum was only possible because advances in technology facilitate international organization and communication among interested actors and organizations. The resulting growth in effectiveness of transnational networks for global mobilizations, together with the increasing capacity among activists and organizations, led to increased participation in large international events (Smith et al. 2008). Such technologies, particularly those associated with the Internet, allow for the rapid diffusion of knowledge and ideas across movement sectors and across national boundaries. In addition, a much broader and more flexible interpretation of what constitutes knowledge is being produced. It goes beyond political theories, analyses, and critical understandings of particular contexts, to include stories, ideas, narratives, and ideologies. Greater stress is also being placed on the capacity of social movements to create, modify, and perform knowledge, identified as "knowledge-practices" and recognized as an important part of what movements do (Casas-Cortés, Osterweil, and Powell 2008). Armstrong and Bernstein (2008) reflect a similar argument with their attention to the significance of social movement challenges to meaning systems, which they argue are as important to social justice goals as are challenges to the distribution of resources.

We propose that in such knowledge-practices it is important to recognize the centrality of sexual politics and its specific meanings and forms in social movements and transnational activism. Thus, in the WSF, the male dominance of sexual politics is evident from the dominant narrative about its origins. Movement scholars and activists have constructed a tale of men with political foresight seizing the historic moment against a background of heroic contemporary images of (male) Zapatistas, Teamsters, radical environmentalists, and anarchists (Alvarez, Faria, and Nobre 2004; Conway 2007; Wilson 2007). These activists sought to provide opportunities for the growing international antiglobalization protest movements to develop visions and processes for achieving an alternative, better world. But short shrift is given to the painstaking decades of activism by feminists in the South, or at the various UN-sponsored conferences and forums on women's rights, or in local communities throughout the world. Rather, published versions of the story have it that the WSF was initiated by individual French and Latin American activist men (Mertes 2004).

According to another widespread narrative of its origins, the World Social Forum would fill the apparent vacuum created for the world's left when the viability of a Marxist revolution disintegrated (Waterman 2004). Neither of these stories takes account of the feminist movements that continued to flourish and create new knowledge-practices. Lessons learned from the era of the Marxist-influenced left, if not from feminist practices, doubtless influenced the design of the forum as an open space where actors from civil society could self-organize within the virtual space of the forum's Web site and at the physical space of the forum itself.

The World Social Forum was not a traditional left-style representative or deliberative body, engaging in hard-fought debates over political programs among its members. Rather, participants would be encouraged to imagine that another world is possible, one without war and violence, one that values the human rights of men and women of all nations and one that protects the environment. Respect for cultural and social diversity *and* a respect for the plural and diverse ways change can happen lies at the core of the forum, encapsulated in its Charter of Principles first issued and endorsed in 2001.[2] These principles gave feminists hope for the possibilities that may be available at the WSF.

Despite the considerable overlap between the principles and politics of the World Social Forum and feminist movements, it is tedious to find that once again, neither feminist organizations nor individual feminist activists were present at the initial discussions of the goals, organization, and logistics of the first forum (Conway 2007; Duddy 2003; Eschle 2005). Nor are feminist ideas apparent in the political discourses or practices of the founding movements, networks, and organizations of the WSF. These social movements appear no more receptive to feminism than do the more traditional organizations of the trade unions.

The labor movement, often characterized as irrelevant to the new era of globalization and to the politics of social movements, was nevertheless involved from the beginning. Through its membership in the Workers Party in Brazil, which had won municipal elections in Porto Alegre, labor helped to host the first forum in 2001. By contrast, feminists faced similar problems of lack of recognition and inclusion in the forum as in other fields. However, feminist commitments and involvement in global justice movements as well as transnational feminist organizations ensured that feminists themselves would be strongly oriented toward the political opportunities presented by the World Social Forum (Alvarez, Faria, and Nobre 2004).

Feminism and the Forum

Despite its limitations, some feminists, us included, believe that the World Social Forum has become an important site for feminist activism. Feminism supports broad antiglobalization goals, and it is vital that gender be integral to political campaigns for global justice. Women in such organizations as Development Alternatives with Women for a New Era (DAWN) and the Women's International Coalition for Economic Justice (WICEJ) worked to increase their presence at the WSF so that by the time of the 2003 meeting, feminist networks and organizations were participating in Forum planning. Two feminist networks, the World March of Women (WMW) and the Articulación Feminista Marcosur, organized two of the forum's five axes or themes: 1) principles and values, human rights, diversity, and equality; and 2) political power, civil society, and democracy (Alvarez, Faria, and Nobre 2004). However, the WMW declared after the forum that women were still only "politely tolerated." There is a long way to go before there is genuine engagement with feminist politics on violence against women, feminist economic alternatives, and issues such as "the ever increasing commodification of women's bodies in the context of globalization" (World March of Women 2003).

It is striking that feminists utilized a long-standing feminist strategy of carving out autonomous space (not unlike the self-organizing of union feminists) to gain purchase within the new global politics of the World Social Forum (Duddy 2003). Feminists participated in its myriad forums, sites, and forms to build transnational alliances and to debate feminist differences, diversities, and strategies. Ara Wilson (2007) argues that transnational feminist activism has adopted the institutional form of the NGO, in parallel with other contemporary social movements, in order to participate in spaces created by the UN and other multilateral agencies and was thus well prepared to engage in the forum process.

It was through this work, ranging from local to international levels, that feminist activism took gender issues to a world scale and developed "their eye for power structures and advanced their fluency in the language of funders and agencies" (Wilson 2007, 20). In this light, the structure and processes of the forum (calling for activities, debates, and networking to be planned by affiliated groups) suited feminist activists, many of whom had more than several decades of experience with working in and around the UN.

Feminists from many of the participating networks began organizing pre-forum strategy meetings. In 2004 a two-day women's forum was held before the World Social Forum that year in Mumbai, India, titled Building Solidarities: Feminist Dialogues (Isis International Manilla 2006). This led to the Feminist Dialogues, a regular pre-forum event established by a coalition of feminist networks and organizations. The initial goal of the dialogues was to strategize about how to be effective as feminists at the forum. The dialogues broadened to become a space in which to reflect and reimagine political strategies, to debate differences and diversities and to establish strategic and politically relevant links with other social movements.[3] It provides opportunities to practice feminist politics at transnational levels that engage material and discursive dilemmas, conflicts, and possibilities. Neoliberal globalization is a central concern, as is the erosion of women's economic security and citizenship. However, our review of the papers and reflections finds that very little direct attention is paid to workers' rights and workers' organizations such as trade unions. This may result from the absence of union feminists at the meetings, as much as from the critical stance taken by many feminists who see the labor movement as a male-dominated institution.

Labor and the Forum

Labor's presence at the World Social Forum takes a variety of forms and is much more formal and institutionalized than that of feminism. Individual unions, peak labor bodies, and Global Union Federations (GUFs) participate directly as well as through movement and network links with the ILO, political parties, left think tanks, foundations, and NGOs. Overviews of those who travel under the labor banner to the forums reveal that male labor leaders play a more prominent role in planning and organizing the WSF than female labor leaders or than the leaders of the women's organizations and movements (Conway 2007; Eschle 2005; Hawkesworth 2006). Here too, sexual politics privileges men's political activism at transnational levels.

The involvement of international labor organizations in the World Social Forum—such as GUFs, the International Confederation of Free Trade Unions (ICFTU)/International Trade Union Confederation (ITUC), European Trade Union Confederation (ETUC), and the Trade Union Advisory Committee (TUAC) of the Organisation for Economic Co-operation and Development (OECD)—stems in part from their critique of the WEF as a place where the voice of labor was not heard. In a clear indication that they felt that labor has a critical role at international levels of governance and global justice, the organizations listed above (calling themselves the Global Union Group) issued a statement, "Democratizing Globalization," to both the World Social Forum and the World Economic Forum before their January meetings in 2003 (ICFTU 2003). The document reproaches all governments and the international community for the dismal lack of progress in reaching any of the objectives of the UN's Millennium Development Goals: "On present policies there is no prospect of eliminating poverty, launching sustainable development, creating more and better jobs, or improving the lives of working women and men" (ICFTU 2003).

International labor believed that both forums could be used as platforms to articulate the case for a more democratic form of globalization with transparent forms of governance that are accountable to all rather than serving business interests. It also argued strongly that the unregulated global market economy favored by the World Economic Forum was exacerbating "financial and economic instability and fuelling intolerance, extremism, xenophobia, tensions and conflicts around the world" (ICFTU 2003). With the global financial crisis beginning in 2007, labor was being far more prophetic than perhaps even it imagined possible.

At the 2003 World Social Forum in Porto Alegre, Marcello Malentacchi of the IMF called for new alliances to oppose the new forms of capitalism, arguing that labor has moved well beyond seeking to link labor standards to trade agreements. Labor campaigns are framed as workers' rights embedded in a development agenda, because they are part of human rights, which in turn are an essential factor in sustainable economic development. As an example, Malentacchi cited the alliances forged between food workers and the European Banana Action Network in support of consumers, small growers, and plantation workers. But alliances are also necessary to mobilize significant and visible support in order to have an impact: "We have made the right arguments in the forums of the powerful for many years, but these have mostly fallen on deaf ears. The world's power elite has no reason to listen, unless we can demonstrate that with the backing of millions who demand a new politics. This is why building new alliances which cooperate ever more closely is central to our task of righting the priorities of global governance" (Malentacchi 2003).

As we saw in chapter 6, Malentacchi had become an advocate for women's rights, so what kinds of alliances do Malentacchi and his colleagues have in mind here? Do such alliances include explicitly feminist organizations? Malentacchi puts the case for the labor movement in terms of "the backing of millions." Union politics has long endorsed the principle that "getting the numbers," through recruiting and mobilizing members, is essential. The problem for feminists revolves around the issue of whether labor recognizes that women workers are also potential new members. Well aware of the value of good member numbers, union feminists therefore make the tactical argument that the labor movement leadership needs to recognize that women constitute substantial numbers of current and potential union membership.

As we suggest in previous chapters, labor can and does have a history of making political and discursive alliances with women activists and feminist networks, but rarely without considerable effort on the part of the women. We searched the sites and documents of the new political spaces of the World Social Forum to observe whether progress might be made at transnational levels of feminist and labor politics. One such example was the launch of the Global Call to Action against Poverty at the 2005 WSF, a worldwide alliance of many organizations, including trade unions and women's groups, as well as NGOs, human rights advocates, and international civil society and faith groups (World Social Forum 2005). Peak labor bodies, such as the ICFTU, joined with advocates, including Wahu Kaara, an African activist and campaigner for women's rights, in calling on governments and international governance structures to become accountable for achieving debt cancellation, just trade, and transparent global governance (World Social Forum 2005).

John Samuel, the director of Action Aid, Asia, speaking on behalf of the alliance said, "We need a shift in national and international policies and agendas. At a time when bombs, security and terror dominate the political agenda it's imperative to bring poverty in the centre of government thinking. We just can't afford to keep quiet when 50,000 people die of poverty related causes every day and the rich and powerful choose to ignore it" (World Social Forum 2005). Taking its cue from the outpouring of support for victims of the Indian Ocean tsunami of 2004, this initiative aims to mobilize popular support for the world's governments to make significant progress on poverty reduction.

Similar to strategies adopted by feminist organizations around the World Social Forum, labor also organized its own preliminary meetings. The Trade Union Forum—organized by the ICFTU, the ETUC, and the World Confederation of Labour (WCL)—is designed to provide trade unionists with opportunities to debate and strategize about their political aims and objectives at the WSF (ICFTU 2004). Common themes of the Trade Union Forum include opposition to war and the WTO, the release of debt burdens for developing countries, and reform of international financial institutions. These are all themes that labor repeatedly articulates as necessary foundations for building alliances with other social movements and with NGOs. While participants debate the value of developing an alternative economic program and the strategies most likely to achieve its implementation, these themes and issues are presented in such a way that gender issues and the state of sexual politics are obscured.

And yet there are possibilities for feminist politics. In arguments that parallel feminist proposals on the significance of gender within the World Social Forum, the labor movement proposes that "decent work" must be central to the forum's claim: another world is possible (ITUC 2008b). The concept of decent work stands in opposition to neoliberal proposals that any job is better than poverty or welfare dependency. Drawing on work such as Richard Sennet's (1998) influential study of the corrosive effects of new capitalism, the decent work campaign is an ILO initiative.

In the campaign's formulation, first articulated in 1999, the ILO broadly defines decent work as "opportunities for women and men to obtain decent and productive work in conditions of freedom, equity, security and human dignity" (ILO 1999). Decent work is an important advance for labor since it goes beyond traditional definitions of workers to include all working people: women and men, young and older workers, nationals and migrants, as well as self-employed farmers, home-workers, and entrepreneurs. An alliance of unions and NGO partners launched the "Decent Work for Decent Life" campaign at the 2007 World Social Forum to underline the global significance of work conditions. In 2008 the campaign was expanded on International Women's Day (March 8) by the ITUC and global unions to call for decent work for a decent life for women (ITUC 2008a).

Unions and Feminism at the 2005 Forum

"We live in a world and in a time where we have to rethink theories and practices, such as the meaning and value of 'work,' including against precarisation, and the way to organize it. We have to raise new questions and try to answer them together with new actors and actions. And the WSF is the right place to do this," says Alessandra Mecozzi.

Alessandra Mecozzi exemplifies union feminism as an insider activist (Armstrong and Bernstein 2008) at the transnational level. Speaking as the international secretary of an Italian trade union, Federazione Impiegati Operai Meallurgici (Metallurgical Employees and Workers Federation, abbreviated as FIOM-CGIL—an affiliate of the IMF), she takes a positive view of the potential of the World Social Forum. She has engaged in union organizing for many years while sustaining a long-standing commitment to the women's movement. She has participated in international women's conferences and taken international positions in her union. Mecozzi has also been actively involved in the forum process, from organizing the Genoa social forum during the G8 meeting in 2001 through to her recent contributions to the 2008 World Social Forum Global Day of Action.

Our interest at the 2005 World Social Forum was in how unions and feminist organizations used the forum as the right place to build alliances. So we looked for those events or sessions where these two movements had organized to come together. We found very few. We also looked for instances where the issues or discourses were shared; again there were very few. Both unions and feminists utilized language that revealed some degree of awareness and engagement with the other: unions sometimes refer to men *and* women workers; feminist organizations recognize the importance of economic security and occasionally note the value of the right of workers to join unions. The 2005 forum included a session called "Change the Economy, Change the Society: Proposals Based on Feminism."

Among the organizations working to develop spaces that brought unions and feminists together was the U.S. Institute for Policy Studies (IPS). We attended the seminars it held on the topic of lessons from working across borders. Members of NGOs and unionists from India, South Africa, and Hong Kong, among others, discussed their concerns about the effects of neoliberal globalization. Borders were defined broadly in metaphorical terms as well as geographical terms. The often unrecognized difficulties that arise in attempting to organize across borders were graphically illustrated.

A woman from the Indian organization, the New Trade Union Initiative elaborated on the difficulties of organizing women garment workers, pointing out that trade union strategies, such as workers' strikes, were frequently impossible to implement. If people's income from their work was very low, the withdrawal of labor in a strike was likely to result in workers and their families coming close to starvation. She complained that mainstream labor organizations avoided these "real" issues, particularly when women were involved. Union speakers acknowledged this concern, attempting to show that their organizing activities were designed to include women.

The speaker from the South African peak union body, Congress of South African Trade Unions, described their plan, Vision 2014, which was aimed at strengthening trade unions in Africa and included building women's union leadership. He, in turn, was dismissive of cross-border support strategies that relied on visits by senior labor leaders, including international officials, something that a participant from the Hong Kong Council of Trade Unions (HKCTU) agreed was largely a waste of everyone's time. His female colleague from HKCTU observed that outcomes were more positive when workers themselves could network across borders. This strategy has greater potential to include women, since most trade union leaderships are still dominated by men. In Asia, where most workers' pay is relatively low, their involvement in cross-border alliances requires the availability of collective resources. Finding ways to work across multiple languages is a further cost. The benefits from such work must be worthwhile on several levels.

Following this session, we were able to interview the young woman from HKCTU about her transnational experiences through the labor movement, including the opportunity to work with a Japanese women's union. She had a high degree of mobility and saw herself as a strong advocate and model for the value of women's leadership in the labor movement. Given her high level of international mobility, we asked how she negotiated her personal life, both in her intimate relationships and with her own family. "I have a partner; he is not from Hong Kong. I also have other relationship as I am not a woman from last century. I cannot only stick to one person for no reason. If we are from the same place, we are always together, OK, we will stay with each other. But as we are not in the same place, it is not necessary to pull each other to be the same place. So that is why I have some other relationships" (Union organizer, World Social Forum 2005). As one of a new generation of women unionists who could work at the international level, this union activist is modeling the political possibilities of a sexual politics of everyday life in which women have gained power to move beyond the still common constraints of family life. Without such relative autonomy, her transnational activism would be severely limited.

A rather more promising space than the seminar organized by IPS discussed above, was the session created by several NGOs, and feminist and union organizations. Titled "The Inter-movement Dialogue," it brought together labor movements, caste and race movements, and sexuality and women's movements from Africa, Sri Lanka, Asia–Pacific, and India, as well as feminist organizations from the North (including ISIS International, DAWN, WICEJ, and FEMNET [the African Women's Development and Communication Network]). The session we observed was held in a large warehouse where the heat was unrelieved by the water misting from ceiling outlets. Language differences made conversation difficult to follow despite translation devices.

Speakers were asked to address the question: What does your movement do in relation to other movements? It rapidly became clear that intermovement dialogue is a demanding practice and one that requires more than single events. Thus, each panelist was keen to ensure that their particular movement's issues and their ways of framing them would be heard. It seemed there was not enough time or space to address the obstacles and opportunities involved in questions about melding political and discursive alliances with other movements. In such a space, addressing perceived conflicts is as necessary and difficult as finding common ground. As Manisha Desai (2005) argues, "the inter-movement session at WSF in 2005 showed [that] movements have not done the serious work of articulating their visions to integrate other visions; reorganizing their movements to include others; and rethinking strategies to address issues of all inequalities, class, race, gender, and sexuality, among others" (9). We can only conclude that a lot more opportunities, spaces, and talking are needed if these goals are to be achieved.

Overall, the physical experience of participating in a global forum of the progressive opponents of neoliberal capitalism, global patriarchy, and international racism was clearly invigorating for participants, us included. Smith et al. (2008), in pointing to the value of the WSF process, observe that it is "manifested in the convergence of activists in set places for rather short times, but that the process itself represents a collection of political and economic activities that have much broader and deeper significance" (123). Some participants focused on the WSF itself, while others were motivated by the need to frame these problems in international terms, as well as local and regional. The global level of the forum makes it possible for organizations to engage with one another around shared issues. For example, unions and feminist organizations share concerns about unorganized and vulnerable workers, the majority of whom are female. However, to work together effectively, both movements must face complex challenges posed by class, race, and sexual politics.

Conclusion

The World Social Forum is deliberately constituted as a movement community that prefigures the just societies its members hope to create (Armstrong and Bernstein 2008, 79). However, experiences at the World Social Forum show that these struggles go on at multiple levels, from the WMW arguing once again that the sexual politics of the forum's own structures and practices must contribute to gender equality, to unions finding ways to engage with feminist organizations to tackle effectively the problems involved in organizing women and children. Although we found that feminists have made fewer gains than we had hoped, we observed (as others have also done) that participants and organizations at the World Social Forum use the space to thrash out agendas and learn from one another (Conway 2007; Smith et al. 2008). We found that discursive alliances between feminists and labor were produced, and even if they are somewhat tenuous, such alliances provide opportunities for making feminist politics with and across transnational labor.

CONCLUSION

The Future of Feminist Politics in Global Union Movements

This book set out to investigate how union women make feminist politics within and through the trade union movement in such ways as to achieve feminist goals, particularly at transnational levels. This is important for feminists and unionists because, as Sylvia Walby (1986) points out, "trade unions are becoming the largest mass organizations of women supporting social democratic projects" (231). Making feminist politics in any sphere of life and at any level necessitates engaging with the sexual politics that prevail. More often than not, it is a sexual politics in which heteronormative masculinity dominates, to the detriment of women and lesbian, gay, bisexual, and transgender (LGBT) people generally. Feminists and others often regard trade unions and the labor movement more generally as inveterate and traditional sites of male dominance, so it is also important to recognize that union women do take up the challenge of sexual politics in trade unions. Women workers as well as the unions have benefited. This is not to suggest that the politics are easy or the success rates are high.

In this chapter, we draw together our argument that making feminist politics involves contesting explicit, but nevertheless complex, discourses and structures of power and that this politics demands an activism that depends on access to material and emotional resources. We suggest that the creation of discursive and political alliances is integral to the political strategies and understandings required to confront the sexual politics of labor movements and of everyday life; and these alliances must recognize the heterogeneity and diversity of women's experiences. We see that feminist union activists build their politics from knowledges and strategies that they find and develop in the women's movement and in labor movements. Likewise, our analysis utilizes and develops a theoretical framework from conceptual resources in feminism, labor, and social movement research fields. We therefore have aimed to work with a focus that can encompass the breadth of historical and transnational analysis of political movements and the closeness and immediacy of everyday life and activism. In our research and analysis, we pay attention to local and transnational political discourses and structures of labor as well as the everyday life issues of activism in order to reach a more comprehensive understanding of the question of feminist politics in the trade union movement.

We argue that throughout its history, the sexual politics of the labor movement has been critical to the rights and conditions of working women. At the same time, union feminists have sought to make feminist politics that challenge the sexual politics within their local unions as well as within and through networks of transnational labor. They have addressed the tensions and contradictions between productive and social reproductive spheres, developing strategies appropriate to their particular material and political conditions. They also advocate for transnational solidarities among workers with awareness derived from their own experiences of gendered differences. However, such understanding of cultural and social differences among workers and unionists are not easily won, as we show in our historical research in chapters 5, "Feminist Politics in International labor," and 6, "Women's Activism in the International Metalworkers' Federation," and in our analysis of the political situation of LGBT workers in what we have called queer organizing in chapter 2, "Sexual Politics, Activism, and Everyday Life." But queer organizing in trade unions also exemplifies the potential of trade unions to adapt and respond to the growing diversity of workers' issues and conditions. Or rather, as we argue, this is a clear example of the potential of feminist politics to tackle sexual politics in trade unions and in workplaces, and to articulate the concerns of marginalized workers.

History and Politics

The labor movement claims a history of over a century of international alliances and political activism, and it is this internationalism that is becoming an increasingly valuable political resource in responding to the growing impact of global capital. We stress that women have always been involved in that history, although with more difficulty than union men have experienced (Boston 1980; Cobble 2008; Drake 1984). Under contemporary conditions, globalization plays a significant role in shaping local, regional, and transnational political mobilization (Hawkesworth 2006; Naples and Desai 2002; Walby 2002). Although the imbalances of power between different types of workers within a country and between workers in different countries are exacerbated by globalization, these same processes create continuities that can become the grounds for mobilizing across asymmetrical differences. For example, the current global financial crisis poses similar threats to different parts of the world, which in turn structures parallel (but not necessarily identical) responses.

Such continuities mean that social movements in different countries take on similar characteristics, an obvious advantage when trying to mobilize across national boundaries (Giugni 2002). "Common postures [of movements] vis-à-vis the state and other international actors help generate shared interpretations of experiences, isomorphic organizations, and complementary activist identities" (Smith and Johnston 2002, 3). This also allows our analysis to connect political experiences and understandings across local and transnational movements. As Armstrong and Bernstein (2008) observe, there is much to be gained analytically from an approach that can examine the diversity of movements for political change.

The emergence of transnational social movements in the twentieth century has contributed new ways of making politics with their more fluid and receptive political networks that provide knowledges, discourses, strategies and tactics, and help to bridge the cultural and spatial divide between activists in different countries. Yet, "the social movement sector does not simply mimic world-system power disparities; but rather, in seeking to transform global inequalities, activists self-consciously act to change how power relations between states impinge on internal SMO [social movement organization] relations" (Smith and Johnston 2002, 6). This lays the foundation for developing political frames and discursive alliances that resonate among activists and movements across borders challenging the problems caused by forces of global capital.

The magnitude of such problems appears impervious to human agency and contributes to a widespread pessimism within progressive politics, including feminist politics. However, activists continue to analyze and campaign against the apparently anonymous forces of the political and global economy. One of our goals in this book is to bring that activism to light, to review and reflect on the knowledges and political strategies that are created in the area of feminist politics and labor movements. Clearly, globalization presents considerable obstacles to progressive politics, including its destructive effects on communities that are constrained by their geographic or political locality. And yet, opportunities for political interventions emerge as the heterogeneity of communities and individuals is recognized and as those on the periphery gain access to new resources via the flows of transnational capital. The processes of globalization are far from impermeable; rather, they present opportunities as well as obstacles for progressive political activism. Thus, we suggest that the trade union movement has the capacity to challenge the appalling effects of globalization on work, particularly women's work, and that union feminists have the tools to revitalize the labor movement.

Activism

Our research has focused on the role played by union feminists as domestic and transnational actors who work within and across unions to build new discursive and political alliances between organized labor and other progressive groups, organizations, and movements. Women and feminists from around the world have become increasingly involved in transnational forms of labor activism. This type of activism brings participants together in a variety of forms—networks, coalitions, organizations, and movements—to focus on a range of issues relevant to securing labor rights and socioeconomic justice for women in global and local economies (Moghadam, Franzway, and Fonow forthcoming). We have observed, traced, and interviewed union women activists who join international campaigns for labor rights, seek pay equity and decent work conditions, advocate for redress from discrimination against workers, and organize as insiders within trade unions, peak labor bodies, and labor and women's rights NGOs.

Not surprisingly, women union activists who have engaged with the politics of the labor movement at international as well as local levels have met with varying degrees of success. Whether at local levels, where union organizations struggle to organize workers and win improved conditions, or at international levels, where peak bodies must also work to meet the very diverse needs of national and transnational organizations, we find that labor and feminism forge discursive alliances through negotiations around the sexual politics of the labor movement. As we show in chapter 7, "Another World Is Possible, If . . ." feminist politics makes gains where it is able to influence and shape the meanings and framing of issues, such as the demand for economic security, the elimination of poverty, and decent work. These issues have a particular impact on women workers. But alliances that involve power sharing and leadership positions for women are much more difficult to establish. For example, we celebrate the achievement of Australian union leader Sharan Burrow in becoming the first female president of the new international body, the ITUC, and now, as of 2010, the first female General Secretary but we must note that of the total leadership (president, deputy presidents, general secretary, and deputy general secretaries), only two of the nine listed are women (ITUC 2009).

This is to suggest that feminist activists concerned with socioeconomic rights for women must depend on more than mobilizing structures (Fonow 2003): activists must contest and refashion the sexual, racial, and heteronormative politics of unions and of the labor movement more generally (see also Armstrong and Bernstein 2008). In addition, women's activism depends on the resources and capacities available in their everyday lives. In the case of union women activists, who are likely to be in the labor force, either in workplaces or in union positions or both, the circumstances of everyday life are as important as their work conditions. In order to integrate this insight into our analysis, we adopt the feminist approach that has brought the sexual politics of everyday life into the public sphere. We draw attention to the ways the circumstances of the sexual politics of everyday life shapes political activism. But we go further than the feminist critique of the largely taken-for-granted assumptions in the West that families are normatively heterosexual and nuclear, and women are central to family care. Such assumptions have a powerful impact on social theory, "family-friendly policies," even feminist politics as well as everyday life. Thus the family understood in these terms plays a contradictory role in the ways political campaigns for women workers' rights have been framed in labor movements (Bailey 2005; Muir 2008).

In chapter 3, "Sexual Politics, Labor, and the Family," we develop the argument that the normative family is a central element in the material and discursive conditions of women's activism. Although the notion of women's "second shift," in which they care for their families after their paid work, has been very influential, it does not recognize women's own needs for care. Once we ask the question about women's care, we find a key difference between women and men, since women generally must manage their own care for themselves. We conceptualize the necessity for women to care for their own bodies in terms of "the laboring body" (Franzway 2001). Thus, questions about resources and capacities for women activists must include not only the ways they negotiate their family responsibilities, but also how they take care of their own bodies. Such care constitutes an integral part of the workload of activism but is a relatively unseen dimension of the work of making feminist politics. We argue that the care of women themselves is critical to feminist theorizing as well as to feminist politics.

Feminist Politics and Labor Movements

Our investigations of the question about feminist politics in labor movements have found that union feminists recognize the potential of labor movements to serve as arenas for political action by women workers of different races, nationalities, and sexualities who are situated differently within the various labor markets. As we show in chapters 5 and 6, union women have been active in campaigning for women's rights and social justice throughout the history of the labor movement. They do not rely simply on the traditional politics of labor movements, but distill knowledge-practices (Casas-Cortés, Osterweil, and Powell 2008) from other political movements, particularly women's movements. However, union women's access to alternative and feminist politics varies according to the times and conditions. For example, the peak period of the early-twentieth-century suffrage campaigns saw working-class women and feminist supporters fighting for the rights of association as well as for equitable conditions (Kessler-Harris 2001; Tax 1980).

In the contemporary period of renewed feminism as well as of globalization, union women activists are using the prevailing discourses of the women's movement, LGBT movements, the civil rights/human rights movement, and the global justice movement to forge a dynamic transnational feminist politics. By building and mobilizing transnational networks of activists and discursive alliances between these various movements, union feminists are creating new political spaces for women workers and new forms of transnational activism. At local and international levels within trade unions and peak union bodies, union feminists have adopted separate organizing strategies to create women's committees, forums, conferences, courses, centers, and solidarity campaigns.

These spaces serve as internal mobilizing structures that can be used to harness union resources, but they also signal the union's recognition that its political objectives cannot be subsumed within agendas based on the norm of the universal worker. By allocating material and political resources to these separate organizing spaces, unions show some recognition of differences among their current and potential members. In addition, separate organizing and the recognition of difference has also proved to be important for LGBT and black workers and union members.

However, as we discuss in chapter 4, "Political Spaces: Centers, Conferences, and Campaigns," these spaces are hard won and difficult to sustain in the face of the often male-dominated sexual politics of labor movements. Nevertheless, labor movements have much to gain from opening up their political agendas in an environment in which the traditional full-time working-class male worker has been forced into relative insignificance in the global economy. We also note that feminists outside labor do campaign for women's rights, including labor rights, but focus more on cultivating political and organizational spaces rather than aiming at union renewal.

By building and mobilizing transnational networks and alliances among these various movements, union feminists create political spaces for new workers and for a new understanding of workers' issues and concerns that arise out of the rapidly changing impact of globalization on both workplaces and intimate lives. For labor to benefit from the work of union feminists, the labor movement must increase and enhance the participation of women within its ranks. This requires rethinking the structures and practices that perpetuate male dominance in the labor movement.

Union feminists are weaving together strengths and strategies growing from labor and women's movements. Their political activism is building at global as well as local and community levels. Despite the considerable obstacles, women's activism and militancy in their workplaces and political commitment are making a significant impact. The minority positions of union women activists and their feminist politics supported by the women's movement provide strong incentives to make creative and useful alliances across state and union borders. As always, progressive political activism demands mutual respect, recognition, and representation of diverse interests and needs. By developing and using union networks, alliances, and community organizations for mobilizing women's participation, union feminists create political spaces for workers' issues and concerns that arise out of the rapidly changing impact of globalization. Transnational union activism is a site of sexual politics as well as a vehicle for transforming sexual politics. Based on our research, we conclude that making feminist politics within labor means contesting explicit but complex structures of power and requires discursive and political alliances to confront the sexual politics of unions, families, and everyday life.

Notes

Chapter 1. Feminist Politics and Transnational Labor Movements

1. Gibson-Graham (1996) cautions us not to replicate conceptualizations and representations of capitalism and of globalization as monolithic, unitary, and fixed. To do so makes it much more difficult to imagine alternatives and to find places where opposition can flourish. Gibson-Graham calls for "queering globalization" (139) as a way to open up new possibilities in our conceptualizations of economic forces, of directing our attention to the gaps, excesses, and lapses in the meaning and logic of capitalism.

2. See chapters 7 and 8 in Fonow (2003) for a fuller account of these structures and how they are being used to mobilize women.

3. The GUFs include International Textile, Garment and Leather Workers Federation; International Federation of Building and Wood Workers; International Federation of Chemical, Energy, Mine and General Workers Union; International Union of Food, Agricultural, Hotel, Restaurant, Catering, Tobacco and Allied Workers' Association; Public Service International; Education International; International Transport Workers' Federation; International Federation of Journalists; International Metalworkers' Federation; Union Network International; International Confederation of Free Trade Unions; and the Trade Union Advisory Committee to the Organization for Economic Cooperation and Development.

4. These include the following: IMF, http://www.imfmetal.org/main/index.cfm; ITUC, http://www.ituc-csi.org/; ILO, http://www.ilo.org/global/lang—en/index.htm; Global Unions, http://www.global-unions.org/; World Social Forum, http://www.forumsocialmundial.org.br/index.php?cd_language=2; GURN, http://www.gurn.info/en/; and Friedrich Ebert Stiftung Archive, http://www.fes.de/.

Chapter 2. Sexual Politics, Activism, and Everyday Life

1. Fa'afafine is a Samoan term that literally means to be like a woman. Takataapui is a Maori term to describe intimate friends of the same sex.

Chapter 3. Sexual Politics, Labor, and the Family

1. Minutes, First Women Workers' International Conference, Vienna, February 25, 26, and 27, 1957, IMF, 5 (11), International Institute of Social History, Amsterdam.

Chapter 4. Political Spaces: Centers, Conferences, and Campaigns

1. Minutes, First Women Workers' International Conference, IMF, p. 12.
2. Ibid., 8.
3. It is important to note that in the Australian system, workers may be members of unions without the whole workplace being organized or unionized. Recruitment may be a much more cumulative process. However, recent legislation, the Workplace Relations Amendment (Work Choices) Bill 2005, has seriously restricted union access to workers and workplaces. The Australian Labor government, elected in 2007, removed some of these restrictions in 2009.
4. Minutes, First Women Workers' International Conference, IMF, p. 4.

Chapter 5. Feminist Politics in International Labor

1. The GUFs were formerly known as the International Trade Secretariats (ITS); the ITUC was formerly known as the International Confederation of Free Trade Unions (ICFTU), and before that the International Federation of Trade Unions (IFTU).
2. See EI's Web page on LGBT issues at http://www.ei-ie.org/lgbt/en/ (accessed July 11, 2010).
3. These activists included Esther Peterson, Frieda Miller, and Mary Anderson, among others.
4. There are exceptions. The International Metalworkers' Federation refused to affiliate with the merged body.

Chapter 6. Women's Activism in the International Metalworkers' Federation

1. International Metalworkers' Federation, "For a Strong International Labour Movement," http://www.imfmetal.org/index.cfm?n=616&l=2 (accessed July 12, 2010).
2. International Metalworkers' Federation, "Milestones in IMF History," http://www.imfmetal.org/index.cfm?n=741&l=2 (accessed August 20, 2010).
3. Minutes, First Women Workers' International Conference, IMF, p. 4.
4. Ibid.

5. Ibid.
6. Ibid., 18.
7. Ibid., 9.
8. See JRank, *Marriage and Family Encyclopedia,* "Women's Movements—Class and Women's Movements in Denmark: Unemployment, Gender, Poverty, and Family," http://family.jrank.org/pages/1765/Women-s-Movements-Class-Women-s-Movements-in-Denmark.html (accessed July 12, 2010).
9. Minutes, First Women Workers' International Conference, IMF, p. 25.
10. Ibid., 22.
11. Ibid., 27.
12. Ibid., 31.
13. Ibid., 40.
14. Ibid., 46.
15. Minutes, First Meeting of the IMF Commission for Women Workers, Vienna, April 19, 1963, IMF 5 (ii), 2, International Institute of Social History, Amsterdam.
16. "Circular Letter, to Members of the IMF Women Workers' Committee," December 16, 1968, IMF 5 (ii), 1, International Institute of Social History, Amsterdam.
17. The Third IMF Conference on Women Workers' Questions, Frankfurt, June 3, 4, and 5, 1970, TBA, International Institute of Social History, Amsterdam.
18. Ibid., 6.
19. Ibid., 9.
20. Ibid., 12.
21. "Summary of Activities for Women, 1970–75," Women Workers' Conference, Geneva, April 1975, IMF Box 19, d-4, 3, International Institute of Social History, Amsterdam.
22. Ibid., 3.
23. Ibid., 5.
24. "Resolution on Women," introduced at the IMF 23rd World Congress, Stockholm, July 2–6, 1974, 12, International Institute of Social History, Amsterdam.
25. Summary of First Trade Union Seminar for Women Workers in India, Jamshedpur, January 26 and 27, 1973, 8, International Institute of Social History, Amsterdam.
26. Summary IMF Fourth Asian Youth and Women's Symposium, Hong Kong, January 29–31, 1975, 10, International Institute of Social History, Amsterdam.
27. Speech by Ilda Simona on International Women's Year in the IMF given at the IMF Women Workers' Conference, Geneva, April 17 and 18, 1975, International Institute of Social History, Amsterdam.
28. Ibid.
29. 1st IMF African Women Workers' Conference, Nairobi, August 4–6, 1980, International Institute of Social History, Amsterdam.
30. Women Metalworkers' Congress, Sao Paulo, Brazil, March 29–31, 1985, 5, In-

ternational Metalworker's Federation archives, Friedrich-Ebert Stiftung Archive, Bonn.

31. Meeting of the IMF Women Workers' Committee, Geneva, April 15–16, 1986, National Report of Federal Republic of Germany, 9, International Metalworker's Federation archives, Friedrich-Ebert Stiftung Archive, Bonn.

32. Ibid., National Report of Japan, 8.

33. Internal Report, IMF Equal Rights Department, November 30, 1994, International Metalworker's Federation archives, Friedrich-Ebert Stiftung Archive, Bonn.

34. Ibid., 4.

35. Asian Sub-Regional Workshop for Women Workers, November 21–22, 1995, Bangkok, Thailand, 2, International Metalworker's Federation archives, Friedrich-Ebert Stiftung Archive, Bonn.

36. Evaluation Meeting of the IMF Special Project "Women and Collective Bargaining" December 11–12, n.d., Geneva, International Institute of Social History, Amsterdam.

37. Ibid., 13.

38. Ibid., 6.

39. Fonow attended this meeting and conducted informal interviews with participants. She also visited the IMF Head Office in Geneva to search IMF documents about women's activism.

40. Fonow observed both the women's meeting and the world congress, where she made field observations, gathered documents, and conducted informal interviews.

41. International Metalworkers' Federation, Minutes, 31st IMF World Congress, Vienna, Austria, May 2005, 79–82, http://www.imfmetal.org/main/files/0511151703177/CONGRESS-MINUTES-2005-english.pdf (accessed July 12, 2010).

42. Ibid., 95–97.

43. Ibid., 95–97.

44. Speech, May 24, 2005, Vienna, IMF World Congress.

45. International Metalworkers' Federation, *Survey on Changing Employment Practices and Precarious Work* (June 2008), 3, http://www.imfmetal.org/main/files/07090410362966/IMF%20report%20on%20precarious%20work%20survey%20-%20english%20-%20revised,%20June%202008.pdf (accessed July 12, 2010).

46. "IMF Holds Workshop on Women and Precarious Work," http://www.imfmetal.org/main/index.cfm?n=47&l=2&c=16988 (accessed July 12, 2010).

47. Ibid.

48. "Change Is Possible," Marcello Malentacchi, March, 5, 2007, http://www.imfmetal.org/main/index.cfm?n=225&l=2&c=15600 (accessed July 12, 2010).

Chapter 7. Another World Is Possible for Women, If . . .

1. World Social Forum, "What the World Social Forum Is," August 22, 2002, http://www.forumsocialmundial.org.br/main.php?id_menu=19&cd_language=2 (accessed July 12, 2010).

2. See World Social Forum, "Charter of Principles," June 8, 2002, http://www
.forumsocialmundial.org.br/main.php?id_menu=4&cd_language=2 (accessed July
12, 2010).

3. See Isis International Web site, "Feminist Dialogues 2009 at WSF," January 20,
2009, http://www.isiswomen.org/index.php?option=com_content&view=article&id
=1175:feminist-dialogues-2009-at-wsf&catid=22:movements-within&Itemid=229
(accessed August 21, 2010). See also the special issue of the *Journal of International
Women's Studies,* 8.3 (2007), for a collection of papers on feminist politics at the
World Social Forum.

References

ACOA (Administrative and Clerical Officers' Association). 1982. *Sexual Harassment in the Workplace: A Union Perspective*. Sydney: ACOA.

ACTU (Australian Council of Trade Unions). 2001. *"Ask a Working Woman": The ICFTU Survey*. http://www.actu.asn.au/public/campaigns/icftuwomensconference/askaworkingwoman.html. Accessed July 13, 2010.

———. 2003. "A Fair Australia. Child Care Policy." ACTU Congress: 1–15.

Adkins, L. 2002. *Revisions: Gender and Sexuality in Late Modernity*. Buckingham: Open University Press.

Adkins, L., and Lury, C. 2000. "Making Bodies, Making People, Making Work." In *Organizing Bodies: Policy, Institutions, and Work*. Eds. L. McKie and N. Watson. 151–66. Basingstoke: Macmillan Press.

Agustín, L. M. 2007. *Sex at the Margins: Mirgration, Labour Markets, and the Rescue Industry*. London: Zed Books.

Alvarez, S. E. 2000. "Translating the Global Effects of Transnational Organizing on Local Feminist Discourses and Practices in Latin America." *Meridians: Feminism, Race, Transnationalism* 1.1: 29–67.

Alvarez, S. E., Faria, N., and Nobre, M. 2004. *Another (Also Feminist) World Is Possible: Constructing Transnational Spaces and Global Alternatives from the Movements*. New Delhi: Viveka Foundation. http://www.choike.org/documentos/wsf_s313_alvarez.pdf. Accessed July 13, 2010.

Anderson, B. 2000. *Joyous Greetings: The First International Women's Movement 1830–1860*. Oxford: Oxford University Press.

Applebaum, E. 2001. "Transformation and Employment and New Insecurities." In *The Future of Work, Employment, and Social Protection: The Search for New Securities in a World of Growing Uncertainties*. Eds. P. Auer and C. Daniels. 17–38. Geneva: Ministry of Employment and Solidarity/International Labour Organization.

Armstrong, E., and Bernstein, M. 2008. "Culture, Power, and Institutions: A Multi-Institutional Politics Approach to Social Movements." *Sociological Theory* 26.1: 74–99.

Atkinson, J. 2005. *Balancing Work and Family: Unions Make a Difference*. http://canadianlabour.ca/index.php/march_2005/Balancing_Work_and_F. Accessed January 20, 2008.

Attenborough, S. 1983. "Sexual Harassment: An Issue for Unions." In *Union Sisters: Women in the Labour Movement*. Eds. L. Briskin and L. Yanz. 136–43. Toronto: Women's Press.

Badgett, M. V. L. 2001. *Money, Myths, and Change: The Economic Lives of Lesbians and Gay Men*. Chicago: University of Chicago Press.

Bailey, J. 2005. "Mothers—And Others—In Union Protest." *Hecate* 31.2: 114–35.

Baker, P. 1993. "Reflections on Life Stories: Women's Bank Union Activism." In *Women Challenging Unions: Feminism, Democracy, and Militancy*. Eds. L. Briskin and P. McDermott. 62–88. Toronto: University of Toronto Press.

Bakker, I., and Gill, S., Eds. 2003. *Power Production and Social Reproduction: Human In/Security in the Global Political Economy*. New York: Palgrave Macmillan.

Banaszak, L. A., Beckwith, K., and Rucht, D. 2003. *Women's Movements Facing the Reconfigured State*. New York: Cambridge University Press.

Bandy, J., and Smith, J., Eds. 2005. *Coalitions across Borders: Transnational Protest and the Neoliberal Order*. Lanham, Md.: Rowman and Littlefield.

Barber, B. 2005. *Don't Play the Race Card*. http://www.tuc.org.uk/equality/tuc-9704-fo.cfm. Accessed July 8, 2010.

Barker, D., and Feiner, S. F. 2005. *Liberating Economics: Feminist Perspectives on Families, Work, and Globalization*. Ann Arbor: University of Michigan Press.

Baron, A., and Boris, E. 2007. "'The Body' as a Useful Category for Working-Class History." *Labor: Studies in Working-Class History of the Americas* 4.2: 23–43.

Barrett, M., and McIntosh, M. 1982. *The Anti-social Family*. London: Verso.

Basu, A. 2005. "Transnational Feminism Revisited." *Feminist Africa* 5: 90–95.

Beale, J. 1982. *Getting It Together: Women as Trade Unionists*. London: Pluto Press.

Beaumont, C. 2006. "Stamping Out Homophobia All over the World." Paper presented at the UK Trades Union Congress Conference—Stamping Out Homophobia. London.

Beccalli, B., and Meardi, G. 2002. "From Unintended to Undecided Feminism? Italian Labour's Changing and Singular Ambiguities." In *Gender, Diversity, and Trade Unions: International Perspectives*. Eds. F. Colgan and S. Ledwith. 113–31. New York: Routledge.

Beck, U. 2000. *What Is Globalization?* Malden, Mass.: Polity Press.

Beckwith, K. 2001a. "Gender Frames and Collective Action: Configurations of Masculinity in the Pittston Coal Strike." *Politics and Society* 29.2: 297–330.

———. 2001b. "Women's Movements at Century's End: Excavation and Advances in Political Science." *Annual Review of Political Science* 4: 371–90.

———. 2007. "Mapping Strategic Engagements: Women's Movements and the State." *International Feminist Journal of Politics* 9.3: 312–38.

Bedford, K. 2007. "The Imperative of Male Inclusion: How Institutional Context Influences World Bank Gender Policy." *International Feminist Journal of Politics* 9.3: 289–311.

Bendt, H. 2003. *Worldwide Solidarity: The Activities of the Global Unions in the Era of Globalization*. Trans. A. Brinkmann. Bonn: Friedrich-Ebert-Siftung.

Benería, L. 2003. *Gender, Development, and Globalization: Economics as if All People Mattered*. New York: Routledge.

Benería, L., and Bisnath, S., Eds. 2004. *Global Tensions: Challenges and Opportunities in the World Economy*. New York: Routledge.

Berger, J. 1968. "The Nature of Mass Demonstration." *International Socialism* 34 (Autumn): 11–12.

Bergeron, S. 2001. "Political Economy Discourses of Globalization and Feminist Politics." *Signs: Journal of Women in Culture and Society* 26.4: 983–1007.

Berkovitch, N. 1999. *From Motherhood to Citizenship: Women's Rights and International Organizations*. Baltimore: Johns Hopkins University Press.

Berry, P., and Kitchener, G. 1989. *Can Unions Survive?* Canberra: BWIU, ACT Branch.

Bezuidenhout, A., and Fakier, K. 2006. "Maria's Burden: Contract Cleaning and the Crisis of Social Reproduction in Post-apartheid South Africa." *Antipode* 38.3: 462–85.

Bianchi, S. M., Milkie, M. A., Sayer, L. C., and Robinson, J. P. 2000. "Is Anyone Doing the Housework? Trends in the Gender Division of Household Labor." *Social Forces* 29.1: 191–228.

Bittman, M. 1991. *Juggling Time: How Australian Families Use Time*. Canberra: Office of the Status of Women, Department of Prime Minister and Cabinet.

Bittman, M., and Wajcman, J. 2004. "The Rush Hour: The Quality of Leisure Time and Gender Equity." In *Family Time: The Social Organisation Of Care*. Eds. N. Folbre and M. Bittman. 171–93. London: Routledge.

Blandford, J. 2003. "The Nexus of Sexual Orientation and Gender in the Determination of Earnings." *Industrial and Labor Relations Review* 56.4: 622–42.

Boston, S. 1980. *Women Workers and the Trade Union Movement*. London: Davis-Poynter.

Bourdieu, P. 1990. *The Logic of Practice*. Cambridge: Polity Press.

Bowman, D. 2007. "Men's Business: Negotiating Entrepreneurial Business and Family Life." *Journal of Sociology* 43.4: 385–400.

Brenner, M. 2002. "Defining and Measuring a Global Living Wage: Theoretical and Conceptual Issues." Paper presented at the Global Labor Standards and Living Wages Conference. University of Massachusetts–Amherst. April 19–20.

Brewis, J. 2000. "'When a Body Meets a Body . . . ': Experiencing the Female Body at Work." In *Organizing Bodies: Policy, Institutions and Work*. Eds. L. McKie and N. Watson. 166–84. Basingstoke: Macmillan Press.

Brickner, R. K. 2006. "Union Democracy and the Struggle for Women's Labor Rights: Reflections from Mexico." Paper presented at the Conference of the Canadian Political Science Association. Toronto. June 1–3. http://www.cpsa-acsp.ca/papers-2006/Brickner.pdf. Accessed July 13, 2010.

Brigden, C. 2005. "Exploring Gender in Peak Union Bodies." Paper presented at the 18th AIRAANZ conference. Sydney. February 9–11.

Briskin, L. 1993. "Union Women and Separate Organizing." In *Women Challenging Unions: Feminism, Democracy, and Militancy*. Eds. L. Briskin and P. McDermott. 89–108. Toronto: University of Toronto Press.

———. 1998. "Autonomy, Diversity and Integration: Union Women's Separate Organizing in the Context of Restructuring and Globalization." Paper presented at the Congress of the International Sociological Association. Montreal.

———. 2009. "Cross-Constituency Organizing: A Vehicle for Union Renewal." In *Unions, Equity, and the Path to Renewal*. Eds. J. Foley and P. L. Baker, 135–54. Vancouver: University of British Columbia Press.

Briskin, L., and McDermott, P. 1993. *Women Challenging Unions: Feminism, Democracy, and Militancy*. Toronto: University of Toronto Press.

Broadbent, K. 2008. "Japan: Women Workers and Autonomous Organizing." In *Women and Labour Organizing in Asia: Diversity, Autonomy, and Activism*. Eds. K. Broadbent and M. Ford. 156–71. London: Routledge.

Broadbent, K., and Ford, M. 2008. *Women and Labour Organizing in Asia: Diversity, Autonomy, and Activism*. London: Routledge.

Brooks, E. C. 2007. *Unraveling the Garment Industry: Transnational Organizing and Women's Work*. Minneapolis: University of Minnesota Press.

Brown, W. 1995. *States of Injury: Power and Freedom in Late Modernity*. Princeton: Princeton University Press.

Buss, D., and Herman, D. 2003. *Globalizing Family Values: The Christian Right in International Politics*. Minneapolis: University of Minnesota Press.

Butler, J. 1993. *Bodies That Matter: On the Discursive Limits of "Sex."* London: Routledge.

———. 2009. *Frames of War: When Is Life Grievable?* London: Verso.

Butler, J., and Scott, J., Eds. 1992. *Feminists Theorise the Political*. London: Routledge.

Buvinic, M., Sabarwal, S., and Sinha, N. 2009. *Impact of Financial Crisis on Women and Families*. World Bank. February. http://portal.unesco.org/en/files/44680/12360162191Mayra_Buvinic.pdf/Mayra%2BBuvinic.pdf. Accessed July 13, 2010.

Caldwell, L. 1983. "Courses for Women: The Example of the 150 Hours in Italy." *Feminist Review* 14: 71–83.

Calhoun, C. 2000. *Feminism, the Family, and the Politics of the Closet: Lesbian and Gay Displacement*. Oxford: Oxford University Press.

Canel, E. 1997. "New Social Movement Theory and Discourse Mobilization Theory:

The Need for Integration." In *Community Power and Grassroots Democracy: The Transformation of Social Life*. Eds. M. Kaufman and H. Dilla Alfonso. 189–221. London: Zed Books and IDRC (International Development Research Centre).

———. 2007. *Assembling Women: The Feminization of Global Manufacturing*. Ithaca, N.Y.: Cornell University Press.

Caraway, Teri L. 2007. *Assembling Women: The Feminization of Global Manufacturing*. Ithaca, N.Y.: Cornell University Press.

Casas-Cortés, M. I., Osterweil, M., and Powell, D. E. 2008. "Blurring Boundaries: Recognizing Knowledge-Practices in the Study of Social Movements." *Anthropological Quarterly* 81.1: 17–58.

Chalfie, D., Blank, H., and Entmacher, J. 2007. *Getting Organized: Unionizing Home-Based Child Care Providers*. National Women's Law Center. http://www.nwlc.org/pdf/GettingOrganized2007.pdf. Accessed July 13, 2010.

Charles, N. 2004. "Feminist Politics and Devolution: A Preliminary Analysis." *Social Politics* 11.2: 297–311.

Charles, N., and Kerr, M. 1987. "Just the Way It Is: Gender and Age Differences in Family Food Consumption." In *Give and Take in Families: Studies in Resource Distribution*. Eds. J. Brannen and G. Wilson. 155–74. London: Allen and Unwin.

Chen, M. A., Vanek J., Lund, F., and Heintz, J., with Bonner, C., and Jhabvala, R. 2005. *The Progress of the World's Women 2005: Women, Work, and Poverty*. New York: UNIFEM.

Clawson, D. 2003. *The Next Upsurge: Labor and the New Social Movements*. Ithaca, N.Y.: ILR Press.

Cobble, D. S. 2004. *The Other Women's Movement: Workplace Justice and Social Rights in Modern America*. Princeton: Princeton University Press.

———. 2008. "Transnational Labor Feminism and U.S. Social Policy, 1914–1957." Paper presented at the Charles Warren Center for Studies in American History. Harvard University. April 17.

Cobble, D. S., and Bielski Michal, M. 2002. "On the Edge of Equality? Working Women and the U.S. Labour Movement." *Gender, Diversity, and Trade Unions: International Perspectives*. Eds. F. Colgan and S. Ledwith. 232–56. London: Routledge.

Cockburn, C. 1991. *In the Way of Women: Men's Resistance to Sex Equality in Organizations*. London: Macmillan.

———. 1998. *The Space between Us: Negotiating Gender and National Identities*. London: Zed Books.

———. 2000. "The Women's Movement: Boundary Crossing on Terrains of Conflict." In *Global Social Movements*. Eds. R. Cohen and S. M. Rai. 51–58. London: Athlone Press.

Cohen, C. 1999. "What Is This Movement Doing to My Politics?" *Social Text* 17.4: 110–18.

Cohen, M. G., and Brodie, J., Eds. 2007. *Remapping Gender in the New Global Order*. Abingdon: Routledge.

Colgan, F., Creegan, C., McKearney, A., and Wright, T. 2006. *Lesbian, Gay, and Bisexual Workers Equality, Diversity, and Inclusion in the Workplace: A Qualitative Research Study*. London: Comparative Organisation and Equality Research Centre (COERC), London Metropolitan University.

Colgan, F., and Ledwith, S. 2002. "Gender, Diversity and Mobilisation in UK Trade Unions. In *Gender, Diversity, and Trade Unions: International Perspectives*. Eds. F. Colgan and S. Ledwith. 154–85. London: Routledge.

Collins, P. H. 2004. *Black Sexual Politics: African Americans, Gender and the New Racism*. New York: Routledge.

Compa, L. A., and Diamond, S. F., Eds. 1996. *Human Rights, Labor Rights, and International Trade*. Philadelphia: University of Pennsylvania Press.

Conley, H. 2005. "Front Line or All Fronts? Women's Trade Union Activism in Retail Services." *Gender, Work, and Organization* 12.5: 479–96.

Connell, R. 1987. *Gender and Power: Society, the Person, and Sexual Politics*. Sydney: Allen and Unwin.

———. 2002. *Gender: Short Introductions*. Cambridge: Polity Press.

———. 2005. "A Really Good Husband: Work/Life Balance, Gender Equity, and Social Change." *Australian Journal of Social Issues* 40.3: 369–84.

Conway, J. 2007. "Transnational Feminisms and the World Social Forum: Encounters and Transformations in Anti-Globalization Spaces." *Journal of International Women's Studies* 8.3: 49–70.

———. 2008. "Geographies of Transnational Feminisms: The Politics of Place and Scale in the World March of Women." *Social Politics* 15.2: 207–31.

Cook, A., Lorwin, V., and Daniels, A. 1992. *The Most Difficult Revolution: Women and Trade Unions*. Ithaca, N.Y.: ILR Press.

Coote, A., and Campbell, B. 1982. *Sweet Freedom*. London: Picador.

Cornfield, D., and McCammon, H., Eds. 2003. *Labor Revitalization : Global Perspectives and New Initiatives*. Vol. 11. Amsterdam: JAI.

Costa, D. L. 2000. "From Mill Town to Board Room: The Rise of Women's Paid Labor." *Journal of Economic Perspectives* 14.4: 101–22.

Crain, M. 2007. "Sex Discrimination as a Collective Harm." In *The Sex of Class: Women Transforming American Labor*. Ed. D. S. Cobble. 99–116. Ithaca, N.Y.: ILR Press.

Creed, H. 1999. "Keeping the Flame Burning." In *Carrying the Banner: Women, Leadership, and Activism in Australia*. Eds. J. Eveline and L. Hayden. 101–10. Perth: University of Western Australia Press.

Crenshaw, K. 1989. "Demarginalizing the Intersection of Race and Sex: A Black Feminist Critique of Antidiscrimination Doctrine, Feminist Theory, and Antiracist Politics." *University of Chicago Legal Forum* 14: 538–54.

———. 2000. "Gender-Related Aspects of Race Discrimination," Background paper for Expert Meeting on Gender and Racial Discrimination. Zagreb, Croatia. November 21–24.

Cross, M. 2004. *The Letter in Flora Tristan's Politics, 1835–1844*. New York: Palgrave MacMillan.

Cruz, M. L. 2006. *Feminists and Money, Transgression and Money, Social Change and Money: Some Final Thoughts from the Money and Movements Forum*. November 9–11. http://www.awid.org/eng/content/download/23258/298990/file/feminists_money_en.doc. Accessed July 8, 2010.

Cuneo, C. J. 1993. "Trade Union Leadership: Sexism and Affirmative Action." In *Women Challenging Unions: Feminism, Democracy, and Militancy*. Eds. L. Briskin and P. McDermott. 109–36. Toronto: University of Toronto Press.

Cunnison, S., and Stageman, J. 1995. *Feminizing the Unions: Challenging the Culture of Masculinity*. Aldershot: Avebury.

Curtin, J. 1999. *Women and Trade Unions: A Comparative Perspective*. Sydney: Ashgate.

Dalla Costa, M., and James, S. 1974. *The Power of Women and the Subversion of the Community*. Bristol: Falling Wall Press.

Dalley, G. 1996. *Ideologies of Caring: Rethinking Community and Collectivism*. 2nd ed. London: Macmillan.

Darcy, J. 1993. "Foreword." In *Women Challenging Unions: Feminism, Democracy, and Militancy*. Eds. L. Briskin and P. McDermott. vii–xi. Toronto: University of Toronto Press.

Deacon, D. 1985. "Political Arithmetic: The Nineteenth-Century Australian Census and the Construction of the Dependent Woman." *Signs: Journal of Women in Culture and Society* 11.1: 27–47.

Deem, R. 1988. "Feminism and Leisure Studies: Opening Up New Directions." In *Relative Freedoms: Women and Leisure*. Eds. E. Winbush and M. Talbot. 5–17. Oxford: Oxford University Press.

della Porta, D. 2005. "Making the Polis: Social Forums and Democracy in the Global Justice Movement." *Mobilization* 10:73–94.

Desai, M. 2005. "The Feminist Dialogues and the World Social Forum." *Perspectives: Women and Gender in Global Perspectives Newsletter* 25 (April): 14–17.

Domínguez, E. R. 2002. "Continental Transnational Activism and Women Workers' Networks within NAFTA." *International Feminist Journal of Politics* 4.2: 216–39.

Downs, L. L. 1995. *Manufacturing Inequality: Gender Division in the French and British Metalworking Industries 1914–1939*. Ithaca, N.Y.: Cornell University Press.

Drake, B. 1984. *Women in Trade Unions*. London: Virago.

Duddy, J. 2003. "How Is a Gendered Perspective Being Placed on the Agenda of the 2004 World Social Forum? An Interview with Carol Barton, Women's International Coalition for Economic Justice (WICEJ)." AWID (Association for Women's Rights in Development). http://www.awid.org/eng/Issues-and-Analysis/Library/How-is-a-gendered-perspective-being-placed-on-the-agenda-of-the-2004-World/%28language%29/eng-GB. Accessed July 13, 2010.

Duffy, M. 2005. "Reproducing Labor Inequalities: Challenges for Feminists Conceptualizing Care at the Intersections of Gender, Race, and Class." *Gender and Society* 19.1: 66–82.

Dwyer, A. 2006. "From Private to Public Bodies: Normalising Pregnant Bodies in Western Culture." *Nexus: Newsletter of the Australian Sociological Association* 18.3: 18–19.

Edwards, P., and Wajcman, J. 2005. *The Politics of Working Life.* Oxford: Oxford University Press.

Ehrenreich, B., and Hochschild, A. R., Eds. 2002. *Global Woman: Nannies, Maids, and Sex Workers in the New Economy.* New York: Metropolitan Books/Henry Holt and Company.

EI (Education International). 2001. *The Rights of Gay and Lesbian Education Personnel, Triennial Report.* Brussels: Education International.

———. 2007. *The Rights of Lesbian and Gay Teachers and Education Personnel. Triennial Report 2004–2007.* Education International. http://download.ei-ie.org/docs/IRISDocuments/Human%20and%20Trade%20Union%20Rights/Gays%20and%20Lesbians/Trienniel%20Survey%20on%20LGBT%202006/2008-00130-01-E.pdf. Accessed July 14, 2010.

Elger, T., and Parker, A. 2007. "Widening Union Agendas? The Case of British Union Policies to Combat Domestic Violence." Paper presented at Work, Employment and Society Conference. Aberdeen: Centre for Comparative Labour Studies, Department of Sociology, University of Warwick. September 12–24.

Elliott, K. A., and Freeman, R. 2003. *Can Labor Standards Improve under Globalization?* Washington, D.C.: Institute for International Economics.

Elliott, R. 1984. "How Far Have We Come? Women's Organization in the Unions in the United Kingdom." *Feminist Review* 16: 64–73.

Elton, J. 1976. "The Organisation of Labour in the South Australian Clothing Trades, 1836–1920." Unpublished Honours Thesis, Flinders University.

England, P., and Folbre, N. 2000. "Capitalism and the Erosion of Care." In *Unconventional Wisdom: Alternative Perspectives on the New Economy.* Ed. J. Madrick. 29–48. New York: Century Foundation Press.

Erne, R. 2008. *European Unions: Labor's Quest for a Transnational Democracy.* Ithaca, N.Y.: ILR Press.

Eschle, C. 2001. *Global Democracy, Social Movements, and Feminism.* Boulder, Colo.: Westview Press.

———. 2002. "Engendering Global Democracy." *International Feminist Journal of Politics* 4.3: 315–41.

———. 2005. "Skeleton Women: Feminism and the Antiglobalization Movement." *Signs: Journal of Women in Culture and Society* 30.3: 1742–69.

Eschle, C., and Stammers, N. 2004. "Taking Part: Social Movements, INGOs, and Global Change." *Alternatives* 29.3: 335–74.

Eveline, J., and Booth, M. 2002. "Gender and Sexuality in Discourses of Managerial Control: The Case of Women Miners." *Gender, Work, and Organization* 9.5: 556–78.

Evertsson, M., and Nermo, M. 2004. "Dependence within Families and the Division of Labor: Comparing Sweden and the United States." *Journal of Marriage and Family* 66.5: 1272–86.

Faue, E. 1991. *Community of Suffering and Struggle: Women, Men, and the Labor Movement in Minneapolis, 1915–1945*. Chapel Hill: University of North Carolina Press.

Ferree, M. M., and Mueller, C. M. 2005. "Feminism and the Women's Movement: A Global Perspective." In *The Blackwell Companion to Social Movements*. Eds. D. A. Snow, S. A. Soule, and H. Kriesi. 576–607. Malden, Mass.: Blackwell.

Ferree, M. M., and Roth, S. 1998. "Gender, Class, and the Interaction between Social Movements: A Strike of West Berlin Day Care Workers." *Gender and Society* 12.6 (Special Issue: Gender and Social Movements, Part 1): 626–48.

Feree, M. M., and Tripp, A. M., Eds. 2006. *Global Feminism: Transnational Women's Activism, Organizing, and Human Rights*. New York: New York University Press.

Field, D. 1983. "Coercion or Male Culture: A New Look at Co-Worker Harassment." In *Union Sisters*. Eds. L. Briskin and L. Yanz. 144–60. Toronto: Women's Press.

Finch, J., and Groves, D. 1983. *A Labour of Love: Women, Work, and Caring*. London: Routledge.

Fine, J. 2006. *Worker Centers: Organizing Communities at the Edge of the Dream*. Ithaca, N.Y.: Cornell University Press.

Firestein, N., and Dones, N. 2007. "Unions Fight for Work and Family Policies—Not for Women Only." In *The Sex of Class: Women Transforming American Labor*. Ed. D. S. Cobble. 140–54. Ithaca, N.Y.: ILR Press.

Folbre, N. 1991. "The Unproductive Housewife: Her Evolution in Nineteenth-Century Economic Thought." *Signs: Journal of Women in Culture and Society* 16.3: 463–84.

———. 2001. *The Invisible Heart: Economic and Family Values*. New York: W. W. Norton.

Folbre, N., and Nelson, J. 2000. "For Love or Money—Or Both?" *Journal of Economic Perspectives* 14.4: 123–40.

Foley, J. 2000. "Developing an Explanatory Framework for the Demise of a Women's Committee." *Economic and Industrial Democracy* 21: 505–31.

Foley, J., and Baker, P., Eds. 2009. *Unions, Equity, and the Path to Renewal*. Vancouver: University of British Columbia Press.

Fonow, M. M. 2003. *Union Women: Forging Feminism in the United Steelworkers of America*. Minneapolis: University of Minnesota Press.

———. 2005. "Human Rights, Feminism, and Transnational Labor Solidarity." In *Just Advocacy? Women's Human Rights, Transnational Feminism and the Politics of Representation*. Eds. W. Kozol and W. Hesford. 221–42. New Brunswick: Rutgers University Press.

Fonow, M. M., and Franzway, S. 2007. "Transnational Union Networks, Feminism, and Labour Advocacy." In *Trade Union Responses to Globalization.* Ed. V. Schmidt. 165–76. Geneva: International Labour Office Press.

Fortescue, R. 2000. "Mardi Gras: The Biggest Labor Festival of the Year." *Hecate* 26.2: 62–65.

Foucault, M. 1979. *The History of Sexuality.* Vol. 1: *An Introduction.* Trans. R. Hurley. Harmondsworth: Penguin.

———. 1980. *Power/Knowledge: Selected Interviews and Other Writings 1972–1977.* Ed. and trans. C. Gordon. Sussex: Harvester Press.

Frager, R. 1983. "No Proper Deal: Women Workers and the Canadian Labour Movement, 1870–1940." In *Union Sisters: Women in the Labour Movement.* Eds. L. Briskin and L. Yanz. 44–66. Toronto: Women's Educational Press.

Frank, D. 2004. "Where Is the History of U.S. Labor and Solidarity? Part I: A Moveable Feast." *Labor: Studies in the Working Class History of the Americas* 1.1: 95–119.

Franzway, S. 2001. *Sexual Politics and Greedy Institutions: Union Women, Commitments, and Conflicts in Public and in Private.* Sydney: Pluto Press.

Franzway, S., Court, D., and Connell, R. W. 1989. *Staking A Claim: Feminism, Bureaucracy and the State.* Sydney: Allen and Unwin.

Franzway, S. and Fonow, M. M. Forthcoming. Book review. *Signs: Journal of Women in Culture and Society.*

Frege, C., and Kelly, J., Eds. 2004. *Varieties of Unionism: Struggles for Union Revitalization in a Globalizing Economy.* Oxford: Oxford University Press.

Friedman, S., and Wood, S. 2001. "Employers Unfair Advantage in the United States of America: Symposium on the Human Rights Watch Report on the State of Workers' Freedom of Association in the United States: Editors' Introduction." *British Journal of Industrial Relations* 39.4: 586–90.

Frundt, H. J. 2005. "Movement Theory and International Labor Solidarity." *Labor Studies Journal* 30.2: 19–40.

Frutiger, D. 2002. "AFL-CIO China Policy: Labor's New Step Forward or the Cold War Revisited?" *Labor Studies Journal* 27.3: 67–80.

Fudge, J., and Owens, R. 2006. "Precarious Work, Women, and the New Economy: The Challenge to Legal Norms." In *Precarious Work, Women, and the New Economy.* Eds. J. Fudge and R. Owens. 3–28. Oxford: Hart Publishing.

Fullagar, S. 2003. "Governing Women's Active Leisure: The Gendered Effects of Calculative Rationalities within Australian Health Policy." *Critical Public Health* 13.1: 47–60.

Gabin, N. F. 1990. *Feminism in the Labor Movement: Women and the United Auto Workers, 1935–1975.* Ithaca, N.Y.: Cornell University Press.

Gallin, D. 2000. "Trade Unions and NGOs: A Necessary Partnership for Social Development." In *Civil Society and Social Movements Programme.* Paper No. 1. 1–47. June. Geneva: UNRISD.

Gamson, W., and Meyer, D. S. 1996. "Framing Political Opportunities." In *Comparative Perspectives on Social Movements*. Eds. D. McAdam, J. D. McCarthy, and M. N. Zald. 275–90. Cambridge: Cambridge University Press.

Gardiner, J. 1975. "Women's Domestic Labour." *New Left Review* 89: 47–58.

Gelb, J. 2002. "Feminism, NGOs, and the Impact of the New Transnationalisms." In *Dynamics of Regulatory Change: How Globalization Affects National Regulatory Policies*. GAIA Books, vol. 1, 1–32. Berkeley: Global, Area, and International Archive, University of California. http://escholarship.org/uc/item/3mr1z2kj. Accessed August 25, 2010.

Genge, S. 1983. "Lesbians and Gays in the Union Movement." In *Union Sisters: Women in the Labour Movement*, eds. L. Yanz and L. Briskin. 161–70. Toronto: Women's Press.

Genge, S. 1998. "Solidarity and Pride." *Canadian Women's Studies* 18.1: 97–99.

Gerstel, N., and Clawson, D. 2001. "Unions' Responses to Family Concerns." *Social Problems* 48.2: 277–97.

Getman, J. 2001. "A Useful Step." *British Journal of Industrial Relations* 39.4: 596–600.

Gibson-Graham, J. K. 1996. *The End of Capitalism (As We Knew It): A Feminist Critique of Political Economy*. Cambridge: Blackwell.

———. 2002. "Beyond Global vs. Local: Economic Politics Outside the Binary Frame." In *Geographies of Power: Placing Self*. Eds. A. Herod and M. Wright. 25–60. Oxford: Blackwell Publishers.

———. 2006. *A Postcapitalist Politics*. Minneapolis: University of Minnesota Press.

Giddens, A. 1991. *Modernity and Self-Identity: Self and Society in the Late Modern Age*. Cambridge: Polity Press.

Gimlin, D. L. 2002. *Body Work: Beauty and Self-Image in American Culture*. Berkeley: University of California Press.

Githens, R. P., and Aragon, S. R. 2009. "LGBT Employee Groups: Goals and Organizational Structures." *Advances in Developing Human Resources* 11.1: 121–35.

Giugni, M. G. 2002. "Explaining Cross-National Similarities among Social Movements." In *Globalization and Resistance: Transnational Dimensions of Social Movements*. Eds. J. Smith and H. Johnston. 13–30. Lanham, Md.: Rowman and Littlefield.

Glickman, L. 1997. *A Living Wage: American Workers and the Making of Consumer Society*. Ithaca, N.Y.: Cornell University Press.

Goward, P. 2006. *Do We Still Need Feminism?* Presented at Human Rights and the Equal Opportunity Commission. Australian Human Rights Commission Web site. http://www.hreoc.gov.au/about/media/speeches/sex_discrim/feminism20060314.html. Accessed July 14, 2010.

Greene, A. M., and Kirton, G. 2002. "Advancing Gender Equality: The Role of Women-Only Trade Union Education." *Gender, Work, and Organization* 9.1: 39–59.

Gross, J., Ed. 2003. *Workers' Rights as Human Rights*. Ithaca, N.Y.: ILR Press.
Gutek, B. A. 1985. *Sex and the Workplace: The Impact of Sexual Behavior and Harassment on Women, Men, and Organizations*. San Francisco: Jossey-Bass.
Hadjifotiou, N. 1983. *Women and Harassment at Work*. Sydney: Pluto Press.
Hakim, C. 2000. *Work-Lifestyle Choices in the 21st Century: Preference Theory*. Oxford: Oxford University Press.
Hale, A., and Wills, J. 2007. "Women Working Worldwide: Transnational Networks, Corporate Social Responsibility, and Action Research." *Global Networks* 7.4: 453–76.
Hanagan, M. 2003. "Labor Internationalism: An Introduction." *Social Science History* 27:4 (Winter): 485–99.
Harcourt, W. 2006. *The Global Women's Rights Movement: Power Politics around the United Nations and the World Social Forum*. Geneva: United Nations Research Institute for Social Development.
Hardt, M. 2004. "Today's Bandung?" In *A Movement of Movements*. Ed. T. Mertes. 230–36. London: Verso.
Hardy, J., Kozek, W., and Stenning, A. 2008. "In the Front Line: Women, Work, and New Spaces of Labour Politics in Poland." *Gender, Place, and Culture* 15.2: 99–116.
Hartmann, H. 1981. "The Family as the Locus of Gender, Class, and Political Struggle: The Example of Housework." *Signs: Journal of Women in Culture and Society* 6.3: 366–94.
———. 1987. "The Family as the Locus of Gender, Class, and Political Struggle: The Example of Housework." In *Feminism and Methodology*. Ed. S. Harding. 109–34. Milton Keynes: Open University Press.
Harvey, D. 2005. *The New Imperialism*. Oxford: Oxford University Press.
Hassim, S. 2005. "Terms of Engagement: South African Challenges [1]." *Feminist Africa* 4: http://www.feministafrica.org/index.php/terms-of-engagement. Accessed August 25, 2010.
Hawkesworth, M. E. 2006. *Globalization and Feminist Activism*. Lanham, Md.: Rowman and Littlefield.
———. 2009. "Institutionalizing Insurgency." *International Feminist Journal of Politics* 11.1: 10–20.
Hawkesworth, M., and Alexander, K., Eds. 2008. "Comparative Perspectives Symposium: Women's Labor Activism." Special issue, *Signs: Journal of Women in Culture and Society* 33.3.
Heagney, M. 1935. *Are Women Taking Men's Jobs? A Survey of Women's Work in Victoria with Special Regard to Equal Status, Equal Pay, and Equality of Opportunity*. Melbourne: Hilton and Veitch.
Healy, G., Hansen, L. L., and Ledwith, S. 2006. "Editorial: Still Uncovering Gender in Industrial Relations." *Industrial Relations Journal* 37.4: 290–98.

Hearn, J., and Parkin, W. 2001. *Gender, Sexuality and Violence in Organizations: The Unspoken Forces of Organization Violations.* London: SAGE Publications.
Heery, E., and Conley, H. 2007. "Frame Extension in a Mature Social Movement: British Trade Unions and Part-Time Work, 1967–2002." *Journal of Industrial Relations* 49.1: 5–29.
Hegewisch, A., with Hammond, S., and Valladares, K. 2006. *Report of the Evaluation of the PSI Pay Equity Campaign 2001–2006.* Geneva: Public Services International.
Hein, C. 2005. *Reconciling Work and Family Responsibilities: Practical Ideas from Global Experience.* Geneva: International Labour Office.
Hensman, R. 2002. "Trade Unions and Women's Autonomy: Organisational Strategies of Women Workers in India." In *Gender, Diversity, and Trade Unions: International Perspectives.* Eds. F. Colgan and S. Ledwith. 95–112. London: Routledge.
Hercus, C. 2005. *Stepping Out of Line: Becoming and Being Feminist.* London: Routledge.
Hill, E. 2008. "India: The Self-Employed Women's Association and Autonomous Organizing." In *Women and Labour Organizing in Asia: Diversity, Autonomy, and Activism.* Eds. K. Broadbent and M. Ford. 115–35. London: Routledge.
Hintjens, H. 2006. "Appreciating the Movement of Movements." *Development in Practice* 16.6: 628–43.
Hochschild, A. R. 1983. *The Managed Heart: Commercialization of Human Feeling.* Berkeley: University of California Press.
———. 1989. *The Second Shift.* New York: Avon Books.
Holcomb, D., and Wohlforth, N. 2001. "The Fruits of Our Labor: Pride at Work." *New Labor Forum* (Spring/Summer): 9–20. http://qcpages.qc.cuny.edu/newlaborforum/old/html/8_article9.html. Accessed July 8, 2010.
Holliday, R., and Hassard, J., Eds. 2001. *Contested Bodies.* London: Routledge.
Holtby, W. 1935. *Women and a Changing Civilization.* New York: Longmans, Green.
hooks, b. 2000. *Feminist Theory from Margin to Center.* Cambridge, Mass.: South End Press.
Hunt, G., Ed. 1999. *Laboring for Rights: Unions and Sexual Diversity across Nations.* Philadelphia: Temple University Press.
Hunt, G., and Bielski Boris, M. 2007. "The Lesbian, Gay, Bisexual, and Transgender Challenge to American Labor." In *The Sex of Class: Women Transforming American Labor.* Ed. D. S. Cobble. 81–98. Ithaca, N.Y.: ILR Press.
Hunt, G., and Haiven, J. 2006. "Building Democracy for Women and Sexual Minorities: Union Embrace of Diversity." *Relations Industrielles* 61.4: 666–82.
Hutchings, K. 2002. "Review Essay: The Human Rights of Women." *International Feminist Journal of Politics* 4.3: 431–49.
Hyman, R. 2002. "The Future of Unions." *Just Labour* 1: 7–15.
ICFTU (International Confederation of Free Trade Unions). 2003. *Democratizing*

Globalization: Trade Union Statement to 2003 WSF and WEF Endorsed by the Global Unions Group ICFTU, GUFS, TUAC, WCL, ETUC. http://www.icftu.org/displaydocument.asp?Index=991216994&Language=EN. Accessed July 13, 2010.

———. 2004. *Report on Activities of the Confederation and Financial Reports, 1999–2003.* ICFTU. http://www.icftu.org/displaydocument.asp?Index=991216994andLanguage=EN. Accessed January 13, 2008.

ILO (International Labour Organization). 1999. *Trade Unions in the Informal Sector: Finding Their Bearings.* Geneva.

———. 2001. *Promoting Gender Equality: A Resource Kit for Trade Unions.* Booklet 5: *Organizing in Diversity.* http://ilo-mirror.library.cornell.edu/public/english///employment/gems/eeo/tu/cha_6.htm. Accessed July 13, 2010.

———. 2004a. *Globalisation Employment Trends for Women.* Geneva: International Labour Office.

———. 2004b. *Towards a Fair Deal for Migrant Workers in the Global Economy.* Geneva: International Labour Office.

———. 2007. *ILO Participatory Gender Audit: A Tool for Organizational Change.* Geneva.

International Metalworkers' Federation. 2005. "Report of the Secretariat." *31st World Congress.* Vienna, Austria.

Irwin, J. 1999. *The Pink Ceiling Is Too Low: Workplace Experiences of Lesbians, Gay Men, and Transgender People.* Available at http://www.arts.usyd.edu.au/centres/aclgr/publications.html. Accessed July 8, 2010.

Isis International Manilla. 2006. *Los Dialogues Feministas/Feminist Dialogues, 2005.* Manilla: Isis.

ITUC (International Trade Union Confederation). 2006. *ITUC Action Programme on Achieving Gender Equality in Trade Unions.* [Electronic Version]. http://www.ituc-csi.org/ituc-action-programme-on-achieving.html. Accessed July 9, 2010.

———. 2008a. *ITUC Report: Global Gender Pay Gap.* Brussels, February. Available at http://www.ituc-csi.org/IMG/pdf/gap-1.pdf. Accessed August 21, 2010.

———. 2008b. *World Social Forum: Trade Union Perspective.* Alternatives International Web site. http://alternatives-international.net/article1968.html. Accessed July 13, 2010.

———. 2009. "ITUC Constitutional Bodies." October. http://www.ituc-csi.org/IMG/pdf/No_66_Affiliates_and_GB___05GC_Constitutional_Bodies___revised_Jan_2010.pdf. Accessed August 25, 2010.

James, S., Foster, F. S., and Guy-Sheftall, B., Eds. 2009. *Still Brave: The Evolution of Black Women's Studies.* New York: Feminist Press.

Jordan, Y. R. Forthcoming. "Labor's Gendered Misstep: The ICFTU Women's Committee and African Women Workers."

Jose, A. V., Ed. 2002. *Organized Labour in the 21st Century.* Geneva: International Institute for Labour Studies.

Juris, J. S. 2005. "Alternative Spaces Within/Beyond Social Forums." In *Global Civil*

Society 2005/6. Eds. M. Glasius, M. Kaldor, and H. Anheier. 208–9. London: Sage.

———. 2008. *Networking Futures: The Movements against Corporate Globalization*. Durham: Duke University Press.

Kaluzynska, E. 1980. "Wiping the Floor with Theory: A Survey of Writings on Housework." *Feminist Review* 6: 27–54.

Katzenstein, M. F. 1998. *Faithful and Fearless: Moving Feminist Protest inside the Church and Military*. Princeton: Princeton University Press.

Kay, T. 2005. "Labor Transnationalism and Global Governance: The Impact of NAFTA on Transnational Labor Relationships in North America." *American Journal of Sociology* 111.3: 715–56.

Keck, M. E., and Sikkink, K. 1998. *Activists beyond Borders: Advocacy Networks in International Politics*. Ithaca, N.Y.: Cornell University Press.

Kessler-Harris, A. 2001. *In Pursuit of Equity: Women, Men, and the Quest for Economic Citizenship in Twentieth-Century America*. New York: Oxford University Press.

Kirkby, D. 1991. *Alice Henry: The Power of Pen and Voice—The Life of an Australian-American Reformer*. Melbourne: Cambridge University Press.

Kirton, G. 2006. *The Making of Women Trade Unionists*. Aldershot: Ashgate.

Krupat, K., and McCreery, P. 2001. *Out at Work: Building a Gay-Labor Alliance*. Minneapolis: University of Minnesota Press.

Lake, M. 1999. *Getting Equal: The History of Australian Feminism*. St. Leonards: Allen and Unwin.

Lawrence, E. 1994. *Gender and Trade Unions*. London: Taylor and Francis.

Ledwith, S. 2006. "Feminist Praxis in a Trade Union Gender Project." *Industrial Relations Journal* 37.4: 379–99.

Ledwith, S., and Colgan, F. 2002. "Tackling Gender, Diversity, and Trade Union Democracy: A Worldwide Project. In *Gender, Diversity, and Trade Unions: International Perspectives*. Eds. F. Colgan and S. Ledwith. 1–27. London: Routledge.

Lee, J. 2003. "A Study of the Emergence of Women's Trade Unions in South Korea." Paper presented at the Cornell ILR Conference on Women and Unions. Ithaca, N.Y. October 20.

Leite, J. C. 2005. *The World Social Forum: Strategies and Resistance*. Chicago: Haymarket Books.

Lenz, I. 2003. "Globalization, Gender, and Work: Perspectives on Global Regulation." *Review of Policy Research* 20.1: 21–43.

Lichtenstein, N. 2003. "The Rights Revolution." *New Labor Forum* 12.1: 61–73.

Liebowitz, D. J. 2002. "Gendering (Trans)National Advocacy: Tracking the Lollapalooza at Home." *International Feminist Journal of Politics* 4.2: 173–96.

Lorwin, L. L. 1929. *Labor and Internationalism*. New York: Macmillan.

Lubin, C. R., and Winslow, A. 1990. *Social Justice for Women: The International Labor Organization and Women*. Durham, N.C.: Duke University Press.

Luce, S. 2004. *Fighting for a Living Wage*. Ithaca, N.Y.: ILR Press.

Luxton, M. 2001. "Feminism as a Class Act: Working-Class Feminism and the Women's Movement in Canada." *Labour/Le Travail* 48: 63–88.

Macdonald, L. 2002. "Globalization and Social Movements: Comparing Women's Movement's Responses to NAFTA in Mexico, the USA, and Canada." *International Feminist Journal of Politics* 4.2: 151–72.

MacKinnon, C. 1979. *Sexual Harassment of Working Women. A Case of Sex Discrimination.* New Haven: Yale University Press.

Maddison, S., and Scalmer, S. 2006. *Activist Wisdom: Practical Knowledge to Creative Tension in Social Movements.* Sydney: UNSW Press.

Maher, J. M., Lindsay, J., and Franzway, S. 2008. "Time, Caring Labour, and Social Policy: Understanding the Family Time Economies of Contemporary Australian Families." *Work, Employment, and Society* 22: 547–58.

Malentacchi, M. 2003. *Trade Unions and Social Movements.* International Metalworkers Federation. Porto Alegre, Brazil. http://www.imfmetal.org/main/index.cfm?id=47andlid=2andolid=2andcid=7840. Accessed November 16, 2007.

Mapedzahama, V. 2008. "Worlds Apart? A Cross-National Comparative Study of Employed Mothers Negotiating Paid Work and Family in Australia and Zimbabwe." PhD Thesis, School of International Studies, University of South Australia. Available for download at http://arrow.unisa.edu.au:8081/1959.8/44403. Accessed July 14, 2010.

Marchand, M., and Sisson Runyan, A., Eds. 2000. *Gender and Global Restructuring: Sightings, Sites, and Resistances.* London: Routledge.

Maroney, H. J. 1983. "Feminism at Work." *New Left Review* 1.141: 51–71.

Mason, A. D., and King, E. M. 2001. *Engendering Development through Gender Equality in Rights, Resources, and Voice.* Washington, D.C.: World Bank.

Masters, M. 2004. "Unions in the 2000 Election: A Strategic Choice Perspective." *Journal of Labor Research* 25.1: 139–82.

May, M. 1985. "Bread before Roses: American Workingmen, Labor Unions, and the Family Wage." In *Women, Work, and Protest: A Century of U.S. Women's Labor History.* Ed. R. Milkman. 1–21. Boston: Routledge and Paul.

McCarthy, J. D. 1996. "Constraints and Opportunities in Adopting, Adapting, and Inventing." In *Comparative Perspectives on Social Movements.* Eds. D. McAdam, J. D. McCarthy, and M. Zald. 141–51. Cambridge: Cambridge University Press.

McCreery, P., and Krupat, K. 1999. "Introduction. Out Front: Lesbians, Gays, and the Struggle for Workplace Rights." *Social Text* 17.4: 1–8.

McDowell, L. 1997. *Capital Culture: Gender at Work in the City.* Oxford: Blackwell.

———. 1999. *Gender, Place, and Identity: Understanding Feminist Geographies.* Cambridge: Polity Press.

Melucci, A. 1994. "A Strange Kind of Newness: What's 'New' in New Social Movements?" In *New Social Movements: From Ideology to Identity.* Eds. E. Laraña, H. Johnston, and J. R. Gusfield, 101–30. Philadelphia: Temple University Press.

Mertes, T., Ed. 2004. *A Movement of Movements.* London: Verso.

Mezinec, S. 1999. *Gender Representation in Australian Unions 1998*. Adelaide: Centre for Labor Research and the United Trades and Labor Council of South Australia.

Milkman, R. 1985. *Women, Work, and Protest: A Century of U.S. Women's Labor History*. New York: Routledge.

———. 1987. *Gender at Work: The Dynamics of Job Segregation by Sex during World War II*. Urbana: University of Illinois Press.

———, Ed. 1985. *Women, Work, and Protest: A Century of U.S. Women's Labor History*. Boston: Routledge and Paul.

Millet, K. 1969. *Sexual Politics*. New York: Avon Books.

Moghadam, V. M. 2005. *Globalizing Women: Transnational Feminist Networks*. Baltimore: Johns Hopkins University Press.

Moghadam, V., Franzway, S., and Fonow, M. M., Eds. Forthcoming. *Making Globalization Work for Women: Women Workers' Social Rights and Trade Union Leadership*. New York: SUNY Press.

Mohanty, C. T. 2003. *Feminism without Borders: Decolonizing Theory, Practicing Solidarity*. Durham, N.C.: Duke University Press.

Molyneux, M. 1979. "Beyond the Domestic Labour Debate." *New Left Review* 1.116: 3–27.

Moon, K. H., and Broadbent, K. 2008."Korea: Women, Labour Activism, and Autonomous Organizing." In *Women and Labour Organizing in Asia: Diversity, Autonomy, and Activism*. Eds. K. Broadbent and M. Ford. 136–55. London: Routledge.

Moses, C. G. 1984. *French Feminism in the Nineteenth Century*. Albany: SUNY Press.

Muir, K. 1997. "Difference or Deficiency: Gender, Representation, and Meaning in Unions." In *Strife: Sex and Politics in Labour Unions*. Ed. B. Pocock. 172–93. Sydney: Allen and Unwin.

———. 2008. *Worth Fighting For: Inside the "Your Rights at Work" Campaign*. Sydney: University of New South Wales Press.

Munck, R., Ed. 2004. *Labour and Globalisation: Results and Prospects*. Liverpool: Liverpool University Press.

Murcott, A. 1983. "It's a Pleasure to Cook for Him." In *The Public and the Private*. Eds. E. Gamarnikow, D. Morgan, J. Purvis, and D. Taylorson. 78–90. London: Heinemann.

Naples, N., and Desai, M. 2002. *Women's Activism and Globalization: Linking Local Struggles and Transnational Politics*. New York: Routledge.

Needleman, R. 1993. "'Comment' on Female Leadership and Union Culture." In *Women and Unions: Forging a Partnership*. Ed. D. S. Cobble. 406–13. Ithaca, N.Y.: ILR Press.

Nicholson, L. J. 1997. "The Myth of the Traditional Family." In *Feminism and Families*. Ed. H. L. Nelson. 27–42. New York: Routledge.

Nimtz, A. 2002. "Marx and Engels: The Prototypical Transnational Actors." In *Restructuring World Politics: Transnational Social Movements, Networks and Norms*.

Eds. S. Khagram, J. V. Riker, and K. Sikkink. 245–68. Minneapolis: University of Minnesota Press.

Nolan, M., and Ryan, S. 2003. "Transforming Unionism by Organising? An Examination of the 'Gender Revolution' in New Zealand Trade Unionism since 1975." *Labour History* 10 (June): 89–111.

Oakley, A. 1974. *The Sociology of Housework*. Oxford: Martin Robertson.

Odih, P. 2007. *Gender and Work in Capitalist Economies*. London: Open University Press.

Offe, C., and Keane, J., Eds. 1985. *Disorganized Capitalism: Contemporary Transformation of Work and Politics*. Cambridge: MIT Press.

Olssen, E. 1996. "Occupational Classification: What the Census Tried to Do and Why It Failed" [Electronic Version]. FRST Caversham, Occupation Working Paper, 1996-3. http://caversham.otago.ac.nz/files/working/occcl1996.pdf. Accessed July 14, 2010.

Ong, A. 1987. *Spirits of Resistance and Capitalist Discipline: Factory Women in Malaysia*. Albany: State University of New York Press.

———. 2002. "The Gender and Labor Politics of Postmodernity." In *Globalization and the Challenges of a New Century: A Reader*. Eds. P. O'Meara, H. D. Mehlinger, and M. Krain, 253–81. Bloomington: Indiana University Press.

Ostenfeld, S. 1998. "Identity Politics and Trade Unions: The Case of Sexual Minorities in Australia." Paper presented at the Association of Industrial Relations Academics of Australian and New Zealand Conference. Waikato, New Zealand. February 3–5.

Owen, M., and Shaw, S., Eds. 1979. *Working Women*. Melbourne: Working Women's Centre.

Parker, J. 2003. "We're On a Road to Somewhere: Women's Groups in Unions." *Industrial Relations Journal* 34.2: 164–84.

Parreñas, R. S. 2001. *Servants of Globalization: Women, Migration, and Domestic Work*. Stanford: Stanford University Press.

Pasture, P., and Verberckmoes, J., Eds. 1998. *Working-Class Internationalism and the Appeal of National Identity: Historical Debates and Current Perspectives on Western Europe*. Oxford: Berg.

Peetz, D. 2006. *Brave New Workplace: How Individual Contracts Are Changing Our Jobs*. Crows Nest, Australia: Allen and Unwin.

Peterson V. S. 2003. *A Critical Rewriting of Global Political Economy: Integrating Reproductive, Productive, and Virtual Economies*. London: Routledge.

Petrović, J. 2000. "Women Save the Union." *South-East Europe Review for Labour and Social Affairs* 3.2: 117–30.

Pettman, J. J. 2001. "Gender Issues." In *The Globalization of World Politics: An Introduction to International Relations*. Eds. John Baylis and Steve Smith, 582–98. Oxford: Oxford University Press.

Phillips, A. 1987. *Divided Loyalties*. London: Virago.

Pocock, B., Ed. 1997. *Strife: Sex and Politics in Labour Unions*. Sydney: Allen and Unwin.

Pocock, B. 2003. *The Work/Life Collision: What Work Is Doing to Australians and What to Do About It*. Annandale: The Federation Press.

Pratt, G. 2004. *Working Feminism*. Philadelphia: Temple University Press.

Presser, H. 2003. *Working in a 24/7 Economy: Challenges for American Families*. New York: Russell Sage Foundation.

Prügl, E. 2004. "International Institutions and Feminist Politics." *Brown Journal of Public Affairs* 10.2: 69–84.

Pyecroft, S. 1994. "British Working Women and the First World War." *The Historian* 56: 699–710.

Quintero-Ramírez, C. 2002. "The North American Free Trade Agreement and Women: The Canadian and Mexican Experiences." *International Feminist Journal of Politics* 4.2: 240–59.

Ragins, B. R., Cornwell, J. M., and Miller, J. S. 2003. "Heterosexism in the Workplace." *Group and Organization Management* 28.1: 45–74.

Romero, M. 1992. *Maid in the U.S.A*. New York: Routledge.

Rooks, D. 2003. "The Cowboy Mentality: Organizers and Occupational Commitment in the New Labor Movement." *Labor Studies Journal* 28.3: 33–61.

Rowbotham, S. 1973. *Hidden from History: 300 Years of Women's Oppression and the Fight against It*. London: Pluto Press.

———. 1989. *The Past Is before Us: Feminism in Action since the 1960s*. London: Pandora Press.

———. 1992. *Women in Movement: Feminism and Social Action*. London: Routledge.

Rupp, L. J. 1997. *Worlds of Women: The Making of an International Women's Movement*. Princeton: Princeton University Press.

Rupp, L. J., and Taylor, V. 2003. *Drag Queens at the 801 Cabaret*. Urbana: University of Illinois Press.

Ryan, E., and Conlon, A. 1989. *Gentle Invaders: Australian Women at Work*. Ringwood: Penguin.

Sassen, S. 1998. *Globalization and Its Discontents: Essays on the New Mobility of People and Money*. New York: The New Press.

Sawer, M. 1999. "Women's Ministries: An Australian Perspective." *Feminist Review* 63: 88–91.

Sayce, S., Greene, A., and Ackers, A. 2006. "Small Is Beautiful? The Development of Women's Activism in a Small Union." *Industrial Relations Journal* 37.4: 400–414.

Sayer, L. 2005. "Gender, Time, and Inequality: Trends in Women's and Men's Paid Work, Unpaid Work, and Free Time." *Social Forces* 84.1: 285–304.

Schmidt, V., Ed. 2007. *Trade Union Responses to Globalization: A Review by the Global Union Research Network*. Geneva: International Labour Organization.

Schroedel, J. R. 1990. "Blue Collar Women: Paying the Price at Home and on the Job."

In *The Experience and Meaning of Work in Women's Lives*. Eds. H. Y. Grossman and N. L. Chester. 241–60. Hilsdale, N.J.: Lawrence Erlbaum.

Scipes, K. 2000. "It's Time to Come Clean: Open the AFL-CIO Archives on International Labor Operations." *Labor Studies Journal* 25.2: 4–25.

Seccombe, W. 1974. "The Housewife and Her Labour under Capitalism." *New Left Review* 83: 3–24.

———. 1986. "Patriarchy Stabilized: The Construction of the Male Breadwinner Wage Norm in Nineteenth-Century Britain." *Social History* 11.1: 53–76.

Seidman, S. 1997. *Difference Troubles: Queering Social Theory and Sexual Politics*. Cambridge: Cambridge University Press.

Sen, G. 1997. "Globalization, Justice, and Equity: A Gender Perspective." *Development* 40.2: 21–26.

Sennet, R. 1998. *The Corrosion of Character: The Personal Consequences of Work in the New Capitalism*. New York: Norton.

Sikkink, K. 2002a. "Infrastructures for Change: Transnational Organizations, 1953–93." In *Restructuring World Politics: Transnational Social Movements, Networks, and Norms*. Eds. S. Khagram, J. V. Riker, and K. Sikkink. 24–46. Minneapolis: University of Minnesota Press.

———. 2002b. "Restructuring World Politics: The Limits of Asymmetrics of Soft Power." In *Restructuring World Politics: Transnational Social Movements, Networks and Norms*. Eds. S. Khagram, J. V. Riker, and K. Sikkink. 300–317. Minneapolis: University of Minnesota Press.

Silver, B. J. 2003. *Forces of Labor: Workers' Movements and Globalisation since 1870*. Cambridge: Cambridge University Press.

Smith, J., and Johnston, H., Eds. 2002. *Globalization and Resistance: Transnational Dimensions of Social Movements*. Lanham, Md.: Rowman and Littlefield.

Smith, J., Karides, M., Becker, M., Brunelle, D., Chase-Dunn, C., della Porta, D., Garza, R. I., Juris, J. S., Mosca, L., Reese, E., Smith, P. J., and Vazquez, R. 2008. *Global Democracy and the World Social Forums*. Boulder, Colo.: Paradigm Publishers.

Smith, T., Sonnenfeld, D., and Pellow, D. N., Eds. 2006. *Challenging the Chip: Labor Rights and Environmental Justice in the Global Electronics Industry*. Philadelphia: Temple University Press.

Smithson, J., and Stokoe, E. 2005. "Discourses of Work-Life Balance: Negotiating 'Genderblind' Terms in Organisations." *Gender, Work, and Organization* 12.2: 147–68.

Snow, D., and Benford, R. 1992. "Master Frames and Cycles of Protest." In *Frontiers in Social Movement Theory*. Eds. A. Morris and C. McClurg Mueller. 133–54. New Haven: Yale University Press.

Snow, D. A., Soule, S. A., and Kriesi, H., Eds. 2004. *The Blackwell Companion to Social Movements*. Malden, Mass.: Blackwell Publishing.

Standing, G. 2001. "Care Work: Overcoming Insecurity and Neglect." In *Care Work:*

The Quest for Security. Ed. M. Daly. 15–32. Geneva: International Labour Organization.

Stepan-Norris, J., and Zeitlin, M. 2002. *Left Out: Reds and America's Industrial Unions*. Cambridge: Cambridge University Press.

Stevis, D., and Boswell, T. 2008. *Globalization and Labor*. Lanham, Md.: Rowman and Littlefield.

Sugiman, P. 1994. *Labour's Dilemma: The Gender Politics of Auto Workers in Canada, 1937–1979*. Toronto: University of Toronto Press.

Tax, M. 1980. *The Rising of the Women: Feminist Solidarity and Class Conflict 1880–1917*. London: Monthly Review Press.

Thomsson, H. 1999. "Yes, I Used to Exercise, But . . . : A Feminist Study of Exercise in the Life of Swedish Women." *Journal of Leisure Research* 31.1: 35–56.

Towart, N. 2002. "Mardi Gras: The Biggest Labour Festival?" *Workers Online* no. 126 (March 1). http://workers.labor.net.au/126/c_historicalfeature_mardi.html. Accessed July 14, 2010.

Traub-Merz, R., and Eckl, J. 2007. "International Trade Union Movement: Mergers and Contradictions." *Friedrich-Ebert-Siftung International Trade Union Program Briefing Papers* 1: http://www.nuso.org/upload/fes_pub/merz.pdf. Accessed August 26, 2010.

Tristan, F. 2007. *The Worker's Union*. Trans. B. Livingston. Urbana: University of Illinois Press.

TUC (Trades Union Congress). 2005. *TUC Equality Audit 2005*. London: Trades Union Congress.

Turner, B. S. 1984. *The Body and Society*. Oxford: Basil Blackwell.

Turner, L., and Cornfield, D., Eds. 2007. *Labor in the New Urban Battlegrounds: Local Solidarity in a Global Economy*. Ithaca, N.Y.: Cornell University Press.

Turner, L., Katz, H., and Hurd, R., Eds. 2001. *Rekindling the Movement: Labor's Quest for Relevance in the Twenty-first Century*. Ithaca, N.Y.: Cornell University Press.

Ungerson, C. 1997. "Social Politics and the Commodification of Care." *Social Politics* 4.3: 362–81.

———. 2003. "Commodified Care Work in European Labour Markets." *European Societies* 5.4: 377–96.

———. 2006. *Cash for Care in Developed Welfare States*. Houndmills: Palgrave Macmillan.

United Steelworkers Canada. 2008. *Steelworkers Humanity Fund Report*. Toronto.

Urban, B. Y., and Wagner, K. C. 2000. *Domestic Violence: A Union Issue—A Workplace Training Resource Kit for Unions*. San Francisco: The Family Violence Prevention Fund.

Vogel, L. 1990. "Debating Difference: Feminism, Pregnancy, and the Workplace." *Feminist Studies* 16.1: 9–32.

Walby, S. 1986. *Patriarchy at Work*. Cambridge: Polity Press.

———. 2002. "Feminism in a Global Era." *Economy and Society* 31: 533–57.

———. 2009. *Globalization and Inequalities: Complexity and Contested Modernities.* London: Sage.
Walker, M. C. 2005. *Speech to the United Food and Commercial Workers (UFCW).* Women's Network Convention. http://canadianlabour.ca/index.php/Marie_Clarke_Walker/681#startcontent. Accessed January 20, 2008.
Waterman, P. 1998. *Globalization, Social Movements and the New Internationalisms.* London: Mansell Publishing Limited.
———. 2004. "The Global Justice and Solidarity Movement and the WSF: A Backgrounder." In *World Social Forum: Challenging Empires.* Ed. J. Sen, 55–66. New Delhi: Viveka Foundation. Available at http://www.choike.org/documentos/wsf_s110_waterman.pdf. Accessed July 12, 2010.
Waterman, P., and Timms, J. 2004. "Trade Union Internationalism and a Global Civil Society in the Making." In *Global Civil Society 2004-5.* Eds. H. Anheier, M. Glasius, and M. Kaldor. 175–202. London: Sage.
Weeks, W. 1994. *Women Working Together: Lessons from Feminist Women's Services.* Melbourne: Longman Cheshire.
Weitz, R., Ed. 2003. *The Politics of Women's Bodies: Sexuality, Appearance, and Behavior.* 2nd ed. New York: Oxford University Press.
Western, B. 1997. *Between Class and Market: Postwar Unionization in the Capitalist Democracies.* Princeton: Princeton University Press.
Wichterich, C. 2000. *The Globalized Woman: Reports from a Future of Inequality.* Melbourne: Spinifex.
Williams, C. 1981. *Opencut: The Working Class in an Australian Mining Town.* Sydney: Allen and Unwin.
———. 1988. *Blue, White, and Pink Collar Workers in Australia: Technicians, Bank Employees and Flight Attendants.* Sydney: Allen and Unwin.
———. 2002. "Masculinities and Emotion Work in Trade Unions." In *Gender, Diversity, and Trade Unions: International Perspectives.* Eds. F. Colgan and S. Ledwith. 292–311. London: Routledge.
Wilson, A. 2004. *Intimate Economies of Bangkok: Tomboys, Tycoons, and Avon Ladies in the Global City.* Berkeley: University of California Press.
———. 2007. "Feminism in the Space of the World Social Forum," *Journal of International Women's Studies* 8.3: 10–27.
Windmuller, J. P. 1995. *International Trade Secretariats: The Industrial Trade Union Internationals.* U.S. Department of Labor. Washington, D.C.: Bureau of International Labor Affairs.
Wintour, N. 2006. "Quality Public Services: The Gender Dimensions." In *Roundtable Report: Women, Socio-Economic Rights, and Trade Union Decision-Making.* Ed. V. Moghadam. 2nd World Forum on Human Rights. Nantes, France: UNESCO.
Wolf, N. 1991. *The Beauty Myth: How Images of Beauty Are Used against Women.* New York: William Morrow.
Wolkowitz, C. 2006. *Bodies at Work.* London: Sage.

Wolmark, J. 2003. "The Pleasure-Pain of Feminist Politics in the 1970s." In *The Feminist Seventies*. Eds. H. Graham, A. Kaloski, A. Neilson, and E. Robertson. http://www.feministseventies.net/wolmark.html. Accessed August 26, 2010. York: Raw Nerve Books.

Workers Online. 2002. *Workers Out for Gay Games*. http://workers.labor.net.au/139/print_index.html. Accessed July 8, 2010.

Working Women's Centre. 1994. *Stop Violence against Women at Work: An Information Guide for Women Dealing with Sexual Violence and Sexual Harassment in the Workplace*. Adelaide: Working Women's Centre.

Working Women's Centres. 2010. "About Us." http://www.wwc.org.au//index.php?page=about-us. Accessed August 18, 2010.

World Bank. 2009. *The Global Financial Crisis: Assessing Vulnerability for Women and Children*. March. http://www.worldbank.org/financialcrisis/pdf/Women-Children-Vulnerability-March09.pdf. Accesed July 14, 2010.

World March of Women. 2003. "Perspective of Women of the World March of Women. Declaration at the 2003 World Social Forum." Viveka Foundation. http://www.choike.org/documentos/wsf_s317_womenmarch.pdf. Accessed July 13, 2010.

———. 2004. *Newsletter 7.1*. http://www.marchemondiale.org/en/bulletin/03-2004.html. Accessed March 29, 2004.

———. 2005. *Women's Global Charter for Humanity*. http://www.1325australia.org.au/textdocuments/Women's%20Global%20Charter.pdf. Accessed June 16, 2005.

World Social Forum. 2005. *Global Action against Poverty*. Porto Alegre, Brazil. http://webmail.horus.at/pipermail/e-rundbrief/2005/000247.html. Accessed July 13, 2010.

Yeo, E. J. 2005. "Constructing and Contesting Motherhood. 1750–1950." *Hecate* 31.2: 4–20.

Yuval-Davis, N. 2006. "Intersectionality and Feminist Politics." *European Journal of Women's Studies* 13.3: 193–209.

Zheng, T. 2009. *Red Lights: The Lives of Sex Workers in Postsocialist China*. Minneapolis: University of Minnesota Press.

Index

activism, 18, 24–25, 27–28, 30; discourses for, 11; and international labor bodies 87–90; and international women's movements 98; and laboring body, 32–34; and LGBT 43–45; mobilizing structures, 15; and practices, 24–26; and sexual politics 27–29; sites of 18–20; and Trade Union Movements 36–41; transnational feminist, 2–3; union feminists 142–44

ACTU (Australian Council of Trade Unions), 19, 74, 88, 97; child care, 63; Rights at Work campaign, 12; Sharan Burrow, 101, 121; Working Women's Charter, 82

AFL-CIO (American Federation of Labor and Congress of Industrial Organizations), in the Cold War, 5; and LGBT alliances, 43

African Labor College, 99

alliances, 38, 71–73; and child care, 62–63; discursive frames for, 11–14; with international labor bodies, 132–33; and networks, 15; with NGOs, 121–22; queer organizing, 42–46; and worker centers, 79–81

Alvarez, Sonia, 16, 126, 128–30

American Federation of Teachers, 42

Anna Stewart Memorial Project, 78

Bailey, Janis, 41, 48, 54, 143

Barrett, Michèle, and McIntosh, Mary, 13, 25, 50

Beale, Jennifer, 30, 77

black sexual politics, 26

body: and care, 62, 66; laboring, 21, 25; practices, 32, 36; in work, 32–33. *See also* laboring body

body/work nexus. *See* Wolkowitz, Carol

Briskin, Linda, 4, 27, 39, 68, 70, 77, 118

Burrow, Sharan, 101, 121, 143

Buss, Doris, and Herman, Didi, 48–49

Butler, Judith, 26, 32

campaigns: for decent work, 92, 106, 107, 134; and family frames, 41, 47–49, 54–56; and family wage, 56–58; by GUFs, Table 1, 93–96; and labor rights, 7, 12, 92, 132; and LGBT rights, 42–45; for pay equity, 56–60; for public childcare, 66; on sexual harassment, 83–85; Working Women's Charter, 82; for work/life balance, 63–66

Canadian Auto Workers, 43

care workers, 10, 61–63

childcare, 9, 60–63, 115, 117

class: and body, 32; and gender, 27, 89–90, 112; intersections of, 44; and race, 6, 8, 26–27, 52, 61; and sexual politics, 26–27; work and, 51–52, 61–62; working class, 15, 32, 58, 89, 98, 112

CLC (Canadian Labour Congress), 43, 63–64, 88, 97

Cobble, Dorothy Sue, 6, 27, 48, 58–59, 62, 98–99, 140

Cockburn, Cynthia, 36, 38

178 · INDEX

Colgan, Fiona, 6, 16, 25, 28, 38, 40, 43, 70
collective identity, 74, 79, 98
Collins, Patricia Hill, 26
Connell, Raewyn, 7, 14, 26–28, 34, 41, 62, 65, 79, 83
Conway, Janet, 2, 15, 125–29, 131, 138
Coors Beer, 44
COSATU (Congress of South African Trade Unions), 88, 135
Cunnison, Sheila, and Stageman, Jane, 29
CUPE (Canadian Union of Public Employees), 43

decent work, 23, 63, 134, 142; campaigns, 92, 106–7; at the World Social Forum, 134
decolonization, 91
Desai, Manisha, 2, 9, 69, 137, 141
discourses, 9–16; of the body, 34; of the family, 48–49, 51, 57, 61, 65; feminist, 21, 116, 121, 124
discursive: alliances, 13, 23, 38; alliances between women and labor, 54, 62–63, 65, 84; alliances produced at the World Social Forum, 133, 137–38; constructions, 32, 56, 143; frames, 11, 38, 68; tools, 13, 88
discursive politics, 24, 37
domestic labor, 31, 33, 36, 55–56; workers, 61, 99, 102

EI (Education International), 28, 44–45, 59, 93, 95, 97
encuentros, 16
equal pay, 55–59; international debates on, 111–12, 114–15. *See also* pay equity
Eschle, Catherine, 2–3, 9–11, 25, 129, 131
everyday life, 9, 24–25, 29–30; and activism, 32–35, 54, 139–40; and family, 48

familialism, 50
family wage, 47; as barrier, 52; debates on, 111; union campaigns for, 57–59. *See also* living wage
fascism, 91
FAT. *See* Authentic Labor Front, 72
feminism, 9–11, 13, 140, 142, 144; and family, 49; union, 88–89, 107–8; at World Social Forum, 129–31, 134–35
Feminist Dialogues, 125, 131
feminization of labor, 53, 99

Ferree, Myra Marx, 2, 62–63, 73
flexibility, 10, 46, 63–65, 119
Folbre, Nancy, 13, 25, 30, 51–52, 62
Fonow, Mary Margaret, 11–12, 40, 77–78, 88
Foucault, Michel, 8, 32
Frank, Dana, 87, 90
Franzway, Suzanne, 9, 26–27, 33, 50, 80–81, 143

GayTUG (Gay and Lesbian Trade Unionists Group), 43
gender, 7–9; audits, 105; and family, 49–50; and globalization, 9–11; and ILO, 104–7; and LGBT workers, 28–29; mainstreaming, 104–16; of sexual politics, 26–27
gender relations, 7, 9, 26–28
Gibson-Graham, J. K., 2, 8, 10, 33
Giugni, Marco, 141
GLAM (Gay and Lesbian Australian Services Union Members), 43
Global Call to Action against Poverty, 133
globalization, 1–2, 8–10, 53, 55, 144–45; antiglobalization, 9, 128, 130; sexual politics of, 121–22; and World Social Forum, 126–32, 135
GLUE (Gay and Lesbian Unionists for Equality), 44
greedy institutions, 41, 62

Hawkesworth, Mary, 2, 103–5, 127, 131, 141
Heagney, Muriel, 58
Heery, Edmund, and Conley, Hazel, 12, 57
human rights, 12, 15–16; campaigns, 93–94; and LGBT workers, 45; and women's rights, 116–17; and World Social Forum, 129–30
husband care, 61

ICFTU (International Confederation of Free Trade Unions), 6, 16, 17, 64–65, 70, 79; merge into ITUC, 100–101; and Sharan Burrow, 121; and women's activism, 98–101; at World Social Forum, 131–33
IFTU (International Federation of Trade Unions), 98–99, 103
IFWW (International Federation of Working Women), 98–99
ILO (International Labour Organization), 6, 102–6; charter, 57; Convention 100, 59,

111; Convention 156, 47, 64; decent work, 134; equal pay, 57, 59–60
IMF (International Metalworkers' Federation), 13, 29, 113–24; first women's conference, 58, 73, 76, 109–13; structure and program 108–9; at World Social Forum, 127, 132,134
intersectionality, 10, 26–27
IPS (Institute for Policy Studies), 135
Irwin, Jude, 28
ITUC (International Trade Union Confederation), 6, 17; and family, 54; and female General Secretary, 143; Organizing Women Workers campaign, 92; structure and programs, 100–102, 131–34

Jordan, Yevette, 99

Katzenstein, Mary, 14, 24, 68
Keck, Margaret, and Sikkink, Kathryn, 14
Kirton, Gill, 76–78

laboring body, 21, 25; and activism, 32–35
labor internationalism, 87, 89–91, 102, 107–8
labor rights, 2, 5–7, 12, 17–18, 28, 37, 42, 87, 106–7, 121; campaigns for, 103, 142, 145
leadership, 4, 6, 38–41; union, 70, 88; women's, 77, 84–85, 119, 135–36, 143
League of Nations, 103–4
Ledwith, Sue, 6, 16, 25, 29, 40, 43, 68, 70, 83–84
LGBT (Lesbian, Gay, Bisexual, and Transgender), 13, 26, 144; and GUFs, see Table 1, 93–96; and trade unions, 42–45, 70, 97, workers, 28–29. *See also* queer organizing
living wage, 57

Maddison, Sarah, and Scalmer, Sean, 35, 37
male breadwinner, 47, 49, 52–53, 61, 112
Malentacchi, Marcello, 123, 127, 132
masculinity, 50; culture of, 41; heteronormative, 39, 61, 139
McCreery, Patrick, and Krupat, Kitty, 38, 44
Mecozzi, Alessandra, 134
Milkman, Ruth, 49, 109
Millet, Kate, 8, 26, 28
mobilizing networks, 11, 20, 89
mobilizing structure, 3, 15, 20, 68–69, 120, 143–44

Moghadam, Valentine, 2, 7, 10, 71–72, 103, 105, 127, 142
mother, good, 56, 58; love, 58
Muir, Kathie, 12, 41, 47, 143

NAFTA (North American Free Trade Agreement), 72, 127
Naples, Nancy, 2, 9, 69, 141
neoliberalism, 4, 6, 53, 55, 57, 64, 119, 128, 131, 134–35, 137
NGOs (nongovernmental organizations), 5, 13, 37, 105; international, 103, 105, 109; labor, 17–18, 100, 121–22; women's, 18, 72–73, 85, 117, 142; at World Social Forum, 131, 133, 136

pay equity, 56–60, 108; campaigns on, 17, 23, 29, 49, 56, 95, 101, 112, 142. *See also* equal pay
Pocock, Barbara, 4, 6, 36, 63
political alliances, 38, 66, 139, 142, 145
political opportunities, 11; in labor, 37, 45–46, 92; and social movements, 13–14, 28–29
power, 8–9, 49, 71, 80, 83, 84, 141; gendered, 13, 14, 83; and sexual politics, 26–28; structures of, 3–4, 41, 118–19, 130, 139, 145
precarious work, 23, 107, 122–23
pregnancy, 33
protectionism, 108, 112
PSI (Public Services International), 4, 44–45, 59–60, 92, 97, 100

queer organizing, 15, 21, 26, 42, 46, 140

race: black sexual politics, 26; and domestic labor, 61; intersectionality, 27, 44, 100; and sexualities, 26, 28–29
reproductive rights, 115, 124
Rowbotham, Sheila, 27, 73, 79, 82
Rupp, Leila, 69, 73, 99, 103

second shift, 21, 25, 30–33, 36, 46, 66, 143
self care, 9, 21, 35
self-organizing, 21–22, 68, 87, 97, 107, 130. *See also* Briskin, Linda
separate organizing, 39–40, 43, 70, 77, 79, 111, 118, 144. *See also* Briskin, Linda
SEWA (Self Employed Women's Association), 39

sexual division of labor, 52–53, 55, 59, 83, 90, 112
sexual harassment, 23, 29, 80, 83–85, 93, 95–96
sexual politics, 7–9, 11, 15, 25, 26–29, 31–32, 41, 121, 128, 139, 143–45; and family, 13, 49–51, 61–62, 65, 70–73; of labor movements, 79, 81, 83, 108, 140, 142; sexual harassment, 83–85; in trade unions, 60, 78, 136
Sikkink, Kathryn, 14–15
Sisters of Perpetual Indulgence, 44
Smith, Jackie, 12, 125, 127–28, 137–38
social movements, 2, 4–7, 11, 67
social reproduction, 9, 13, 21, 30–31, 51, 53
solidarity, 16–17, 39, 68–69, 74, 88, 90–91, 109, 144
sustainable harmony, 38

trade, 2, 11, 16–17, 121–22, 127, 132–33
transnational: activism and alliances, 20, 36, 44, 55, 72, 104, 116, 119, 128; feminism, 3, 7, 98, 103, 105, 126, 129, 133–34, 144; labor movements and politics, 2–7, 9, 13, 23–24, 46, 48, 64, 81, 87–88, 107, 108, 138, 140–41; networks, 14, 45, 71, 75, 100, 128, 145
Transport Employees Union, 43
Tristan, Flora, 89–90
TUC (Trades Union Congress), 42–43, 47, 57, 60, 82

UNESCO (United Nations Educational, Scientific and Cultural Organization), 19–20, 117

union feminism, 3, 22, 88, 108, 134
United Nations, 116–17
United Steelworkers, 18, 72

wages for housework, 51, 55
Walby, Sylvia, 2–4, 7–9, 55, 57, 139, 141
Waterman, Peter, 5, 91, 103, 129
WEF (World Economic Forum), 127, 131–32
WICEJ (Women's International Coalition for Economic Justice), 100, 130, 136
Williams, Claire, 6, 34, 52, 83
Wilson, Ara, 10, 128, 130
Wolkowitz, Carol, 32–34, 61
Women in the Authentic Labor Front or Frente Auténtico del Trabajo, 72
Women of Steel, 40, 77
women's committees, 40–41, 68–70, 99, 107, 121, 144; IMF and, 114–16, 118; union feminists and, 3, 17, 88; within GUFs, 92, 93–96; within ICFTU and ITUC, 99–102, 107
women's policy machinery, 104
work/family balance, 23, 65
World March of Women, 15, 92, 126, 130
WSF (World Social Forum), 18–20, 23, 67, 92, 100, 109, 125–38; and charter of principles, 129
WTO (World Trade Organization), 97, 127
WWC (Working Women's Centres), 18–19, 75, 80